W. G. BUTLER SC. N.Y.

City of Middletown, in 1825.

CENTENNIAL ADDRESS,

BY

DAVID D. FIELD, D. D.

WITH HISTORICAL SKETCHES OF

CROMWELL, PORTLAND, CHATHAM, MIDDLE-HADDAM,

MIDDLETOWN AND ITS PARISHES.

MIDDLETOWN, CONN.:

WILLIAM B. CASEY.

1853.

MIDDLETOWN:
NEWS AND ADVERTISER PRINT.
1853.

CENTENNIAL ADDRESS

AND

HISTORICAL SKETCHES.

CONTENTS.

HARTFORD, July 15, 1850.

MY DEAR SIR:

I have postponed, until this time, my final reply to the invitation received from yourself and the other gentlemen of the Committee for that purpose, to deliver an address at the ensuing Centennial Celebration of the settlement of Middletown, in hopes that I should find myself able to comply with your request, but I have ascertained, that the arrangement of the terms of the courts during the Summer and Fall will not allow me the leisure necessary for a suitable preparation for the service to which you have invited me; and I am therefore under the necessity, (reluctantly for the reasons mentioned in my last interview,) of declining its performance.

Grateful for the compliment implied in the invitation of the committee, I am, with sincere regard, yours,

WM. L. STORRS.

To JOHN JOHNSTON, Esq., Middletown, Ct.

NEW HAVEN, Nov. 8th., 1850.

WM. B. CASEY, M. D.

Chairman Committee of Arrangements.

DEAR SIR:

I received some days since, your favor of the 4th, conveying to me from the Committee of Arrangements for the Centennial Anniversary, an invitation to be present and to share in the exercises of the celebration.

I have delayed my answer in the hope that I should be able to say positively that I would come. It is still, however, so uncertain whether my engagements will admit of my coming, that it will not be safe to depend on me for any active share in the work of the day, or for being in Middletown, in the body at all

I say this very unwillingly, for I do not know of any other appointment of the kind which it would give me so much pleasure to make and fulfill. I am respectfully, yours,

WM. H. RUSSELL.

INTRODUCTORY REMARKS.

THE Second Centennial Anniversary of Middletown, should have been celebrated in October 1850; but owing to the infirm health of Rev. Dr. FIELD, who delivered the ADDRESS on that occasion, it was deferred until November. At a meeting of the citizens of Middletown held in July 1850, at which Doct. WM. B. CASEY, then Mayor of the City, presided, a Committee was appointed to make arrangements for the approaching Anniversary, which Committee was constituted as follows:

WM. B. CASEY, *Ex-Officio Chairman.*
PROF. JOHN JOHNSTON,
DOCT. CHAS. WOODWARD,
DOCT. J. BARRATT,
FREDERICK HALL, ESQ., *Portland.*
HON. JOHN STEWART, *Chatham.*
ASA HUBBARD, ESQ., *South Farms.*
EDWARD SAVAGE, ESQ., *Cromwell.*

Invitations were sent to Hon. W. L. Storrs, now of Hartford, Judge of Superior Court; To Wm. H. Russell, Esq., of New Haven, and other gentlemen, natives of the Town, inviting their presence and assistance on the occasion of the Anniversary, but their engagements were of such a nature, as to prevent their acceptance of the invitation. Their letters are herewith subjoined.

Rev. Dr. Field having finally notified the Committee of his improved health, and ability to discharge the duties of his appointment, the 13th day of November was fixed upon as the time for holding the celebration, and notice given accordingly. Mr. Russell's letter informing the Committee of his inability to attend and participate in the exercises of the day, having been received at so late a date, that it was impossible to provide a substitute, the duty of supplying his place, so far as might be, devolved upon Doct. Casey, the Chairman of the Committee, and he accordingly prepared a short introductory Address, a copy of which is printed in the following pages.

An Ode, hastily written for the occasion by one of our townsmen, was set to Music by Mr. John Porter, and effectively sung by the Choir of the North Church.

In conclusion, the Committee would remark, that it was extremely doubtful for some time, owing to Dr. Field's state of health, whether the celebration would be held at all; and therefore the preparations and arrangements for the occasion were suspended. Consequently, when the Committee received notice from Dr. Field that he was ready to fulfill his appointment, there was but little time, before cold weather, in which to make the necessary preparations.

The doings of the day, and the order of exercises, were described in the Daily News, a small paper just started, and from that we copy an account of the proceedings.

Centennial Celebration

OF

MIDDLETOWN.

THE celebration of the second Centennial Anniversary of the settlement of Middletown took place in the city of Middletown, Nov. 13th, 1850, and the condition of the notification in regard to the favorableness of the weather proved to be quite unnecessary, as it was one of the most pleasant days with which this remarkably genial fall season has been crowded. At the hour appointed, considerable numbers of our citizens and visitors from the neighboring towns, assembled in the vicinity of the Post Office to witness the forming of the procession. At half past ten o'clock, a walking organization was effected under the direction of John N. Camp, Marshal of the day. The following was the arrangement of the column:

The excellent Brass Band from New Haven.

The Mansfield Guards under the command of Gen. E. W. N. Starr, (a very thoroughly drilled company, and as gentlemanly, as it is military in its appearance.)

The Committee of Arrangements.

The Rev. Dr. FIELD, the Orator of the day, (and whose external personality is said strongly to resemble that of Ex-Minister Guizot.)

The Rev. Clergy of the city and vicinity.

The City Fathers.

Invited Guests.

The Faculty and Students of Wesleyan University.

Members of the Friendly Association of Cromwell.

St. John's Lodge of Free and Accepted Masons, (whose charter, we think, dates back as far as 1787.)

Central Lodge, No. 12, Independent Order of Odd Fellows.

Sons of Temperance, from the Mattabesett and Mamooson Divisions, decorated in simple white.

Putnam Chapter of the Order of United Americans, (with a very tasteful regalia.)

Town Officers and Citizens.

The Procession was formed in front of the North Church, and proceeded on its march up Main to Washington, thence to High, thence to Church, thence again through Main street, to the North Church. The exercises in the Church were introduced by music from the New Haven Band. A very appropriate prayer was offered by the Rev. Dr. CRANE, the senior resident settled clergyman, and pastor of the oldest congregation in the city. Dr. WM. B. CASEY, Chairman of the Committee of Arrangements, made a few pertinent remarks, in which he took occasion to remind us of some of our advantages and wants. The choir of the North Church then sung, in a very chaste and effective manner, the following

ODE.

Two Hundred Years ago here, and Autumn leaves were falling,
And the woods to woods were calling here, Two Hundred Years ago;
And their roaring sounds like thunder, made the forest seekers wonder,
When stirred by blasts of Autumn winds, Two Hundred Years ago.

Two Hundred Years ago, there were Indian footsteps roaming
O'er the hills, they heard them coming here, Two Hundred Years ago;
They were from our Western Mountains, they'd been quaffing at the fountains,
And were wending hither homeward here, Two Hundred Years ago.

Two Hundred Years ago here, the deer were wildly bounding,
And the partridge wing-drum sounding here, Two Hundred Years ago;
On the tree-tops gaily prancing, was the merry squirrel dancing,
At his prey the wolf was glancing, here, Two Hundred Years ago.

Two Hundred Years ago, here, there flowed a noble river,
And its finny tribes were sporting here, Two Hundred Years ago;
And like God, the glorious giver, this same water faileth never,
But is passing now as ever here, Two Hundred Years ago.

Two Hundred Years ago, here, the Red Man broke his arrow
And his bow in silent sorrow here, Two Hundred Years ago,
And he left his Fathers buried here, and shrunk his heart in silence there,
And the White Man ploughed their graves here, Two Hundred Years ago.

The Rev. Dr. FIELD, of Higganum, gave a characteristic Address, interesting, in the main, for its historical facts and reminiscences.

The Church, we believe, was filled to the extent of its capacity with an apparently interested audience; and we doubt not the occasion will be long held, by all who were present, in pleasing remembrance. The Band permitted us to depart under the touching strains of *Auld Lang Syne.*

The celebration is over. Hereafter let it be remembered that Middletown is a matron with the weight of Two Hundred Years upon her brow. May Heaven watch over her, and her children forever.

Our City, in the evening, presented a very brilliant appearance. Many of the stores, public buildings and private dwellings were splendidly illuminated, by way of a finishing up of the Centennial Celebration.

The side-walks, of course, were somewhat thronged with observing and happy promenaders. With modest bonfires, burning balls, and intrusive fire-crackers, and an occasional adventurous sky-rocket, and the unrevolving lights of the windows, the crowd appeared to be well entertained.

This celebration, on the whole, which was anticipated with but little interest by not a few, has passed off in a commendable manner. Enthusiasm is sometimes of a slow growth. Imagine that "an hundred years are gone," and give us another demonstration to-morrow, and the thing shall be done up in a manner entirely satisfactory.

ADDRESS OF DR. CASEY.

An interesting and important occasion has this day called us together. We have assembled within these walls to celebrate the Two Hundredth Anniversary of the settlement of our town. Yes, two hundred years have passed, since first the white man here took up his abode. What thronging fancies crowd upon the mind as it wanders back over this vista of years, and pictures to itself the long series of incidents and changes, extending throughout this period. Let us indulge ourselves with the retrospect. I do not intend to trespass far upon the province of my venerable and learned friend, who is to address you this day, nor will I detain you long from the pleasure, which his rich and matured production will afford. As Chairman of the Committeee of Arrangements, it devolved upon me to make some introductory remarks, and I have therefore hastily thrown together a few crude and unconnected reflections, which have occurred to me in the midst of absorbing professional duties; and merely regretting that the task had not been committed to abler hands, I proceed to discharge its requirements.

In the year 1650, this fair and beautiful town, (then lying on both sides of the river, and embracing within its limits the present townships of Portland and Chatham,) was little better than a wilderness, inhabited solely by the wild red man, and by beasts of prey, scarcely more savage than the natives who pursued them in the chase. The hills were clothed with dense forests, and the valleys and plains, covered with the rank luxuriance of the native plants and grasses, save here and there a spot under tillage, which glistened and rejoiced with its burden of maize. From no hospitable chimney the smoke ascended up to heaven, or spread its cloud over the landscape. The adventurous sons of the Pilgrims, who travelled hitherward, might have caught sight of the thin wreath of blue vapor, which curled lightly upward from the wigwam of the Sachem, or the council fire of his chiefs. They might have heard from afar off the wild yells and the shrill whoops of the braves, as they engaged in the war dance, meditating, it may be, even then, the destruction of the pale faces, of whose approach they were doubtless aware ; or perhaps, they might have paused in their journey and listened with wondering and not unfearful attention to the wild dirge of the women, mourning the departure of some loved one, in their plaintive and wailing death-song. No white sail gleamed through the trees that skirted the banks of our beautiful river ; and no keel parted its gentle waves ; nought ruffled its surface, save the frail birchen canoe, which danced lightly over its waters, scarce leaving a ripple in its wake. Here and there dusky forms glided about with stealthy and noiseless tread ; and anon came upon the ear the shrill laughter of Indian boys and maidens, engaged in their primitive sports. Such was the state of things at the advent of our forefathers : a few years passed, and then there might be seen by the sides of the Sebethe, an occasional rude hut or log house, with its little clearing, and the more substantial fortress or block-house, which the early settlers invariably built, as a place of refuge from the murderous attacks of their savage neighbors; and now, too, began to appear the fruits of advancing civilization. The forests bowed beneath the vigorous blows of the sturdy axe-men, and the sunlight glanced upon earth that for years had not felt its summer rays; rich fields of waving grain rose in its season; the varied sounds of busy industry were heard, blended with the songs of praise and thanksgiving, which pealed from the lips, aye and the hearts, of our pious forefathers; for they failed not to worship the Being who had led them hither, though their meeting house had to be surrounded by high palisades, and sentries with loaded muskets kept watch and ward at its entrance. In some places, the picture we have sketched was tinted with darker hues; quarrels and conflicts were not wanting, and the terrible war-whoop of the savage sometimes burst forth, startling from their midnight slumbers the early inhabitants, who considered themselves abundantly fortunate to escape with life from their burning dwellings, and find safety and refuge in the fortress. Then followed retaliation, and the helpless women and children of the natives were occasionally involved in the punishment dealt out, unsparingly, by the murderous rifle and musket. Such events, however, were exceedingly rare in the early history of our own place; few, or no feuds existing between our pioneers and their Indian neighbors. But the red race was doomed, and its inevitable destiny was to fade before the white; in vain with desperate courage, they essayed to stem the tide which was slowly, but surely, bearing them down. With all their bravery, their strength, and their cunning, they could not resist the current which swept them away. Here and there a scattered handful obstinately maintained their ground for a brief period, but they too were forced at last to abandon the contest and the field, and their dearly loved hunting grounds passed forever from their possession. The smoke was no more seen floating from their huts; their war-whoop no longer startled the ear; their council fires have long since died out, and their very bones are disturbed from their resting place to make room for the white man's invention. And in our day, as you all know, the strong hold of their most powerful Sachem, is dedicated to the sacred object of receiving the remains of those who have descended from the very pioneers, whose advent that Sachem witnessed. But time rolls on, and now on either bank of the river and at some distance from it, there are scattered about houses of goodly size, at least, if not pleasingly shaped and proportioned; meeting houses and school houses too, occur, as you travel along the beaten paths which at this time traversed the country—and vessels of considerable size are not wanting to add attraction to the river scenery. Everywhere are evident the signs of peace and prosperity. Alas, that they should be so soon interrupted.

Something over a century had passed, when the sound of war is again heard through the land, and the earth trembles beneath the tread of marching columns and lumbering artillery; the fierce rattle of musketry and the heavy booming of cannon in different quarters, announce the impending conflict. It is not now a contest between different races, but brother meets brother in the field of strife, and the blood of hostile kindred and neighbors is mingled upon the plain. Drawn from their quiet homes and peaceful occupations, our ancestors shouldered their muskets, and hastened at the call of their country, to meet and resist that country's oppressors. Bravely they bore themselves in the various battles, and stoutly they endured and went through the hard trials and struggles of the Revolutionary period; and no better soldiers served through those campaigns than the troops of Connecticut. But the war at last is ended, and those brave men return to their homes, and resume their accustomed toil; the sword is exchanged for the plough-share, and the bayonet for the sickle, and again the tide of prosperity sets onward; and gradually but steadily our town increased in extent and population; numerous ships and smaller craft were built at our wharves; manufactories of various kinds were established and put in operation; persons of wealth and distinction here sought a home, and Middletown was known far and wide, as a beautiful and thriving place. But once again the note of preparation is sounded; our former enemy has made new aggressions, and ever ready at the call of duty, our town furnishes its quota of men and means. Many a battle witnessed the good conduct of our townsmen, and Lake Champlain added its crowning glory; for the result of that engagement immortalized the gallant commander, whose name and whose descendants yet live amongst us.

Turn we however from war and its praises. A speedy peace having been wrested from our antagonists, its results are quickly apparent, and once more we are engaged in those pursuits and occupations more congenial to our taste. It is unnecessary for me to dwell upon the period succeeding the war of 1812, as most of those now before me are familiar with its history. I pass rapidly by it, merely remarking that the town remained nearly stationary. During this time, however, was established the Military Academy, which was the nursery of many who have since been distinguished in the different pursuits and occupations of life. It may be proper to allude again in this connection to military matters, for the purpose of reminding you, that our place was, as before, well and ably represented on the fields and waters of Mexico, wherever and whenever there was need of efficient service.

We are brought now in the course of events, to the present point of time, respecting which I design briefly to offer a few observations, which, I trust, will not be deemed out of place on this occasion. Further, I claim your respectful attention, not on account of their own intrinsic excellence or profundity, but because they concern us all, as inhabitants of the place, and consequently participators in its fortunes and reputation. We seem to have reached a stopping place, and I fear, are in some danger of paralysis, even if not threatened with decline. Let us briefly inquire into our condition.

On most accounts we have reason to be proud of our town. Blessed with all the advantages of nature and art; with a fertile soil and salubrious climate, easily accessible by land and water, and delightfully situated, the Sun in his daily circuit shines on no lovelier place than our own. Washed along its eastern border by the 'long' and beautiful river, and embraced on the west by a chain of picturesque hills; serried in every direction by rivulets, that afford an abundance of manufacturing power; from every valley, and from almost every hill side there goes up unceasingly the sound of industry and activity. The seat of an excellent Literary Institution; abundantly provided with Schools and Churches; the earth in most places yielding a rich increase; the very rocks furnishing a source of wealth,—what can we want more, to fill our cup with blessings? Our townsmen are heard of and known in all quarters of the globe; they may be found in the golden mountains of

California, and in the frozen seas of the Arctic Circle; they have visited the Celestial Empire, and sipped their tea in its native gardens. In benighted Africa you will find them, engaged in their labors of love and benevolence; amid the ruins of Central America they have left their traces; they have sailed up the Nile, and stood upon the top of the Pyramids; and it is told, though the account may be somewhat apochryphal, that they have opened a house of refreshment on the track through the Great Desert! In short, wherever the stars and the stripes have been unfolded to the breeze, there have some of our adventurous brethren been present, to salute the flag. They have graced the saloons of the noble and the wealthy in other lands, and have given high character to the national Councils of our own. The products of their talents, ingenuity and industry, have found their way wherever civilization has entered; and the very heathen have had reason to bless the existence of our people. Do we lack any thing, then, it may be asked, which would alike contribute to our happiness, and advance our prosperity? Bear with me a moment, while I enumerate a few requisites, yet wanting, to perfect the character of our town. And first, we want more public spirit; that feeling, which induces individuals to sacrifice some merely personal or local interest, for the promotion of the general good. More liberality of sentiment, and action too, which after all is the true secret of advancement. More enthusiasm, more union and harmony, on all matters of public interest and welfare. We want, moreover, to get rid of various little local and sectional jealousies, which detract from our character, and place obstacles in the way of our improvement. We want a more lively faith in the indisputable fact, that what is for the benefit of one portion or class of our citizens, extends its beneficial influence throughout the whole community. We want also, somewhat more of reverence for age and antiquity. One of the great characteristics of the present generation is a fondness for novelty, and unquestionably this is often a useful stimulus; but in grasping after and adopting everything that is new, let us not on that account, affect to despise everything that is old. Hundreds of years ago, the Hebrew sage asserted that there was nothing new under the sun; and if we are not disposed to receive this as a literal verity, we must nevertheless acknowledge, that human affairs move very much in circles; what, years ago, was at the bottom of the wheel and almost forgotten, again comes to the top, and with a new dress and a different name, is eagerly run after as something entirely new. Now, one great effect of such celebrations as the present, is to draw off the mind from a too eager pursuit of novelty, and by carrying us back a century or two, to make us sensible of the fact, that every thing before and around us, is not our own work, and due to our own exertions, and did not all at once start into perfection, but was the slow growth of ages, and only attained after much toil and suffering. Let us not speak lightly then, but rather with reverence and respect of our forefathers; let us remember how much they had to encounter, upon their entrance into this now highly favored place; and let the contemplation of its past history diminish our self-complacency, while it enlarges our views, and stimulates us to greater and more united exertions.

There are many other advantages arising from these celebrations, which I will barely allude to. They encourage a love of home: by increasing its attraction, they draw back the wanderer to his birth-place, and quiet in a measure that restless spirit of change, which is somewhat too striking a feature of the New England character. They revive old and pleasing associations, and brighten the chain of past friendships, which time's rust had well nigh severed. They foster a spirit of enquiry and investigation; they add to our stores of knowledge, by leading to the collection of historical facts, many of them perhaps just on the point of being lost forever; they serve as connecting links between different ages and periods, and as landmarks, by which future generations can trace back their progress from infancy to maturity.

They change the current of our feelings, running perhaps too strongly upon the perishable things of earth—they elevate the mind above the mere present, and carry the thoughts far forward beyond its fleeting limits; for in the faithful mirror of the past, we see, as it were, ourselves projected into the future, and can infer from the reflection there presented, the estimation in which coming ages will hold the now existing race. They thus serve as a medium of comparison, by which we should not only learn to judge, but also to improve ourselves; and the result of this voluntary self-examination, when carefully and candidly instituted, must diminish our self-esteem and expand our charity.

What can be more delightful, what more beneficial, than the re-unions effected by such occasions, as that which has this day brought us together!

Every county, nay, every town in New England, may be considered as a nursery, wherein are reared those individuals, whose genius, talents, and virtues, have so strongly impressed their characteristics upon the whole American people. Acquiring the rudiments of education in the district schools of their native places; improving their minds, and their powers, by the steady, but varied use of every faculty; with habits of industry and keen observation, and great facility of adapting themselves to almost any situation and circumstances, in which they may be placed, they leave the paternal roof, and spread themselves over the length and breadth of the country, in search of a wider field for the exercise of their talents, or in the hope of more speedily acquiring the means of indulging their tastes and fancies. You will find them everywhere; engaged in every variety of occupation, and filling every kind and degree of private and official station.

They teach our schools—they edit our papers—they navigate our ships—they extend our commerce abroad, and our trade at home—they regulate our time—and they make our laws. In the workshop, the counting house, or the legislative hall, they are equally at home. From them chiefly, are recruited the ranks of the various professions; and when you hear of any one in either of them, who has acheived a lofty and commanding reputation, or who has distinguished himself by any particular excellence, you may be almost certain, *that* man is a Yankee.

The course of time rolls on, and year after year adds to the number of expatriated New Englanders. Think you, that during all this time, their hearts have not yearned, again to behold their birth places, and once more to revisit the scenes of their childhood and early associations? Think you, they do not often in fancy, play over their youthful sports upon their native village green, and tread again the well-remembered roads and paths, through which their youthful feet so often strayed? Think you they do not recall to mind their former playmates and associates, and ardently long for some occasion, which should revive those friendships, and restore those early days? Aye, do they: and right gladly and promptly do they obey the summons, and embrace the opportunity, which such a celebration as the present furnishes them. Joyfully they hasten to the old home, and heartily they greet their early companions; and through many a year afterwards, will memory love to linger upon this happy meeting; and in many an hour hereafter, amid the cares of business, the whirl of pleasure, or in the intervals of engrossing occupations, will such a scene, and such an occasion come back to the mind, soothing its perplexities, alleviating its sorrows, and refining its enjoyments. Like an oasis in the desert, will it serve not only for present delight, but as a perpetual theme for grateful recollection; and not until the shades of life's evening gather around them, and the palsying hand of decay obscures their failing faculties, will they cease to remember, or be thankful for, the privilege which you have this day enjoyed.

Few, or none of those now before me, it may safely be said, will ever witness the return of another Centennial Anniversary; but a hundred years hence, your children, and your children's children will celebrate it, doubtless, on a scale of magnificence, of which, we who are here, can now form no conception. Instead of the hundreds, who have this day assembled together, to do honor to the occasion, there will be thousands and tens of thousands, gathered within some vast and spacious edifice, to listen to the history of their forefathers' advent. The now quiet little place which is our residence, will then, perhaps, be transformed into an extensive and busy city, and from its lofty mansions and comfortable dwellings, will pour out a countless multitude, all animated with the zeal and spirit which such an occasion should call forth. From all quarters of this wide-spread and mighty continent, will be collected the descendants of those now on the stage, and those who have preceeded them. From the South and the West, aye, even from the very borders of the Pacific Ocean, it may be, will the iron horse speed them to the land where their first breath was drawn. And here, where we are now making this humble endeavor to cherish and preserve the memory of our simple hearted, but earnest and persevering ancestors, and to perpetuate the record of their trials, and struggles, and sufferings, will another generation perform the same pious and grateful duty for us. Then, when we are "sleeping that sleep which knows no waking;" when our bones shall have mouldered into dust, and our ashes lie mingled with those of our predecessors; when our very names shall be old; then, I say, will those, our descendants, turn with pride and gratitude, to the printed record of this day's proceedings, and rejoice that this, our feeble attempt at the commemoration of Middletown's nativity, was not suffered utterly to fail; that the facts, which, for this occasion have been gathered, and garnered up with so much care and patient research, were rescued from the obscurity which was fast enshrouding them, and snatched from an oblivion, which would, ere long, have been irretrievable.

HISTORICAL ADDRESS;

DELIVERED AT THE

SECOND CENTENNIAL ANNIVERSARY

IN THE

CITY OF MIDDLETOWN, CONN.,

November 13, 1850,

BY DAVID D. FIELD.

HAD the author of the following Address, when requested to deliver it, foreseen the sufferings before him from a long and distressing rheumatic affection, prudence would have prevented the undertaking; and after it was delivered, and a copy requested for publication, all attempts to prepare one with so many and long notes as were deemed desirable to accompany it. His error was, that he flattered himself with the hope of a speedy recovery, and so has occasioned disappointment and long delay. But now that the work is about to be put to press, he feels it a privilege to express his gratitude to God, for restoring him, in a good degree, to health; to the Committee, and his numerous friends in Middletown and vicinity, for their patient waiting, and help, in many instances, in furnishing him with facts. Should the work contribute to help them and their children to keep in remembrance the privations and hardships, the zeal and piety of their ancestors, and stimulate them to the imitation of their Christian virtues, it will be a rich reward.

D. D. F.

December, 1851.

ADDRESS.

The English Colonists who removed, in 1636, from the vicinity of Boston to the townships of Wethersfield, Hartford and Windsor, were invited to these places by the Indian inhabitants, from the expectation that their settlement among them, would be a protection from the Mohawks, whose very name was a terror to them on the one hand, and from the Pequots, who were their more immediate dread on the other. How well founded was their expectation, is attested by the wisdom with which the Pequot war was soon undertaken, and the valor and success with which it was prosecuted. The destruction of these malicious and dangerous enemies was not effected fully by the ruin of the Mystic fort, nor by the fight immediately after, with Sassacus and his men, as the victors were marching to their vessels in Pequot harbor. These were sufficient to move the Pequots at the Fort of Sassacus, to burn their wigwams and disperse in rambling parties; a dispersion, which did not wholly secure them; for the General Court appointed Capt. Mason, and furnished him with men to prosecute the war: some forces were sent from Massachusetts for this purpose; and Indians, who had been inimical to the Pequots, willingly came forward and assisted in destroying them. One of their parties was taken by the Massachusetts troops, united with some of the Narraganset Indians. Another party crossed Connecticut river, and some English scouts had a skirmish with them on a hill in Saybrook, whence they fled into a neighboring swamp, from which the hill is called Pequot Hill, and the swamp Pequot Swamp, to this day. Their course was near the Sound. A few of them were pursued by some English soldiers and by some Mohegans, down the eastern shore of the harbor west of Guilford Borough. They swam across the harbor, but were taken as they ascended the opposite bank. Among these was a Sachem, whom Uncas shot with an arrow. He cut off his head, and put it in the fork of an oak, where the skull remained many years. From this transaction the harbor has ever since been called Sachem's Head. The fugitives generally, proceeded to a large swamp in Fairfield, whither they were pursued and surrounded; about 20 were killed and 180 taken prisoners. By these various attacks and losses, the destruction of the Pequots as a tribe was completed, though numbers escaped and fled to the Mohawks. It was probably well for the Colonists that these did escape, for their melancholy and forlorn condition told that their tribe was no more. It told also, what bold and desperate fighters those Englishmen were, who had come to Connecticut, and how hazardous it would be for the Mohawks to contend with them, and those whom they had undertaken to protect.

The destruction of the Pequot tribe was of the greatest importance to the settlement at Saybrook, and to the other settlements on Connecticut river. It struck a general terror into the Indians in Connecticut, and beyond it, and prevented their rising in great numbers against the English, for nearly forty years. It opened fine sites for the Colonists on the Sound; at Guilford, Branford, New Haven, Milford, Stratford and Fairfield; sites which were speedily occupied.

Between the Pequot war and the war of King Philip, settlements in New England were multiplied, and acquired strength for the exigences of this long and horrid contest, in which the Connecticut people, by reason of the union of New England Colonies had to bear their part in furnishing men and means; a union, which, in addition to the benefits to the colonies themselves for the time being, may have suggested the importance of the union of thirteen colonies a century afterward. But though they bore their part, they retained the friendship of the Connecticut Indians, and some of them opposed the course of Philip.*

But why was not Mattabesett† at once settled after the Pequot war? Those who passed down the river saw the lands from the banks. But along these were no such wide alluvial grounds as there were further up the river, nor such flat and clearly arable lands, specially important at the time, as appeared in some places on the Sound. For a mile or more immediately north of the present city, the lands seemed to be too low and wet to be drained and converted, even into meadows; too much covered and entangled by thickets to be reclaimed by persons in the circumstances of the colonists. They were regarded doubtless as a dead swamp, as the low lands were at the Nooks in the Upper Houses. The beauty and richness which strike the eye in the great amphitheatre before us did not appear. The river itself and its graceful turn eastward, were obscured by immense trees, which had been striking their roots into the banks for ages, and stretching out their branches till they drooped in the stream. The cliffs of the Portland stone

* Trumbull, vol. 1., pp. 368, 9.

† The Indian name for Middletown.

also stood shelving and frowning over it. Industry and art were needed to remove the primeval forests and let in the rays of the sun upon the water and the land, that this glorious scenery might be revealed. Numerous sections of good lands west, and back from the river, had not then been examined, probably by any English eye.

Another cause concurred to prevent an early settlement. A large Indian tribe existed here, who were more than suspected of being enemies to the English. Their great sachem, Sowheag, had his castle on the high ground, back from the river, in the north part of the city, and was able thence to call around him many warriors, whose wigwams stood thick on both sides of the Connecticut, at points particularly desirable for settlements. His authority spread over a large territory, over the Piquaug or Wethersfield Indians, over a clan on the north-western branch of the Little River in Berlin, if he had not some right and sway among the Farmington Indians.* In April 1647, some of his Indians had conducted and aided the Pequots in the excursion which they made into Wethersfield, where they killed six men and three women, and took two maids captive. Sowheag entertained the murderers and treated the people of Wethersfield in a haughty and insulting manner. It seems that they had previously offered him some provocation.

* In the His. Discourse, by Rev. Noah Porter, jr., now Professor of Moral Philosophy in Yale College, delivered at Farmington in 1840, after stating how that large township was obtained from the Indians, and how the title was confirmed by two successive agreements, the first in 1650, and the second in 1673, he observes, that "in 1651 Massacope gives a quitclaim deed of all this land, that he was probably a Mattabesett Indian, and with his son signs the agreement for valuable considerations and gratification at the time of sale." Not satisfied with the "limits as specified in the deed, he went out and for himself examined and marked the boundaries."

The General Court were therefore disposed to forgive him, and appointed a committee to compromise all difficulties. But he wholly refused to give up the murderers, even after the destruction of the Pequot tribe, and continued his outrages against the English. The Court therefore, in August, 1639, determined to send one hundred men there to take the delinquents by force. They notified their friends at New Haven of their determination, both that they might receive their approbation in an undertaking of such general concern, and that they might make the necessary arrangements for defending themselves. Governor Eaton and his council viewed it important the murderers should be brought to punishment; but in existing circumstances deemed the measures proposed inexpedient, and dissuaded the Connecticut Colony from executing their purpose. In such circumstances, it is no wonder that a few English emigrants were unwilling at once to come and settle near Sowheag and his warriors, who had all the lurking places for mischief many miles around, especially as those who wished to settle in Connecticut could find good lands among the planters above on the river, or in the settlements which had sprung up on the Sound.

A settlement however, was contemplated in Mattabesett, before the session of the General Court in October, 1646; probably some months before, for on the 30th of October in that year, the General Court appointed a Mr. Phelps to join a Committee for the planting of Mattabesett. The Committee already existed. What the enlarged Committee did for the accomplishment of the object; how soon and thoroughly they examined the grounds, fixed on sites for the beginning of settlements, and had the names of persons enrolled, who had engaged and were preparing to come and put up dwellings, we are not expressly informed. They do not appear to have made rapid progress, for on the 20th of March, 1649–50, (1650 according to our mode of dating,) Samuel Smith, sen., of Wethersfield, was appointed a member of the Committee in the place of one that would not act. This year the settlement is understood to have been commenced, but by how many precisely, and in what part of the year we are not informed, for a few of the first pages of the Town Records are lost, and others are nearly obliterated. Few came at first, but a considerable number before the close of the next year, for on the 11th of September, 1651, the General Court "ordered that Mattabesett should be a town," and that the inhabitants should make choice of one of their number to take the oath of Constable. This year too, the town was ordered to be rated. In the Autumn "of 1652 the town was represented in the General Court, and in November, 1653, the General Court further approved that the name of the plantation, commonly called Mattabeseck, should for time to come, be called Middletown." The number of taxable persons in 1654, was thirty one. It has been suggested, that the name of Middletown was given to the township, because it lay between the towns up the river and Saybrook at its mouth; but it is far more probable that it was taken from some town in England, for which the settlers had a particular regard.

Before the commencement of the settlement, Sowheag had given to Mr. Haynes, Governor of Connecticut a great part of the township, for which a consideration was given in return. But the Indian title was not wholly extinguished until about twelve years after. Then Sowheag having probably deceased, or become imbecile, certain chiefs, knowing what he had done, for a further and full consideration, gave to Samuel Wyllys and others, acting in behalf of the town, all the land between Wethersfield, (then including Glastenbury,) and Haddam," to run from the great river the whole breadth east, six miles, and from the great river west as far as the General Court of Connecticut had granted the bounds should extend;" a distance which will be noticed as we proceed; excepting a tract on the west side of the river, previously laid out to Sawsean to remain his forever, and three hundred acres reserved for the heirs of Sowheag and Mattabesett Indians to be laid out on the east side.*

When Indians sold lands, they were in the habit of reserving, besides the exclusive right to small definite tracts, the right of hunting and fishing where they pleased, and of cutting saplings for their simple articles of manufacture, so that the lands were nearly of as much value to them after they were sold as before, until the Colonists made very considerable advances in clearing and cultivation. Though such reservation is not mentioned in the deed of the Indians to Mr. Wyllys and others, the right was probably considered as remaining.

The reservation on the west side of the river was in the neighborhood called Newfield, and up that street the Indians had a cemetery previously to the settlement of the English among them, with rude monuments placed over their dead; on them were drawn such devices as corresponded with their superstitions, and such as they were able to prepare with their rude instruments. Some of these remained on the ground, or in a stone wall fencing it, within the memory of a few persons now living. The Aborigines were numerous about the north-west part of the city, long after the English settlements began.

The Little River, where the bridge crosses it from the city to Newfield, was the head of navigation for their

* Note A.

water craft, as they returned from trips up and down the Connecticut, loaded with game, peltries and fish. They held lands there until 1713.

The reservation east of the river, was laid out partly on Indian Hill, and partly a little eastward of the first Congregational Church, built in what is now Portland.—This was held by them until 1767, when having dwindled to a small number, they sold their right and united with the Farmington Indians.

At Indian Hill was a famous grave-yard, where in some instances, monuments were erected over the graves with inscriptions after the English manner. The early chiefs and principal men were doubtless buried on the west side of the river. But after the settlement of the remnant of the tribe in Portland, some in whose veins ran a portion of noble blood, were doubtless buried at Indian Hill.*

Here as elsewhere, they buried their dead sometimes in a sitting posture; and believing that those whom they regarded as good men, would have wants and enjoyments in a future world corresponding with those possessed here, they buried with them for their gratification on their way to eternity, or their enjoyment after their arrival there, food, utensils, arms, ornaments and wampum.†

---

* The Mohegans it is understood used to visit the Mattabesetts, at least after the collection of the remnant of the tribe in Portland. There is a tradition that one of the Mohegans, supposed to be a descendant of the great Uncas, or Onckous, visited them and died among them of the small pox. A grave stone which once stood on Indian Hill, not long since found, is confirmatory of the tradition; for on this it is written: "Here lies the body of John Onckous, who died Aug. the 30, 1722, aged 26 years.

† As specimens of this, the contents of three graves opened in the Spring of 1808, may be mentioned—one of a man, and two of children. The man was placed sitting, wrapped in a blanket, (which was not entirely consumed, but upon exposure to the air became as burnt straw); in his

Besides the cemeteries just mentioned, evidences of the burial of the natives have been found on the left bank of Taylor's Creek, as it enters the Connecticut. Their bones have also been found recently, west of the river in excavations made for the Branch Railroad from the city.

The Indians east of the river were sometimes called Wongonks or Wongums, but the reservation being for the heirs of Sowheag and Mattabesett Indians, those are only other names for the same tribe, or a remnant of it. A class also that inhabited or frequented the region about Pokatapaug Pond in East Hampton, and had a favorite place of rendesvous on the principal island which the pond incloses, were in all probability Mattabesetts. The island * is sometimes said to have been owned by an In-

---

lap were two small brass kettles, probably filled with soup or succotash at the time of burial, one of which had sunk down into the other, in which were a spoon, knife, phial, and pipe. His arm was extended round the kettles, and where the flesh came in contact with the brass, from the elbow to the wrist, the flesh was preserved. In the hand of one of the children was found a brass cup of the size of a tea cup, and here again the flesh on the fingers was preserved, where they came against the brass. Around the wrist was wampum strung on deer skin, and near by, beads supposed to have been placed about the neck. In the grave of the other child was a copper box containing wampum.

The Indians like other men, wished to live on earth as long as they could, believing as they did in a future state; and to cure a cold and many other complaints, they used to stand on a hot stone rolled into a hole dug in the earth, until they were brought into a profuse sweat, and then plunged into water A lot at Indian Hill is called Hot House lot, because it had one of these holes in it.

* When the water is high, it flows over the middle of this Island and makes it two islands It contains about nine acres, though it has been reported as much less. On the western side are steps visible when the water is low, supposed to have been laid there by the Natives, for their convenience in visiting it. That they were much about the pond is evi-

dian whose name was Tarramuggus, and the name of such an Indian is appended as a witness to the deed of which we have spoken. He may have been the principal man of the class; but the deed signed by others, conveyed to the English this and all their ponds in Middletown.

In closing these remarks about the Indians, it is but simple justice to add, that bad as Sowheag and his men were thought to be for a time, it is not known that they were unusually troublesome to the English after the settlement commenced. But they are gone from this region, long since extinct as a tribe, and who knoweth that their blood runs in the veins of any living creature.

And now the question arises, who were the first colonists? and how did the settlement proceed?

In reply to the first question, we are only able to say with certainty, such being the defects of the records, who were among the early settlers, rather than who were certainly the very first. The earliest remaining entry on the town books, is dated Feb. 2, 1652; and that is a vote for building a meeting house. There were people enough before, to constitute a little assembly for the worship of God, and when neither the season nor the weather drove them to one of their temporary dwellings or shantees, the shade of that vast elm which had stood for ages unknown, at the entrance of the old grave yard, was their temple. Thus saith tradition.

The vote for building a meeting-house was speedily executed. The edifice was only twenty feet square, ten from sill to plate, and was enclosed with palisades. It stood on the open green, (which may have been larger

---

dent from the relics of their implements often found on the shores. It is a fine sheet of water, which white people love to visit in summer, both for the pleasure of sailing and fishing.

than now,) a little west or north-west of the first English grave yard. This sufficed the people eighteen years; eight after the second grant of land from the Indians.

From this house some important surveys were made, for in March, 1663, the General Court "granted that the bounds of Middletown be extended to *four* miles to the south from the meeting-house, *five* miles from the said house westward, and *three* miles from the great river eastward." Afterwards the territory was extended eastward three miles more. By this grant we are not to understand, however, that the township through its whole length from Wethersfield [the part of it now Rocky Hill] southward, was to be uniformly five miles in breadth west of the Connecticut, and six miles east. The western boundary is a north and south line; so that by this course, and the great bend in the river eastward, the breadth some part of the distance below the aforesaid starting point, expands to about ten miles. The breadth directly opposite, across the river, is much more than six miles, though less from Middle Haddam Landing, but more than six on an average.

In January, 1659, the General Court granted to Middletown, Wethersfield and Farmington, all the vacant lands between their bounds and the bounds of Wallingford, (then including Meriden and Cheshire,) for the purpose of making a new plantation. This grant covers the tract generally now constituting Berlin, to which a small section from the north-west corner of Middletown has been annexed.

As for the early settlers, John Hall, William Cornwall, William Smith, Samuel Stocking, Robert Webster, and Thomas Wetmore, were settlers in 1652, and settlers probably, some or all of them from the beginning.—Thomas Allen, Andrew Warner, Nathaniel Bacon, William Markum, Nathaniel Brown, George Hubbard, Henry Cole, Giles Hamlin, George Graves, William and Daniel Harris, Thomas Miller, and a man by the name of Martin, supposed to be John Martin, were settlers early in 1654, and probably earlier; they may have been here as early as the settlers first named. John Savage, Samuel Stow, Robert Warner, John Wilcox, William Bloomfield, Matthias Treat and Nathaniel White, were early settlers; and so were persons by the name of Cheney, Clements, Bow, Eggleston, Lucas, Tappin or Tapping, Turner and some others.

Most of the very early inhabitants settled in or near the city. The largest collection was about the Meeting-House Yard, and on the northern end of Main street, above Washington street. These were Thomas Allen, William Smith, Andrew Warner, Nathaniel Bacon, William Markham, Nathaniel Brown, Samuel Stow, George Hubbard, Thomas Wetmore and John Hall. Others settled further south on Main street, several about the southern end of it. With these, new colonists were intermingled from time to time.

A part of the early inhabitants settled in the Upper Houses, and almost all these erected their dwellings in the lower part of the village, on the street, midway between Middlesex Turnpike and the river. These were Nathaniel White, Samuel Stocking, George Graves, Robert Webster, Joseph Smith, Daniel Harris, John Martin, John Savage, Thomas Ranney, David Sage, and John Kirby. Between the upper and lower settlements intercourse was maintained by a ferry across Little River.

In 1670 there were only fifty-two house-holders in the town, and but thirty-five surnames, those of the same surnames being generally relatives. These house-holders had come here at different periods, but it was agreed that all should be considered as proprietors; and as very many of the present inhabitants have descended from them, and not a few who retain their surnames, it may be well to give here the entire catalogue. This is as follows: Thomas and Obadiah Allen, Nathaniel Bacon, William Briggs, Alexander Bow, William Cheney, Jasper Clements, Henry Cole, Samuel and Nathaniel Collins, William, John and Samuel Cornwall, and William Cornwall, jr., George Durant, Samuel Eggleston, Edward Porter, John, Richard and Samuel Hall, and John Hall, jr., Giles Hamlin, William and Daniel Harris, George, Joseph, Daniel and Thomas Hubbard, John Hurlburt, Isaac Johnson, John Kirby, Isaac Lane, William Lucas, Anthony Martin, Thomas Miller, Thomas Ranney, David Sage, John Savage, Samuel Stocking, Samuel, Thomas and John Stow, James Tappin, Edward Turner, John and William Ward, Andrew, Robert, and John Warner, Thomas Wetmore, Nathaniel White, and John Wilcox.

It will be perceived that in this catalogue, some early settlers who have been mentioned, do not appear. This is true of William Bloomfield, Nathaniel Brown, George Graves, William Markum, John Martin, William Smith, Joseph Smith, Matthias Treat, and Robert Webster. These either removed from the town or died before 1670. With two or three exceptions, the fifty-two house-holders were of English extraction. They came hither directly from the British Isle, from towns in the east part of Massachusetts, or from earlier settled towns in Connecticut.*

After 1670 the population of the town gradually in-

* Note B.

creased, and on the 11th of November, 1679, "the town by vote, agreed to build a new meeting-house, thirty-two feet square, and fifteen feet between joints"; and seems to have gone forward the subsequent winter, and made preparations for fulfilling their agreement; but in the meanwhile the people in the Upper and Lower Houses, entertained different views as to the site on which it should be raised. In May 1680, however, they mutually condescended for peace' sake, and jointly agreed to set it on ground which they minutely described. It was south of the first meeting-house, on Main street, on the east side —but standing in the street—and about opposite what is now Liberty Street. In this all the inhabitants worshipped at least twenty-three years, and the greater part of them more than thirty-five.

By the time this was opened for religious worship, Wm. Roberts and John Cotton became inhabitants. Solomon Atkins, Maybe Barnes, Samuel Bidwell, Daniel Markham, Job Payne, William Southmayd, and Comfort Starr, not far from this time, became inhabitants also; others settled here at different times. Among those who became settlers before the close of the 17th century, were Thomas Andrews, James Bennet, Jonathan Gilbert, Edward Higbee, Edward Shepherd, and William Sumner, John Gill, Richard Goodale, John Stancliff, John Clarke, Joseph Rockwell, John Thompson, George Phillips, Abraham Bartlet, Daniel Prior, and Benjamin Hands, though they may have come in an order varying much from that in which their names are given. These, with the descendants of earlier settlers, spread themselves extensively over the limits of the Lower and Upper Houses.

The inhabitants of the Upper Houses became so numerous, that in January, 1703, "the town agreed they might settle a minister and build a meeting-house, provided they settled a minister within six, or at most twelve months from that time." The Legislature incorporated them as a parish in May following.

The settlement of Middlefield was begun about 1700, and of Westfield about 1720, the settlers being mostly from the two first parishes. The former was incorporated in October 1744, and the latter in May 1766.

Though forty rights of land were laid out to the proprietors on the east side of the river in 1675, (the remaining twelve being laid out on the west side, in the neighborhood called Maromas;) though some of these rights covered land of a fine quality, on which improvements were soon made; though the Wongonk meadows early attracted the attention of the people, both in the Lower and in the Upper Houses, only two families are known to have lived on the east side of the river before 1700. Another settler was there about 1703, and there were nine or ten settlers in 1710. In May, 1714, thirty-one persons petitioned for parish privileges most of whom may have been heads of families. From their names it is apparent many of them were from the west side of the river. The petition was granted and the parish was named East Middletown.

The settlement in Middle Haddam was commenced about 1710, but had a slow growth. In October 1748, twenty-six persons, with twelve from Haddam Neck, a part of Haddam, petitioned for incorporation as a parish and their desires were gratified in May 1749. A smaller proportion of the settlers here were from the west side of the river than in East Middletown.

The three miles granted to Middletown in 1683, constitute the parish of East Hampton, and a small section attached to Westchester, a parish in the town of Colchester. A long time after this was granted the question arose how it should be divided among the inhabitants; the proprietors of the town, or their representatives, claiming it wholly, while others insisted upon a share of it as it was given to the town after their fathers became settlers. At length this friendly compromise was adopted, that it should be divided to the proprietors of the town according to their original list, and the list of 1714 united, and to others according to the latter list only.

On this tract no settlement was made until 1743, when thirty-two persons came into the place, many of whom were doubtless heads of families. They were drawn thither particularly by the excellent mill-seat at the outlet of Pocotopogue Pond, where a forge was established. The people were formed into a separate parish in May 1746.

Thus the population spread, and five entire local parishes were formed in the township, and most of a sixth before 1750. Westfield, as already stated, was incorporated some years later.

All these were Congregational parishes; and before 1750 a Church was organized by inhabitants of the first parish of Middletown and Westfield, called a "Strict Congregational Church," which *as such*, years since ceased to exist.

Ship building had become a great business in East Middletown, and had begun to flourish at the landing in Middle Haddam before the incorporation of these parishes, in connection with East Hampton, as a town, in October 1767. The name of Chatham was therefore given to it, in allusion to Chatham in England, by reason of the extent and importance of this branch of industry and enterprise. East Middletown became the first parish of Chatham. But in 1841 when this parish had increased so much in population and business, that it was formed into a separate town, it was necessary it should have a new name. Ship building had not ceased, but the quarrying business had become the more important concern. The new town therefore was called Portland from Portland in England, whence free stone in immense quantities is transported to London and other parts of that country, as the free stone from our Portland is carried to New York and other cities and towns in the United States. And who knows but Middle Haddam landing may so resume ship building and carry it on, that the name of Chatham will be very appropriate hereafter. The site and population of the village favor the suggestion, and a few enterprising spirits may carry it into execution. Should the manufacturing enterprise of East Hampton cast big guns on the site of the old "Iron Works," this will render the name still more appropriate.

A company are now again zealously working the "Cobalt Mine." The probable mineral riches of the hill in which this is found, excited the attention of the celebrated and philosophical John Winthrop, Governor of Connecticut, before there were any settlements in Chatham, and the story was that precious discoveries were made. It may have engaged the attention of his son, John Fitz Winthrop, afterwards Governor. Several companies and individuals at different times have collected quantities of the ore, and sent it to foreign countries. The present company have gone further, and made preparation for extracting its contents, and done so to a limited extent. Should operations prosper here, as it is hoped they will ere long, the Mine will augment the business of the landing, and increase the population of the town.

Reference has just been made to the increase of inhabitants in Portland. The United States census now being taken, shows a very considerable increase of population in this place for the last thirty years, and also in the city of Middletown; but as a general thing the increase of population in all the six parishes of which we have been speaking has been slow. The population of what is now Middletown, Portland and Chatham in 1756 was five thousand six hundred and sixty-four; in 1820, sixty-four years afterwards, nine thousand six hundred thirty-six; it is now, thirteen thousand two hundred and twenty-one.* Why is it not twice and thrice this number? The descendants of some of the early settlers, and in truth of some of the later settlers, are now very numerous. The general reason is, the temptations to emigrate have been so many. At first families went off from time to time to the newer settlements in Connecticut where lands were cheaper, to Western Massachusetts, to Vermont, where one of the towns is called Middletown after this town, because some of the settlers went from this place, and to the borders of New York. They then went to Central New York, whither Hugh White, a native of the Upper Houses, led the way. He has drawn fame after him, because he was the first American who ventured beyond the German Flats, to the region of the Oneidas, soon after the Revolution, in the Spring of 1784. The town called Whitestown, in honor of him, at first had jurisdiction over all the western portions of the Empire State, bordered south and south-west by Pennsylvania, and thence by Lake Erie, Niagara river and Ontario. At Mr. White's death, in 1812, the ter-

* In Middletown there are eight thousand seven hundred and ninety-one inhabitants, in the city four thousand two hundred and fifteen, in other parts four thousand five hundred and seventy-six; in Portland two thousand nine hundred and five, Chatham one thousand five hundred and twenty-five.

ritory had nearly three hundred thousand souls and has many hundred thousand more souls at the present time. It is a territory intersected by canals and railroads, contains cities, large villages and charming townships, churches, colleges, academies and schools and great Lake ports, from which numerous steamers traverse our inland seas. How many think you, from Middletown, Portland and Chatham are now dwelling within the first limits of Whitestown? An honored native of this town,* was in the company that settled Marietta, the first town settled by the English in Ohio. A native of this place also,† was commissary in the first surveying company that went to the Reserve in the same State, and landed at Coneaut Creek. The large rude log building, which they erected on the east shore of the stream, and which served both as a store-house for their provisions, and a dwelling for their families was called "Stow Castle." A town also in Summit county bears the surname of the same individual. How many think you from the different parts of the ancient town of Middletown, are now dwelling in the great State of Ohio? And how many in the great West beyond, which has seemed to be receding and spreading as settlements have advanced towards it? Your kindred and friends are scattered in all directions through the country.

The character of the early settlers of Middletown may be given in few words. It is not pretended they were a perfect community. They had their faults as other early settlers of New England. But their faults were not peculiar to themselves; they pertained to the

---

* Col. Meigs.

† Joshua Stow, Esq.

age in which they lived, and are susceptible of much palliation from the circumstances in which they were placed. This admitted, they were as a body, a very religious people, possessed of much practical knowledge, not derived altogether from experience and observation, but also from reading and intercourse with literary and well informed men; friends of liberty, constitutional liberty, regulated by righteous laws.

They were a very religious people. All attended public worship. Before they had a meeting-house, they worshiped God under the boughs of a tree, and in less than two years they built them a Sanctuary, and eighteen years after, another. These were humble structures it is true; but they were grateful for the accommodations they afforded. They secured regularly the services of a minister of the gospel. Not long after the settlement commenced, the people employed Mr. Samuel Stow, a native of Concord, Mass., and graduate of Harvard College as a candidate for the ministry. He preached to them a number of years. Mr. Nathaniel Collins succeeded him as a candidate, and was ordained the first pastor Nov. 4th, 1668. At this time the church was organized, consisting of ten male members, including himself, a nucleus around which others were gathered.

In the early settlements of Connecticut, people were assembled for public worship by the beat of a drum, and the place was guarded by armed men, as a security from attacks by the Indians. The smallest guard allowed by law consisted of eight soldiers with a sergeant, and this was the number on guard here for a time. The beat of the drum was necessary to collect the soldiers, and it collected also the congregation. Mr. Giles Hamlin gave a drum to the town and to the train bands, and never did a chime of bells sound sweeter. The people did not need it, that they might know that the Sabbath had come. It was on their minds through the week, and before the sun sunk in the west on Saturday, wordly concerns were laid aside that their minds might be free to keep the day in a holy manner. But this told them when the time arrived to start for the sanctuary; and while there was danger from the Indians, when they might go with safety. A drum was used in the Upper Houses more than sixty years after the settlement began.

The people were mindful of the great duty of living in peace. This is apparent from their plans and measures, when difficulties were rising, to have them adjusted. When different views were entertained by the people of the Upper and Lower Houses about a site for the second Meeting-house, for "peace sake" they condescended to each other, and agreed upon a place for setting it. When the question arose how the lands granted to the town in 1683 should be divided among earlier and later settlers, the matter was arranged by concession. Another fact illustrates this characteristic in regard to the inhabitants of the first society. After the people in Upper and East Middletown had become distinct parishes, they undertook to build a new Meeting-house, much larger than either of the houses which had previously existed within their limits. Different portions of the inhabitants wished for its location at the north, west and east corners of the great square, lying between Main and High streets; but lest their preferences should lead to abiding alienation, they agreed the point should be decided by lot. But as there were four corners to the square, it was suggested it would be well to put them all to the solemn trial. This was done and the south corner was drawn, which none had really desired. But as the lot was considered as expressing the divine will, the people went forward and built there, and there they worshipped more than eighty years.

The original mode of singing among the Puritans was Congregational, and the psalms were lined. But into this house a choir was introduced. It was large and admirably trained. The elder President Adams, who attended worship here in 1771, says of the singing: "I heard the finest singing that I ever heard in my life: the front and side galleries were crowded with rows of lads and lasses, who performed all their parts in the utmost perfection—a row of women all standing up and playing their parts with perfect skill and judgment, added a sweetness and sprightliness to the whole, which absolutely charmed me."

The settlers possessed much practical knowledge, the result of observation and reading, and intercourse with the wise and good. The early clergy were superior men, men of talents and learning, and the magistrates and public men were well informed. The people themselves were able to read; most of the males at least to write and keep accounts, and they united their efforts with those of their superiors for the right training of the young. Family worship and government were maintained with strictness. Attending public religious instruction with their children, they welcomed their ministers to their dwellings and ordered their families so as to have their visits the most profitable to their entire households. The Bible, that inexhaustible source of knowledge, and what other books they had, were more read, more studied at home by old and young, and their contents made the subjects of more reflection and conversation, than are found now in the abodes of their descendants.

Nor let us think too meanly of the common schools

which were established by law, and the people were required to maintain. All deemed them indispensable to the diffusion of knowledge through the entire community. Hence we find the town in March 1676, when their means were small, agreeing to pay a Mr. Webb twenty-five pounds for keeping school a year. Mr. Samuel Stow, who was so many years a candidate for the ministry, Nathaniel White and Jasper Clements, three of the proprietors of the town, made bequests for the support of common schools, the benefits of which are felt to the present time. Parents were glad to send their children to school; ministers visited the schools and encouraged the children to learn; yea, they often took youth into their own houses and instructed them themselves.

Common schools have accomplished unspeakable good here and through the State, and wherever they have been established.

Our common schools are now improved in some instances, here and there, and it is encouraging to witness their advancement. Where circumstances admit of it, let a High School be established for the older children, as has been done in this city, and the means of a higher education opened to all, and the happy results will soon be felt.

In places of far less population and wealth much may be done. Let a few energetic and decided men take hold of the subject, and they will arouse their neighbors to the importance of improving the schools, and as these become what they should be, the minds of the young will be filled with a thirst for knowledge, which will seek gratification when the period of schooling is passed. They will be ready to form associations and use means which will diffuse an enlightening and elevating influence around them.

Some measures have been adopted in the Upper Houses for advancing education, which deserve public commendation. I allude especially to what has been done by the "Friendly Association," a literary society, which has been regularly kept up about forty years, which flourishes still, and is accomplishing much good.

The settlers were the friends of Constitutional liberty, and of righteous laws well administered. They came here under the wing of the constitution which went into operation in 1639, allowing them to elect their own officers, and to unite with others in the election of officers for the commonwealth. That Constitution was superceded by the charter of Charles the second; a charter liberal for a monarch to grant, and which showed the adroitness of Governor Winthrop in obtaining it. Thus the people had what they wished, the privilege of managing legally their own concerns, whether of town or society, school district or any other corporation with which they were connected, while they took a part with others in elevating men to higher stations, and more extensive trusts.

They knew their rights. Though for more than twenty years the public laws were in manuscript, copies of them were sent to the towns, publicly read and left for examination by the inhabitants; and then they were printed and bound in a volume with blank leaves, and every family was required to purchase a copy. The new laws, made from time to time, were sent to the towns, that after being publicly read, they might be copied into the same book with the printed laws. Thus the people had the laws continually before them, and were probably more conversant than the people now are with the existing statutes.

One trait of the early settlers was, that when they

found public men very faithful, they elected them repeatedly to office, sometimes for long periods, and to old age. Perhaps there were not among them as many qualified for office as among their posterity, in proportion to the population; but they did not judge it best to drop tried and good men on slight grounds. It was no part of their policy to throw aside men merely to make way for others; especially such as had become conversant with the duties of a high station, for the sake of experimenting on raw hands. Their principles and their circumstances both prompted them to union, and to seek the general welfare in distinction from party objects. A remarkable illustration of this is found in the elections of Mr. Nathaniel White, who resided in the Upper Houses; a man of high religious character, and sound judgment. He was one of the first magistrates of the town, and held military commissions. From 1659 to 1710 the year before his death, he was chosen representative to the General Court, the elections being then semi-annual, eighty-five times. Among the men settled in the Lower Houses, whom the people delighted to honor were Mr. Giles Hamlin, his son John Hamlin, and his grandson Jabez Hamlin. The first mentioned and Mr. White were appointed commissioners, or justices of the peace in 1669, and in 1684 commissioners for Middletown, Haddam and Meriden. Mr. Hamlin, though

"Near fifty years crossing the ocean wide,"*

was elected representative to the General Court twenty-two times; and in 1685 was elected an assistant, and thus annually until his death, except as the privileges of the freemen were interrupted by the usurpation of Maj. Andros.

---

* From the epitaph on his Monument.

John Hamlin was a member of the General Court as a representative seven sessions, and then an assistant twenty-six years.

Jabez Hamlin, besides being advanced in military life to the rank of a Colonel, was put into the commission of the peace as early as 1733 or 4; was a justice of the quorum for Hartford county, from 1745 until 1754, and then judge of that court thirty years. He was elected a representative to the General Assembly forty-three times, and was repeatedly Speaker of the Lower House. He was also for a time a member of the Council of safety. He was judge of probate from the formation of Middletown district in 1752 till 1789, and mayor of this city from its incorporation in 1784 until his death.

The excellence of Giles Hamlin may have contributed to bring forward his son John Hamlin, but the son could not have received and retained the confidence of the people in those times, had he not been a superior man: and the excellence of John Hamlin, combined with that of his father, may have had more influence in bringing forward Jabez Hamlin; but all three were capital men. Jabez Hamlin was publicly educated and possessed a well informed and well balanced mind, unusual sweetness and uniformity of temper, and courtliness of manners. He took an active interest in the welfare of persons of every class, exercising a benevolence through a long life, which was seen and felt by all. Thus he descended to his grave, rich in the esteem of men, and beloved of his God.

Seth Wetmore was a lawyer in this town, and a justice of the peace sometime before the middle of the last century. He was elected a representative to the Legislature forty-eight times, and was a judge of Hartford county court.

Samuel W. Dana and Asher Miller were long elected to public offices: and the clerkship held by the late John Fisk Esq., shows that the people have not forgotten altogether to continue correct and faithful men in office. Still in recent times, some offices have passed rapidly from one person to another. The court of Probate for this District has existed ninety-eight years. By the first three judges it was held sixty-nine years. Since the death of the last of these, it has been held by eleven judges.

As for Ministers, they were not hastily settled nor hastily dismissed. Mr. Samuel Stow, and the first settled pastor, were employed as candidates longer than was common in the early days of Connecticut. But long candidateships were usual, and when ministers were settled, they were considered as settled for life. The first four pastors of this Church died in office, and including the time of their being candidates, they supplied the people nearly one hundred and fifty years. The first two pastors in Upper Middletown died in office; the first in Westfield; the first three in Portland; the first in Middle Haddam, and the first three in East Hampton.

It has been said that the early ministers were superior men, men of talents and learning.

Mr. Collins, the first pastor, was a native of Cambridge, Massachusetts, and was educated at the College in that town, as was an elder brother by the name of John, who was a minister in London. Both were famous ministers in their day. The church or people here were united and happy during Mr. Collins' life; he died in 1684. Cotton Mather says of him, in his Magnalia.—"The church of *Middletown* upon *Connecticut* River, was the golden *candlestick*, from whence this excellent person illuminated more than that whole colony; and all the qualities of most exemplary *piety*, extraordinary integrity, obliging affability, joined with the accomplishments of an extraordinary preacher, did render him truly excellent." He also wrote an elegy on him, in which he describes his virtues in quaint rhymes:

"I sigh the *fate* for which our broached eyes
Spend floods of *brine;* at which a dire surprise
Of a soul chilling horror doth invade
The *soul* not *stone* before; at which are made
In serious minds, as many wounds as were
To Cæsar given. Reader, shake to hear;
THE DEATH OF COLLINS, 'tis. He dead,
Without a *paper* sheet to lay him out!
O shame. O that *Egyptian odours*, and
Embalmers too, were now at my command!
I want them. But *hyperboles* withdraw,
Begone *licentious poets.* What I saw
On this occasion, let some country rhymes
That call a spade a *spade*, tell after times."

* * * * * * * * * *

Pity, the Church of Middletown bespeaks
Set in the midst of swoons and sobs and shrieks.

* * * * * * * * * *

The second pastor was Rev. Noadiah Russell. He was one of the founders and trustees of Yale College, and one of the framers of Saybrook Platform, and of course held high rank among his brethren. Two of his sons, William and Daniel, were educated at the seminary which he had assisted in founding, and became ministers of the gospel. Daniel settled in Stepney in Wethersfield, now the town of Rocky Hill.

Rev. William Russell succeeded his father in the ministry here, and it is a remarkable fact that he labored in the work just forty-six years, dying on the same month, and on the same day of the month on which he was ordained. He preached the election sermon before the Colony Legislature in 1730. The celebrated George Whitfield, being entertained at his house over night in Oct., 1740, says of him: " I think him an *Israelite* indeed, and one who has been long mourning over the deadness of professors. *Oh!* that all ministers were like-minded." He also expresses his admiration " of the simplicity of his host and the order wherein his children attended on family devotion." Mr. Russell was a member of Hartford South Consociation, when that Consociation was called in 1758, to act with the Consociation of New Haven County in the " Wallingford case, and he manifested much concern for the peace and union of the church and society in Wallingford, and to effect an accommodation of the difficulties which had arisen." " He was a gentleman," says Dr. Trumbull, " of great respectability for knowledge, experience, moderation, and for pacific measures, on all occasions."

Rev. Enoch Huntington was the fourth pastor of the first church in this town. While a member of Yale College, (of which institution he was a trustee many years,) he was distinguished for ripe scholarship, and was a successful candidate for the Berkeley prize. When he began to preach he was a popular candidate. A congregation on Long Island sought him for their pastor. The people in Pittsfield, Mass., invited him to settle with them, but he deemed it his duty to settle in this place, where he had a call at the same time. His ministry was more extended than that of his immediate predecessor, and during the greater part of this long period, besides discharging his official duties, he instructed young men while fitting for college, or who without a collegiate course were looking forward to the learned professions, and to important stations in business. The town being then greatly concerned in commerce, and having extensive connections, youths from abroad, as well as from this place and vicinity, were placed under his tuition. Had we a full catalogue of his pupils, which has been much sought for, we should find the names of many literary, distinguished and useful men. President Dwight of Yale College, was one of his early pupils, and had such respect for him, that some thirty years afterwards he placed a son under his care. The first families in Middletown, of different denominations, sent their sons to him. The Rev. Elijah Parsons of East Haddam, and the late Dr. Sheperd of Lenox, Mass., studied theology with him.

It is rare to find four ministers in succession, in any church for so long a time, of such standing and influence as the four now noticed. As the early settlers of the town, and their descendants for generations, had superior men for their ministers, so they had very worthy men for deacons. One of their three first elected and ordained deacons was John Hall, son of the first John Hall, one of the early clerks of the town. He died Jan. 22, 1694, aged 75, and his epitaph declares his virtues.

"Here lyes our Deacon Hall,
Who studied peace with all,
Was upright in his life,
Void of malignant strife;
Gone to his rest, left us in sorrow
Doubtless his good works will him follow."

These rhymes are as quaint as Cotton Mather's, and not a whit quainter than some epitaphs found on gravestones in old England; but the ideas cannot be mistaken. In the subsequent list of deacons, we find the names of

Jabez Hamlin, Chauncey Whittlesey and Matthew Talcot Russell.

We are assembled to celebrate the Second Centennial Anniversary of the settlement of Middletown. For two hundred years, the worship of God has been celebrated in this congregation, according to the views and forms of the Congregationalists. And here some rather striking coincidences occur. It is very near one hundred and fifty years since Congregational worship was commenced in Upper Middletown, and from these churches went forth colonists, to form the other Congregational churches and societies generally, which have sprung up within the original limits of the township. This too is the first Centennial Anniversary of christian worship here, according to the rites of the church of England, and with this Episcopal church have been somewhat connected the origin and growth of the same denomination in Portland and Middle Haddam. The Baptist church in this city has existed a little more than half a century: the Baptist Society in Upper Middletown was formed in January, 1801. The Methodist congregation in the city was formed in 1791, but was small until 1800 and after.

The economy and customs of the three denominations now mentioned, provide better for the frequent change of ministers than those of the Congregationalists, and comparing the whole existence of all the churches, they have actually changed their ministers more frequently. Rev. Abraham Jarvis, one of the early rectors of the Episcopal church here, served it many years, and while here, was raised to the highest station in the Episcopal churches of the commonwealth, which his brethren could give him. Some, among the long list of rectors following, have been much esteemed, several have been raised to eminent stations.

Rev. Mr. Miles served the Episcopal congregation in Portland many years. But so many have been the Episcopal ministers; so many the Baptist and Methodist; and so many recently the congregational, that they cannot be even named on this occasion. The trials and the prosperity of their churches cannot be stated, much less can any thing be said about more recent congregations, and this is the less important, because their origin and progress are so well known. We are assembled to hear old and forgotten things, rather than those which are late and familiar.*

The settlers generally, rich as they were in faith, had little property, and every thing to begin anew. At first their dwellings were wretched, hardly sheltering them from the rage of the elements: they had but little furniture, and the articles generally of the plainest forms. They manufactured nearly all their clothing in the family, and very imperfectly, having no provision for fulling, shearing and pressing their woollens. They were inexperienced in subduing a forest; were deficient in implements for cultivating the ground; had scarcely any teams, horses, cattle or sheep. There were but few mechanics among them. They anticipated difficulty in procuring so necessary a mechanic as a blacksmith, and reserved an hundred pound lot to tempt one to come among them. It was not until Sept., 1661, that one appeared, who pledged himself to do the town's smithing, at least for four years. At a subsequent time they induced a blacksmith to settle among them in a similar way.

Our citizens who go to the West, entertain us by the story of their privations and hardships, and yet these are hardly a tythe of what the Colonists suffered. Besides

* Note C.

having greater means and resources in the outset, they can almost fly on cars, or steamboats to their destinations; carry what they wish with them, and at little expense; can go right on to a prairie, or if they enter a forest, they may have the light which experience has shed during two centuries, in turning a wilderness into a fruitful field.

The settlers were poor half a century; and for half a century more, they did not rise much above the condition of comfortable livers. Framed houses they had, but with few rooms and often never finished. Almost all looked to their clearings and forests for the means of support. From the former, they got their food and a few articles to barter; from the latter, they got materials for boards, staves and hoops, which were also to barter; and the bartering was for groceries, and a few finer articles of clothing. In 1680, but one vessel was owned and that only of 70 tons; only one more was owned on the river, and that at Hartford, of 90 tons. The trade was carried on in these vessels, and in a few coming rarely from Boston. Two vessels only were owned here in 1730; both united, rated at 105 tons.

There was probably but one merchant here in 1680, and the merchants in the colony, then 24 in number, are spoken of by Gov. Leet in his report to the Board of Trade and Plantations in England, as doing but little business. There were probably not more than two merchants here, in 1730. One of these was James Brown, an excellent Scotchman, from Edinburgh, who used to cross the country to Boston on horse-back, once or more in a year, to make his contracts. Some years after this, there were only three or four merchants. But in the latter half of the last century, a very profitable trade was opened with the West Indies, and some accumulated large estates. The most successful in this trade was Richard Alsop, who had been educated a merchant in the store of Philip Livingston in New York. George Phillips, Col. Matthew Talcot and others were engaged in it.

This trade stimulated agriculture; and by this time the best lands in all the parishes were brought under cultivation, and yielded abundant crops of wheat, rye, barley, oats, flax, maize, and English grasses. Great quantities of provisions; and great numbers of cattle and horses were sent to the West Indies; and great quantities of rum, (an article *then* believed to be useful as a beverage, and necessary to men engaged in arduous labors,) were imported, together with sugar, molasses and salt. Great quantities of provisions were sent from the river to New York, to be consumed there, or re-shipped for foreign markets, and thence various articles of merchandize were brought back in return: for by this time most of the trade which had gone eastward, and mainly to Boston, had changed its course.

The West India trade, and almost all other trade, the Revolutionary War deranged, or rather suspended. It was resumed, however, and flourished when the war was over. Some of the principal traders at this time, were Elijah and Nehemiah Hubbard, and Col. Lemuel Storrs, George and Thompson Phillips, sons of the George Phillips before mentioned, Gen. Comfort Sage, and others, took a part, and some of them an important part in it. Joseph W. Alsop, a younger man, also succeeded in it. Before the close of the last century, however, this trade was annoyed and injured by the principal belligerent powers of Europe; evils which led on to a temporary controversy with France, then to the restrictive system, and the more serious war with Great Britain. During that system and war, our seaports presented lines of naked masts. Vessels, old and new, were laid up on the sides of this river, and as another item in the calamities of people on the Connecticut, twenty-two vessels of various descriptions, estimated at a hundred and sixty thousand dollars, were burnt by the enemy at Essex. The sons of the ocean were driven to almost every expedient to get their bread, sold too at an enhanced price.

Since the last war with Great Britain, almost all the commerce from this place is domestic, and this is still limited. Under this change many enterprising men have invested property in factories, and hundreds, who might otherwise have exerted their strength and their skill in following the seas, are now engaged in mechanical and manufacturing operations. In these factories, the cultivators of the soil too, find a market for their products.

Wars try men's souls. The Pequot war, and King Philip's war, tried the men of Connecticut. Queen Ann's war at the beginning of the last century, tried them, and pressed them with a heavy debt.* The

* The fruitless undertaking against Canada, in 1709, says Trumbull, "was a capital loss and expense to the Colonies." One quarter or more of the troops died. Connecticut only sustained the loss of 90 men. The expedition occasioned the first emission of paper money in Connecticut.

Besides the assigned quotas raised by the colonies, independent companies were raised and sent on to the army. The following persons were volunteers from Middletown, viz. "Nathaniel Gilbert, Benjamin Cornwell, John Allen, Samuel Doolittle, Nathaniel Hobart [or Hubart,] Jonathan Gilbert, Waite Cornwell, Edward Bow, John Lane, entered, (but by reason of the death of his father, hired another in his room,) Charles Butler, Jacob Conte, and Thomas Stevens," all of whom "served under Capt. Moses Demming." "Jacob Doude, and Jeremiah Leman" who "served under Capt. Andrew Ward."

In May, 1722. the Assembly passed an act requiring all the arms "received upon the Canada expeditions," including "those lodged in any

French war of 1744, and especially that of 1755, continuing for a longer period, tried them. In both, Connecticut furnished more than her proportion of men. In the latter, some went to Ticonderoga, some to the Havanna, and some elsewhere, and many never returned. A number from Upper Middletown did not. How many then from all the parishes west of the river? The only son of the first minister in Chatham fell in battle in this war. How many then in all the parishes east of the river? But we are accustomed to speak of the Revolutionary war as trying men's souls, particularly in 1776. This did try them, in various respects. It was a war with Englishmen, whose blood we shared, and for the redress of wrongs, which it was believed, fathers should never have inflicted; a war with an ancient, rich and powerful nation, that thought at first they could overawe us, and then that they could subdue us. It was a long, bloody and expensive war, in which hope sometimes rose high, then sunk, but lived on, rose again and again, until in eight years the glorious triumph arrived.

But little can be said on this vast subject now—a few things only, to show how your fathers felt and acted at that time, in conjunction with the people of other towns in our beloved State.

The news of the passage of the Boston Port Bill, and the arrival of Gen. Gage in May, 1774, to enforce it by stopping the trade of that important town, and with it to a great extent, the trade of Massachusetts and New Eng-

---

town or in the hands of any person in the government" to be brought to and lodged at the State House in Hartford. This appears to have been done—but in May 13, 1725, the volunteers from this place asked the General Assembly, to grant liberty for the delivery of the arms to each of them, which had been taken away by a former order, and the request was granted by both Houses.

land, excited alarm and indignation in Connecticut. "The House of Representatives, then in session at Hartford, passed strong resolutions against the unrighteous act." Many towns did the same, and pledged their cooperation in defense of the rights of the people. On the 15th of June in this year, more than five hundred inhabitants of this town assembled and gave such a pledge. The following are their deliberate and comprehensive resolves:

1. "That we will heartily concur in any salutary measures, that may or shall be devised and come into, or recommended by a General Congress, from all or most of the Colonies, or by the greater places of trade or commerce on the continent, or by the inhabitants of this Colony, for the preservation of the rights of British Americans.

2. That Messrs. Matthew Talcott, Richard Alsop, and Titus Hosmer, be our Committee of correspondence, whose duty it shall be to collect all such intelligence, as may be necessary to enable us to act our part presently, and to good effect in the system of America; to communicate such intelligence to others, as may be useful to them and the common cause, and in our behalf to cooperate with the Committees of other towns, in concerting or executing any general plan of proceeding for the good of the whole."

It is not known that Chatham formally passed such resolves, but there is evidence enough that they cherished the same sentiments, and it is scarcely possible that any towns should have been more faithful than these two were, in sustaining them.

One measure, which was the subject of much consideration about this time, was the breaking off from all trade with the mother country, so long as she should continue her arbitrary proceedings. How the people felt on this point, is clear from an incident which occurred, when the delegates from Massachusetts were on their way to the first Continental Congress. Stopping in Middletown, Dr. Eliot Rawson, Mr. Alsop, Mr. Mortimer and others, the committee of correspondence, Mr. Henshaw and many other gentlemen, called upon them to pay them their respects, and to assure them that they thought that all was in their hands, and that they would abide by whatever should be determined on, *even to a total stoppage of trade to Europe, and the West Indies.*" This assurance is the more noticeable, because the wealth of the town at that time, was mainly derived from foreign commerce, and some of the gentlemen present were principals in carrying it on. Congress assembled, and formed an association for non-importation, non-exportation and non-consumption "of British goods." The Colonial Assembly approved and recommended it, and before the year was closed, the people here heartily concurred in it, and appointed a committee of inspection, consisting of seventeen persons, "to see the same duly observed, to publish the names of any willful transgressors of said association, and generally to do every thing necessary to the carrying into execution the objects of the association, according to the true intent and meaning of said Congress." The people of Chatham did the same, and appointed a committee of eleven, larger in proportion to their population, for the same purpose. Such committees were appointed from time to time, in both towns, through the Revolution. This measure, thus pursued here and elsewhere, was designed to show Great Britain, that the Americans were determined not to submit to oppression, and that if they could not live peaceably with her, they would endeavor to live without her.

But what other things did the towns of Middletown and Chatham do, under all the motives which were brought to bear upon them? They met very often, considered the measures recommended and urged upon them by the General Assembly, or by the Governor or Council of Safety in behalf of the Commonwealth; approved them, and took promptly the steps necessary to their execution.

One thing which they did, was to see that the inhabitants took the oath of fidelity to the State, and the records of both towns year after year, abound with such subscriptions.

Another thing was to provide that sundry articles, necessaries of life specified by a law of the State, should be sold at certain fixed prices. This law the town of Middletown approved February 10th, 1777, soon after it was passed, and all informing officers were charged "to be very circumspect and diligent in their inquiries after all breaches of said act." The binding force of this law is repeatedly recognized. The town of Chatham on the 1st of April in the same year, voted, "That the inhabitants with one consent, will join with, and support to the utmost of their power, the authority, selectmen and all informing officers in carrying into execution the laws made for the regulation and affixing the prices of certain articles therein mentioned." The law thus approved was followed by another, and a very severe one, against monopoly and the engrossing both of agricultural products and imported goods, entitled an act to encourage fair dealing, and to restrain and punish sharpers and oppressors."

Early this year it was seen and felt to be of the last importance, that the army of Washington should not be obliged to depend as much as it had been upon militia; but should have soldiers enlisted for three years, or during the war; and Continental battallions were ordered to be raised in the State. That the respective towns might fill their quotas, all classes were earnestly exhorted, by an appeal to their patriotism, to procure the enlistment of men. Such orders and exhortations found a speedy and full response in the feelings of the people, both of Middletown and Chatham. But it would be tedious to repeat all the votes they passed, and measures they took to engage soldiers.

Both towns did much for the support of the families of these soldiers, sometimes by assigning them to the care of large committees, or the care of particular families to individuals. They also did much to supply the soldiers themselves with clothing.

In the course of the year 1777, Middletown voted that the selectmen distribute to the officers and soldiers families, the salt belonging to the town as they should think it needed, and the remainder to the poor at their discretion. Chatham made a similar donation.

In December 1779, Middletown voted that every man in the town that has a team, be desired to furnish the light dragoons with wood, at least one load, as soon as possible. This was doubtless much needed, for the winter proved exceedingly cold.

But to revert to the year 1774. It was thought very possible then, that Gen. Gage might use force against those whom he regarded as rebels against the British Government, and on such an occurrence, that it would be the duty of Americans far and near to help their injured brethren. Military men in Connecticut accordingly prepared to start at once, upon the knowledge of an attack. All this is evident from the rush of hundreds and thousands of armed men towards Boston, upon what is termed the "Boston alarm," in Sept. 1774. This was a premature report that the "English ships of war were cannonading Boston, and the regular troops massacring the inhabitants without distinction of age or sex."

At the October session, this year, the General Assembly resolved, "That the several towns in this Colony be and are hereby ordered to provide as soon as may be, double the quantity of powder, balls and flints that they were heretofore by law obliged to provide, under the same directions and penalties as by law already provided."

The circumstances of the Bostonians grew worse and worse. Deprived of their trade, want and suffering pressed them. The rich in Connecticut and elsewhere contributed liberally, and those of smaller means added to the amount, and forwarded relief. But as more was learned continually of the oppression they were enduring, the higher rose the spirit of resistance.

Titus Hosmer Esq., gave to this spirit the sanction of his enlarged mind. As the difficulties with Great Britain were becoming more serious, at a session of the General Assembly in Hartford, a secret meeting was held by the members, in which a long and thorough discussion was carried on by appointed debaters, whether in the controversy, Great Britain was in the right, or the Colonies. In this discussion Mr. Hosmer was conspicuous; great light was imparted, the members became satisfied that the right was with the Colonies, and that they would be justified in resisting their oppressors in war, should war come. The members scattered the light among their constituents, and the grand result was, that when the time for decided action arrived, the people of Connecticut were remarkably united, and so continued through the long contest, which has effected so much good for our country and the world.

Blood was shed at Lexington in April 1775, and then the war commenced. Return Jonathan Meigs and others of Middletown, on petition, had been constituted a company of light infantry the preceding year, and Mr. Meigs became their captain. Comfort Sage commanded a company of light horse. Immediately upon the news of the battle at Lexington, Capt. Meigs marched his company "completely uniformed and equipped," to the environs of Boston. Capt. Sage was there with his troop, and Capt. Silas Dunham with a military company from Chatham.

In this month the General Assembly held a session, and enacted a law "to raise one fourth of the militia, for the special defense of the Colony; formed into companies of one hundred men each, and into six regiments." The Assembly "also authorized the purchase of three thousand stand of arms." About this time the companies in Middletown and Chatham were formed into a regiment.

Large sums of money had been expended upon a lead mine in this town by foreigners; and when the Revolution commenced, it was in the hands of Col. James, a British officer, who had raised a quantity of the ore, and prepared it for exportation. This mine, and this ore, the government of Connecticut now seized for their own use.

The plan for the brilliant enterprise of taking Ticonderoga was formed in Connecticut, in the same month in which the war commenced at Lexington. In this, Samuel Holden Parsons, whose family resided here in the Revolution, was prominent; for he informed the General Assembly afterwards by a memorial, that he, together with Samuel Wyllys, Silas Deane and others, did in April 1775, undertake the suprising and seizing the enemies' fort at

Ticonderoga, without the knowledge of said Assembly, and for that purpose took a quantity of money from the treasury, giving their receipts for the money, all which [£810] had been expended in said service, and prayed the Assembly to cancel said notes and receipts. The memorial was honored, and this enterprise which Mr. Parsons did so much to start and effect, inspired the Colonists in Connecticut and elsewhere with confidence, that in the war with Great Britain, they should triumph: and this triumph he himself did much to secure.

In the memorable battle of Bunker Hill, which occurred the following June, officers and soldiers from Connecticut participated. Gen. Putnam showed his usual intrepidity. This battle fired the whole country. Hundreds of our men were about Boston months afterwards. Many of the militia were directed to points upon our own coast, and to co-operate with the faithful in and about New York.

But while the preceding events and transactions served to keep up, and strengthen the opposition to Great Britain in Connecticut, it must be admitted that there were some among ourselves, who doubted the propriety of the course which the Colonies were pursuing, and who were in heart opposed. Some took refuge in Nova-Scotia, or other parts of the King's dominions. But tories, or semi-tories, were not so numerous in Connecticut as in some other colonies, as in Southern New York and in the Jersies, particularly after the British had possession of New York, and began to issue their proclamations. It was rather the colony, whither tories were sent for safe keeping; so that the people were called to watch and guard tories, as well as to the more pleasant service of showing hospitality and kindness, to such as fled to them from Long Island to escape the flatteries, and the arms of the enemy. The tory mayor of New York city was sent hither, and many smaller tories. William Franklin, the last royal Governor of New Jersey, though the son of Dr. Benjamin Franklin, "the genius of the day, and the great patron of American liberty," and possessing much of his ability and shrewdness, was a tory, and so remained. A convention of New Jersey, after an examination, declared him "a virulent enemy to his country," and a person that might prove dangerous; and sent him to Gov. Trumbull, who was desired to take his parole; and if he should refuse to give that, "to treat him agreeably to the resolution of Congress respecting prisoners." The very day that the Representatives of the Thirteen United Colonies of America declared, "that these Colonies are, and of right ought to be free and independent States," Mr. Franklin entered Connecticut. The next morning a parole was prepared for him, by Gov. Trumbull and the Council of Safety. He moved for an alteration in the parole, and for liberty to return to New Jersey, which was refused. He then asked permission to go to Stratford. This was not granted, but he was informed that he might go to Wallingford, to which he finally consented, "and signed his parole accordingly." In a few days "he applied to be removed from Wallingford to Middletown, which was granted on the same parole." Here he came and remained until the people were alarmed by his influence; for in a town meeting, January 7th, 1777, they appointed Capt. Samuel Russel, Col. Comfort Sage and Seth Wetmore Jun., to prefer a petition to Gov. Trumbull, to remove Gov. Franklin from the town, for the safety of the town and State. What Gov. Trumbull at once did is not ascertained, but it is probable he consulted the Congress of the United States: for on the 22d of April "Congress resolved, That Gov. Trumbull be informed, that Congress have received undoubted information, that William Franklin, late Governor of the State of New Jersey, and now a prisoner in Connecticut, has, since his removal to that State, sedulously employed himself, in dispersing among the inhabitants the protection of Lord Howe and Gen. Howe, styled the King's commissioners for granting pardons, &c., and otherwise aided and abetted the enemies of the United States; and that he be requested forthwith to order the said William Franklin Esq., into close confinement, prohibiting to him the use of pen, ink and paper, or the access of any person or persons, but such as are properly licensed by Governor Trumbull.*

The year 1776, was rendered remarkable by the departure of the British from Boston, their approach to New York, and eventual occupation of the city, which they held until the cessation of hostilities, and the arrival of the treaty of peace. It was rendered remarkable also, by the almost incessant calls for the services of our men within our own borders and beyond them, as appears in part from the records of the commonwealth now before the public, in part from other histories, and from tradition. After 1776 indeed, until the close of the war, our whole seaboard was exposed to alarms and attacks, and how seriously, let the incursions of the enemy into Danbury and New Haven; the burning of Norwalk, Fairfield and New London tell, and the accursed massacre at Groton. But as to the scenes of that most trying year.

In May "large detachments of militia were ordered to hold themselves in constant readiness to march at the

* Journals of Congress, Vol. III. pp. 121.

shortest notice, for the defence of any portion of Connecticut, or other adjoining Colonies."

In June, seven regiments were ordered to march immediately, and join the Continental army in New York," and at this time James Wadsworth Jun., of Durham was appointed Brigadier General, and among the seven Colonels then appointed, was Comfort Sage of this town, who as Captain, went with a company of light horse to the neighborhood of Boston the preceding year.

In August following, the whole of the standing militia of the State west of Connecticut river, together with two regiments on the eastern side, were ordered to march to New York city, and about the same time a large proportion of the remainder, were sent to aid the inhabitants of Suffolk county on Long Island. In the beginning of September, the standing militia together with the light horse on the east side the river, were ordered to march with the utmost expedition to Westchester, near New York. These drafts of course included the militia of Middletown and Chatham. In the operations in the months of August, September and October, on Long Island, in and about New York, "the Connecticut forces comprised a large portion of Washington's army. The regular troops were formed into a division, comprising two brigades. The division was commanded by Major Gen. Joseph Spencer" of East Haddam and by Brig. Gen. James Wadsworth of Durham, just mentioned, and Samuel H. Parsons of this place. "They signalized themselves in all the achievments," and were distinguished for their sufferings, as well as for their valor. Capt. Jabez Hamlin, who had been an ensign under Capt. R. J. Meigs the year before, died of sickness this year at East Chester. Col. Sage remained at or near White Plains in November in the same year, and it is understood was in the service of his country long afterwards.

The standing militia of the State were subjected to five heavy drafts in 1776, and were sent to Rhode Island, to Long Island, to New York, to the High Lands, and to the western borders of this State. Instead of asking therefore who went into the war from Middletown and Chatham this year, we may rather ask, who did not go?

The privations and hardships of militia men this year were great. They sacrificed the sweets of home for a large portion of time, and their business was deranged or suspended. These things however were as nothing compared with the sufferings of those who were taken prisoners, particularly of such as were confined in New York. A letter from a prisoner of distinction, belonging to Connecticut, dated New York, December 26th, 1776, declares, "The distress of the prisoners cannot be communicated by words. Twenty or thirty die every day; they lie in heaps unburied. What number of my countrymen have died by cold and hunger, perished for the want of the necessaries of life. I have seen it." Samuel Clark of this town "stated to the Assembly, that he was one of the unfortunate men taken at fort Washington, and confined in New York until December 1776, and then with others nearly dead, liberated on parole."*

---

* It is impossible to ascertain at this time, all who died during the Revolution, from battle and other evils connected with it. Some idea may be formed of the mortality from the statements following. John and James Smith, Abijah Kirby, Nathan Edwards and Reuben White, from Upper Middletown died in prison in New York. Some escaped from prison there, while others remained until released. What numbers then from different parts of Middletown must have felt the horrors of imprison-

In describing the events of this trying year, Marshall says, " While the seat of war was in New York, very essential aid was given by that State," but, he adds, the main force of the army was drawn from New England. Such was the zeal and unanimity of those States, that while the enemy remained in their neighborhood, requisitions for militia were unformly complied with, and they enabled the American army to keep up a

---

ment in that city ? Moses Pelton, a soldier from Portland is said to have been killed in the war. David Sage, Timothy Cornwall, Isaac Buck, Bartlett and Lemuel Lewis and others, are said to have died of sickness or in prison. Jacob Norton from East Hampton died in prison in New York. In a bill of mortality kept in Middle Haddam by Rev. Benjamin Boardman, Asa Brainerd is mentioned as dying in the camp in 1775; Heman Higgins as dying in the army, of sickness in 1778; Jesse Higgins also as dying in the army the same year: Nathaniel Rich was killed in the action of Norwalk, July 11th, 1779, and the same year Jabez Arnold Jun., died in a tour in the militia at East Haven. Jonathan Cook Jun., and Seth Higgins are mentioned as dying prisoners in New York in the latter part of 1777, and not far from the same time, Jesse Swaddle, Elisha Taylor, Seth Doane Jun., and John Snow are mentioned as dying on their way home from captivity. And it should be added here, that not only great numbers of captive soldiers suffered in prison, but a considerable number of captive privateersmen, out of the many living on Connecticut river, who engaged in this tempting and hazardous concern. This was true of the officers and crew of the Sloop of War Sampson, built at Higganum, some of whom, about one hundred in all, are understood to have been from Chatham, some were probably from Middletown. These were consigned to the old Jersey. In the records just referred to, and under date of June 4th, 1782, Capt. David Brooks, the commander of the sloop, Nathaniel Stocking, Jonathan Brainerd Jun., William Akins or Atkins, Elihu Cook, Elijah Green and James Stocking are mentioned as dying in New York. Shubael Brainerd, the first Lieutenant, is known to have died in the prisonship, it is believed many others did. Tradition declares that numbers belonging to the sloop, died in New York about the time of the death of the Commander and first Lieutenant.

respectable appearance."* To a liberal share of this commendation Connecticut is justly entitled.

Nor did the services of the militia of New England, and especially that of Connecticut close with 1776.— The enemy were too much in our neighborhood afterwards, and among us. The campaign of 1777 opened with the invasion of Connecticut, and the march of the enemy to Danbury. Their services were needed this year in Pennsylvania, and in the Jersies; in Rhode Island, which was invaded; particularly in the State of New York, while a junction of the British forces in the city with the army of Burgoyne was apprehended; and years after his surrender, they were needed about the Hudson river. We needed them long in our own State; for in addition to the continual exposure of the coast, the burning of Norwalk and Fairfield, and the attack on New Haven, occured in 1779; the burning of New London, and the massacre at Groton in 1781.

But as much as militia men suffered by frequent and sudden marches, absence from home and the derangement of business, by cold and storm, sickness and conflict, the Continental soldiers had a harder lot. They were called to greater distances, and kept longer from their families, were more exposed to sickness from change of climate, and the more they learned of the military art, the more liable to have a position assigned them in the hottest of the battle. Much compassion was felt for them, and much was done for the relief of their wives and children in their absence, and yet when the war was over, many returned poor to their homes.

Among the families helped in Middletown, were those of Colonels, Return Jonathan Meigs, John Sumner, and

* Washington's Life, Vol. III. pp. 53.

Jonathan Johnson; Captains, Robert Warner, Edward Eells, Abijah Savage, David Starr and William Sizer; Lieutenants, William Henshaw, Hezekiah Hubbard, John Hubbard and Othniel Clark, which renders it probable, that all these for a time were in the Continental service, many of them certainly were. But how many more officers from Middletown were in the continental line, it would be difficult at this late period to ascertain. And it is more difficnlt to ascertain the like fact in regard to Chatham; for though the people of that town were prompt and liberal in providing for the families of those who were in the regular army, they were not so particular in naming them. Another thing which increases the perplexity is, that persons enlisted at different times, some after they had served in the militia. Some, about the commencement of hostilities, enlisted into the service of their country during the war. A recruiting officer appeared then in one of the neighborhoods of Middle Haddam, as an aged man now living distinctly remembers, procured several enlistments there, and more in the surrounding neighborhoods; a thing which was probably done in other parts of ancient Middletown. But as the number of these was diminished by death, by loss of health or limbs; or as the war raged more, or regular soldiers were more valued, new enlistments were called for, for the residue of the war, or for given periods. From what information has been received, it is believed, that Col. John Penfield, Capt. Joseph Blague, afterwards Col. Blague, Capt. John Cooper, Lieut. Daniel Stewart, and Ensign Daniel Shepherd were commissioned officers in the Revolution, from that part of Chatham which is now Portland, and more or less in the service of their country. Several of them may have been continental officers. Capt. Blague was for a time, and commanded a company in the battle at Saratoga. On some occasion, Gen. Lafayette as an expression of esteem for him as an officer, and it is said in the presence of Washington, gave him a beautiful sword.* Captains Silas Dunham and Stephen Brainerd, Lieut. Marcus Cole, his son Ensign Abner Cole, breveted Lieutenant, from what is now Chatham, were in the war. The Coles were Continental officers, and some of the other officers may have been, and others still, not now specified.

First or last, almost all that could, in some capacity, took part in the long contest. Continental soldiers went where they were commanded. Militia men by regular drafts and orders, or on the report of danger, flew to the places where the enemy came, or was apprehended. Old men, exempted by age from service, showed a disposition to do what they could. About sixty here formed themselves into a company, to learn more of the military art, with a determination to preserve the liberty of their country. They marched in these streets. The drummer of the company was over eighty, and was as much engaged and alert as in his younger days. Lads sympathized and imitated. Mothers, wives, daughters and sisters, while laboring more in the house for the comfort of those gone to the camp, entered themselves into the field, and did the work of men.

To tell all that the people of Middletown and Chatham did, during the protracted struggle, were all the facts collected and arranged, would require much time. They are not collected and cannot be now, as many records have perished since they transpired, and the performers of them almost entirely, and most of their immediate de-

* Now in the hands of his son-in-law, Col. Covil.

scendants have already gone to the grave. Still some further ideas may be gathered from sketches of a few individuals, for which there are more ample materials.

Capt. Return Jonathan Meigs has been spoken of. He was born in this town. The family was from that part of Guilford which is now Madison. In the capacity of major, he accompanied Arnold up the Kennebec river to the city of Quebec, and wrote the best account that exists of that perilous and suffering expedition. Abijah Savage of the Upper Houses was with him, and probably others from Middletown and Chatham. Mr. Savage was then an officer, afterwards a continental captain, as just noticed. The provisions for the expedition were scanty, and a part of the corps were obliged to stop on the way, and return to avoid starvation. The rest kept on, and at the end of sixty-three days, on the night of the 13th of December 1775, crossed the St. Lawrence at Wolf's Cove, without being discovered by the guard boats from the men of war, and formed in good order on the Plains of Abraham, near the city of Quebec, while the British sentinels were articulating "all is well." But successfully as they had accomplished their journey, the soldiers were emaciated by fatigue and hunger; their clothes were nearly worn out or rent from their bodies; their time of enlistment was expired; they were penniless, and in these circumstances could not but think of wages, kindred and home. But when Gen. Montgomery arrived with his force by a different route, he was anxious in the emergency of the case, that the men should re-enlist. They were marched in front of his quarters, and he addressed them "like a father, like a brother, and like a soldier," and in less than twenty minutes gained their hearts, and to a man they volunteered their services. The storming of the city followed on the last day of the year, and the result is known. The New England men fought most bravely. Maj. Meigs entered with a battallion within the walls of the city, but was made prisoner with captains Morgan and Dearborn, afterwards American Generals. Upon his exchange and return in 1777, he was appointed Lieutenant colonel, with authority to raise a regiment. Having raised it in part, he marched to New Haven, and was then designated by Gen. Parsons, to execute a project for the surprisal and capture of a body of the enemy at Sag Harbor, L. I. He embarked with about two hundred and thirty men, in thirteen whale boats, and proceeded eastward as far as Sachem's Head in Guilford, that he might the better cross the Sound. At that place he re-embarked one hundred and seventy of his detachment, May 23d, at 1 o'clock P. M., and landed within three miles of Sag Harbor at 1 o'clock at night. Having made arrangements for attacking the enemy at five different places, they proceeded with the greatest order and silence within twenty rods of them, and then rushed with fixed bayonets upon their barracks, guards and quarters, while Capt. Throop with a party under his command, at the same time, took possession of the wharves and vessels lying there. The alarm soon became general, a schooner of the enemy, of twelve guns, within one hundred and fifty rods of the wharves, opened an incessant fire, but with little effect. Twelve vessels, brigs and sloops were destroyed, a great amount of forage and provisions; six men were killed and ninety taken prisoners. Col. Meigs returned to Guilford with his prisoners in twenty-five hours from his departure, having transported his men by water and land in that time ninety miles, without the loss or injury of a single person. Such is the substance of two accounts of that memorable exploit. In view of it Congress resolved; "That Congress have a just sense of the merit of Lieut. Col. Meigs, and the officers and men under his command, who distinguished their prudence, activity, enterprise and valor, in the late expedition to Long Island; and that an elegant sword be provided by the commissary general of military stores, and presented to Lieut. Col. Meigs." Probably numbers from Middletown and Chatham were in this expedition.

"In 1779 Col. Meigs commanded one of the regiments under Gen. Wayne which stormed and carried Stony Point." Probably many individuals from Middletown were in that regiment. One who was in it from Middle Haddam, used to say that he determined and strove to be the first to lay hold of the flag-staff. In this he failed, but always affirmed that he helped the more successful aspirant pull the flag down. His honest character is evidence that he spoke the truth. His name was John Strong.

After the peace, Col. Meigs returned to this town and lived a few years, but in 1787 went with the very earliest emigrants to Marietta, the first town, (as has been mentioned,) settled by the English in the great State of Ohio. Though an ordinance had been provided for the government of the Northwest Territory, and a Governor and Judges were appointed, yet they had not arrived, and the emigrants were without civil law and authority. Col. Meigs drew up a concise system of regulations which were adopted by the emigrants until the proper authorities should arrive. These regulations spread upon a sheet, were attached to the side of a large oak from which the bark was cut off to receive them, standing at the confluence of the Muskingum with the Ohio. They were as frequently consulted, it is affirmed, as the oracle of ancient Delphos, and very happily regarded.

In the latter years of his life he was Indian agent at the Cherokee station, and was so beloved and trusted by the Indians, that they denominated him emphatically "The White Path." At this station he died, Jan. 28, 1823, in his 83d year. It is said his death was serenely happy in the assurance of christian hope, and that at his funeral a petition ascended to heaven, that his successors at the Cherokee station might walk in the *White Path.* His remains were interred amidst a concourse of friends, with the honors of war.

Col. Meigs had three younger brothers who lived to adult age, Giles, John and Josiah.

Giles Meigs lived and died in this town, and is remembered by the people. He was a captain of militia in the Revolution, and went with his company to New London.

John Meigs entered the army a volunteer at the beginning, and served through the war. He was attached to the regiment of Col. Webb, was appointed adjutant, and for a time acted as brigade major. He soon received a commission, and serving a few months as a Lieutenant, was advanced to a captaincy. During a part of the war he was stationed in Rhode Island, and two or three years in the neighborhood of the High Lands. He was a very active officer, and much beloved by his regiment. In 1797 he removed to New Hartford, where he died in 1826, aged 73 years.

Josiah Meigs was a graduate and tutor of Yale College, subsequently a lawyer, in which capacity he resided and acted for a time at Bermuda, where he had an opportunity to observe how our vessels and men were treated by the English, and to plead in their behalf in the court of Admiralty. For years afterwards he was Professor of Mathematics and Natural Philosophy in Yale College; then President of the University of Georgia at Athens, and then Surveyor General of the United States. At last he was placed at the head of the U. S. Land office at Washington, where he died in 1822 aged sixty-five.

Gen. Parsons has been repeatedly mentioned. He was born at Lyme, and was the third son of Rev. Jonathan Parsons, an eminent clergyman, for some years minister of Lyme, and then at Newburyport, Mass. He was graduated at Harvard College in 1756, and read law with his maternal uncle, Hon. Matthew Griswold, afterwards Governor of Connecticut. He commenced the practice of law in Lyme, and represented that town ten or twelve years consecutively in the Legislature. Having been appointed King's attorney for New London county, he removed to the town of New London in 1774. He had an elevated standing at the bar, but resigned his appointment as King's attorney at the opening of the Revolution. About the time of his agency in forming the plan for taking Ticonderoga, he was made a colonel, marched his regiment to Roxbury, and remained there until the enemy evacuated Boston. He was in the battle on Long Island in August 1776, about which time he received an appointment as Brigadier General. He was subsequently in many important military transactions under Washington and Putnam, about New York, the Hudson river and the western section of Connecticut, in which he showed great activity, judgment and courage.

In 1780 he was one of the judges on the trial of Major Andre, and about that time became Major General. For his successful attack on the British troops in Morrisania in 1781, Congress requested the Commander-in-chief to express to him their thanks. In the latter part of this year, the Governor and Council of Safety of Connecticut, requested him to take the command of the State troops and coast guards, and to dispose of them as he should judge necessary, to protect the inhabitants against desultory expeditions of the enemy.

Upon the establishment of peace, Gen. Parsons opened a law office in this town. He was sent to the Legislature, and in the measures for the formation of Middlesex county, was more active and influential than any other man. In 1785, the year in which this was formed, he traveled to Ohio, and in January following held a treaty with the Indians, in connection with Gen. Richard Butler and Gen. George R. Clark, near the mouth of the Great Miami. In this treaty the Indians ceded to the United States a large and valuable tract of country. He returned home the following spring, and in October following, (1787,) he was appointed by Congress first judge of the territory northwest of the Ohio, but did not go forward and enter upon the duties of his office, until he had taken a part in the Convention of Connecticut, which in January 1788 adopted the National Constitution. His associates were Gen. James M. Varnum of of Rhode Island, and the Hon. John Cleves Symmes* of New Jersey. In 1789 Gen. Parsons took a journey to the Western Reserve, to make arrangements for forming a treaty with Indian tribes, who claimed lands in that portion of Ohio. In the contemplated treaty, Oliver Wolcott of Litchfield, the first Governor of that

---

* Mr. Symmes was a son of Rev. Timothy Symmes, the first minister of Millington, in East Haddam, and father-in-law of Gen. Harrison late President of the United States.

name, and James Davenport Jun. Esq., of Stamford, were appointed by the government of Connecticut to act with him. But in that treaty he did not take a part; for in returning to his residence in Marietta, he was drowned in descending the rapids of the Great Beaver Creek, Nov. 17, 1789, aged 52.

Nehemiah Hubbard, a direct descendant of George Hubbard, one of the earliest settlers of this town, was born April 10th, 1752, O. S., and at the age of fourteen, went to live with Col. Matthew Talcott, as clerk in his store, where he continued until he was twenty-one years of age. He then went to the West Indies, first as supercargo, and afterwards as captain and merchant.

Early in 1776, he entered the army, and in May of that year, was appointed by Gov. Trumbull paymaster to the regiment, commanded by Col. Burrall, and which was sent on service to the shore of Lake Champlain. He first went and paid the troops at forts Stanwix, Schuyler, Herkimer, on the Mohawk, and then joined his regiment at Ticonderoga, where he remained some time.

"In May, 1777, he was appointed by Major General Greene, who was at that time quarter-master general of the United States, his deputy for the State of Connecticut; which post he filled until the resignation of Gen. Greene. He was again appointed by Colonel Pickering, then acting as quarter-master general, but he declined. He continued, however, to discharge the duties of deputy-quarter-master general, till relieved by another person, when he entered into the service with Wadsworth and Carter, who supplied the French army. This he accompanied to Yorktown, and was present at the siege and surrender of Lord Cornwallis."

"As a provider of public supplies, all his movements were marked by decision, promptness and punctuality.

The resources of Connecticut were brought forward at the most critical juncture; and while the army was enduring the greatest privations, it was frequently relieved by this State, through his energy and extraordinary exertion. As a specimen of the confidence reposed in him by such men as Washington, Green, Trumbull, and Hamilton; it ought to be mentioned that after the organization of the present government, Colonel Hamilton, while Secretary of the Treasury, was pressingly urgent to have him take the management of an institution which he wished to establish, for promoting the manufactures of the country."

"After the Revolutionary war, he settled here as a merchant, where he continued the remainder of his life. As a proof of the confidence reposed in his ability and integrity, it may be mentioned, that he was justly placed at the head of two of our most important monied institutions. He was President of the Middletown Bank, from 1808 till 1822, when he resigned, being then seventy years of age. He was also the first President of the Savings Bank, and held that place until his death."

"Many instances have come to the knowledge of the writer, in which he showed the most enlarged liberality, in furnishing young men and other persons with money, to enable them to begin and advance in business."

"The person of Mr. Hubbard was rather above the ordinary stature: his appearance very commanding, and he retained a very erect form till the last, with an uncommon exemption from most of the infirmities of age. His memory and judgment seemed to be unimpaired to the last. His judgment was quick, discriminating and rarely erroneous. In his deportment there was always a most noble frankness, nor did he fail honestly to reprove, when he saw rebuke required. A reproof from him carried a sting to the conscience, that in the end worked for good, instead of being productive of rancorous resentment."

"As a man of business, he was uncommonly methodical and was altogether, one of the first merchants of his day. In his private walk and character, were beheld all the stern virtues that adorned the lives of some of the best of the New England Pilgrim fathers. He was a faithful attendant on public worship, in one society, during fifty years, and for the last eighteen years an exemplary professor of religion. And it must be known to the citizens generally, how unremitted were his exertions for the cause of christianity, and for the spread of the gospel abroad, as well as for its support at home, together with the deep interest which he took in the welfare of the church to which he belonged."

"He gave liberally to all engaged in good works, and the calls of the present day are not few. He was, indeed, ever conspicuous, though unostentatious in every good work. Than he, Middletown never possessed a citizen of more sterling worth or purer patriotism."

Many of his ancestors and relatives, were distinguished for longevity. He died February 6th, 1837, aged eighty-five years, and we trust ascended to the eternal rest, prepared for the righteous.

His numerous relatives, descendants and connections will look back with veneration to his memory.*

Other respected inhabitants of Middletown, who helped forward the Revolution in one capacity and another, deserve more notice than can now be given them.

Matthew Talcott settled in Middletown as a merchant about 1750, and was advanced in the militia to

* Obituary in Sentinel and Witness, Feb. 15th, 1837.

the rank of a colonel. When the Revolution commenced he warmly espoused the cause of his country. When Middlesex county was organized, he was appointed a Justice of the Quorum, and afterwards Judge of the County Court. He died August 29, 1802, aged 89.

Chauncey Whittlesey was educated at Yale College, studied theology and licensed to preach, but relinquished the ministry as his profession without relinquishing his attachment to the gospel. He entered into mercantile concerns, and was distinguished for correct business habits. In 1776 he was on a committee "to procure and purchase such articles of refreshment and clothing, as should be directed by the Governor and his Council of Safety," and in that and in the succeeding year, thousands of dollars were expended by him in procuring and purchasing such articles. From December 1797, until August 1801, he was collector of customs for the port of Middletown. He died in March 1812, aged 65.

Elijah Hubbard, in May 1777 was appointed by the Governor and Council of Safety "commissary and superintendent of the stores provided by the State, for the Continental troops." From the instructions given him for the collection of supplies, the drafts upon him for them, and the various references to him in the doings of that committee, it is apparent that great confidence was reposed in him, and that the support and comfort of the soldiers depended much upon his proceedings. He was a justice of the peace, and for the last six years of his life a justice of the Quorum. He died suddenly at Hartford, while attending the General Assembly, May 30, 1808, aged 62; of which body he had been a member in more than thirty sessions.

John Pratt, a native of Hartford, entered into the army at the commencement of the Revolution, and rose to the rank of captain. He served his country through the war of the Revolution, and through the Indian war which followed and which raged in Ohio, was under Gen. St. Clair and Wayne, sharing in the mortification of the former from defeat, and the gratification of the latter from victory. Having been long in military life and further services from him being less needed, he resigned his commission near the close of 1793. He settled soon after in Middletown, where his gentlemanly manners, his good sense and integrity, gained the affections and confidence of the people. He was a magistrate, and repeatedly elected Representative to the Legislature, sometimes by the votes of both parties in politics. He died December 27, 1824, aged 71.

What the people did for physicians for half a century, I know not unless those who had the cure of souls, undertook to cure the body, which ministers did then frequently. Dr. John Cooper, whose name is honorably associated with medical skill, lived here about 1700. Dr. John Arnold came from Haddam some thirty years after, and lived here until his death in 1754. He was probably instructed by the Rev. Phineas Fiske of that town, who was an eminent physician as well as divine. Before his death Dr. Abijah Moores was here, who died in 1759. Contemporary with these two men, and surviving them, was Dr. Eliot Rawson, a direct descendant of the celebrated Edward Rawson, long Secretary of the Commonwealth of Massachusetts. Contemporary with the two physicians last mentioned for a while, though dying sooner than the latter, was Dr. John Osborne.—Medical authority pronounces him "a very respectable physician."* He ranked higher as a scholar than most

* Thatcher's Medical Biography, pp. 413, 14.

of the literary men of his day, and was also a poet. When in College at Cambridge he was distinguished for mathematical investigations, and for his Latin verses. One of the professors pronounced his hexameters truly Virgilian. Before he was graduated in 1737, he wrote an elegy on the death of a young sister, and addressed it to an elder one. It was written in the Spring of the year, and he begins by describing with great beauty the charms of the season, and then addresses his bereaved and sympathizing relative;

"But, Sister, all the sweets that grace
The Spring, and blooming nature's face,
The chirping birds,
Nor lowing herds,
The woody hills,
Nor mumuring rills,
The Sylvan shades,
Nor flowering meads
To me their former joys dispense,
Tho' all their pleasures court my sense,
But melancholy damps my mind;
I lonely walk the field
With inward sorrow filled,
And sigh to every breathing wind.
I mourn our tender Sister's death
In various plaintive sounds,
While hills above, and vales beneath
Their faultering note rebounds.
Perhaps when in the pains of death
She gasp'd her latest breath,
You saw our pensive friends around
With tears bedew the ground;
Our loving father stand,

And press her trembling hand,
And gently cry, my child adieu,
We all must follow you.

After Mr. Osborne was graduated, he was offered a tutorship in Harvard College, but declined the honor. About this time residing at his father's house in Eastham, Mass., and in the midst of companions accustomed to a sea-faring life, he wrote his Whaling Song, which is as sportive, as the elegy, from which we have quoted, is plaintive. It has been sung with rapture by our hardy adventurous whalemen in all latitudes, whither they have gone to harpoon the monsters of the deep. Besides these poetic effusions, there are a few stanzas, which our author wrote upon his death bed, which are religious, expressing his resignation to death, and anticipations of heaven.

Dr. Osborne died May 31, 1753, aged 40, leaving a widow and six children.

Dr. John Osborne, son of the preceding, studied medicine at Hartford, under Dr. Morrison, an eminent physician from Scotland, and in 1758, before he had attained his majority, he went with the army that attacked Ticonderoga in the second French war, and in a subordinate capacity was in the medical department of the Provincial troops." He practised in this place more than sixty years, about as long a space as was occupied by all his predecessors, if we except Dr. Rawson. He was a man of very extensive reading, and for many years possessed the best medical library in the State. His knowledge of the materia medica was accurate and extensive, and he excelled in chemistry. He exerted himself greatly to remove the prejudices against inoculation for the small-pox, and to improve the treatment of that distressing disease. About one thousand and two hundred persons were inoculated here in the winter 1777 and '78. He was one of the founders of the medical Society of the State, and gave instruction to students in medicine. As a practitioner he was eminent. He appreciated the worth of well-bred and faithful physicians, but held quackery in the utmost abhorrence. He had great sensibility, quick apprehension and strong passions; he spoke his mind fearlessly when and where he pleased, and it was not safe for any to attack him in words, for none better understood the retort *keen*. The numerous anecdotes still circulating respecting him, when well told, present him directly before our eyes, and yet his heart was not a stranger to kind emotions. Among his patients were the poor and unfortunate, and to these he was merciful. He died in the summer of 1825, aged eighty-three.

Dr. John Dickinson, son of Rev. Moses Dickinson of Norwalk, was a well informed physician. He began to practice in Wallingford, but removed to this town upon an invitation from the selectmen, and was here liberally patronized, and repeatedly sent a Representative to the Legislature in the time of the Revolution. Soon after that period he declined professional business, but acted as a magistrate and influential man in the town. In 1793 he was appointed a Judge of Probate, and in 1796 Judge of the County Court, both which offices he held until 1807. He died in 1811, aged eighty-two.

It sometimes occurs, that superior talents are found in the same family through several successive generations. Two physicians by the name of Osborne, father and son have been described. The latter had four sons who were all literary men, John Chevers and Samuel Osborne physicians, and Joseph and William Franklin Osborne, merchants.

Dr. John C. Osborne, received his classical education under that eminent teacher, Rev. Enoch Huntington, and his medical education exclusively under his father. He began practice in Newbern, N. C., in 1787, and continued there twenty years. He was well known as a successful practitioner, and was repeatedly placed at the head of the Medical Society of that district. From Newbern he removed to New York, and was soon after introduced to a large practice; was created professor of the Institutes of medicine, in the Medical Faculty of Columbia College, and upon the union of that faculty with the College of Physicians and Surgeons, was again appointed to a professorship. He died of pulmonary consumption in the island of St. Croix, upon the day of his landing, March 5th, 1819.

Dr. Thatcher, to whom I am indebted for these facts, observes further concerning him:

"With his professional erudition Dr. Osborn united great literary acquirements, and his knowledge of books was varied and extensive. These acquisitions he often displayed in his course of public instruction. His view of the materia medica as a science, was equalled by few, and his knowledge of the actual medical qualities of the native productions of our soil, was a subject which he delighted to investigate, and in his practice, and by his instructions, he earnestly enjoined an acquaintance with these important medical agents."

"Dr Osborne was a man of much more science and eminence in his profession, than either his father or his grandfather, and possessed a very fine taste for poetry, Belles-letters and painting. While quite a young man, Mr. Barlow submitted to him and his friend, the late Richard Alsop Esq., the manuscript of the "Vision of Columbus," for their correction and revision, previous to its publication. His taste in painting was highly cultivated, and he might have attained to great eminence as an artist."*

Dr. Samuel Osborne, was a physician of quite respectable standing, first in Brooklyn, and then in New York city

Joseph Osborne and William Franklin Osborne, both were endowed with poetic talents.

I have seen three pieces of the former. Two of them were written to be spoken by lads at an exhibition following the examination of a school, one at the beginning and the other at the close, at which parents were expected to be present. They express finely the feelings of children and parents on such occasions. The third piece is a paraphrase on the third chapter of the Epistle of James. As a specimen of this, take the first stanza:

"Him mayest thou deem a perfect man, whose word,
To give offence or pain was never heard:
Who rules his tongue; is master of the art,
To rule his passions and control his heart."

A number of deceased physicians, besides those already mentioned, practised here. But most of these died so recently that they are still remembered, and we have not time now to speak of them particularly.

Dr. Nathaniel Little resided in the Upper Houses from 1742 to 1746; who, after the latter date is supposed to have removed to Lebanon. Of his practice and skill nothing is known.

Between 1757 and the close of the last century, Dr. Aaron Roberts, and four or five other physicians, practised in the Upper Houses for shorter or longer periods.

Dr. Asher Ward, a native of the parish, practised in

* Thatcher's Medical Biography.

Middlefield, probably some eight or ten years, and died there in 1788. Dr. Jehiel Hoadley, after a much longer practice, died there in 1810. About 1785, Dr. Josiah Hatch practised for a short time in Westfield. He afterwards practised in New Hartford, but spent the latter part of his life in Grandville, Miss., where he died in August, 1834, aged 80.

It is probable that the settlers in Portland employed physicians from this side the river, for more than thirty years. The Rev. Moses Bartlett, who was settled there in 1733, and died in 1766, was a physician; as was also a son of his who bore his name, and lived until 1810. The former studied both theology and medicine, with Rev. Phineas Fiske of Haddam, his father in-law; and the latter, with Dr. Benjamin Gale of Killingworth, now Clinton. Contemporary with this physician for some years, was Dr. Thomas Wells, and also Dr. Elisha Phelps.

Dr. Joshua Arnold, brother of Dr. John Arnold, and probably instructed by Mr. Fiske, was a physician in Middle Haddam at an early period, and was succeeded by Jeremiah Bradford and Amos Skeele.

Dr. Robert Usher was a native of Millington, in East Haddam, and a student of Dr. Huntington of Windham. He settled in that part of Chatham which was attached to the parish of Westchester, in 1762. Upon the breaking out of the Revolution, he went as a volunteer to the vicinity of Boston, and in Jan., 1776, "was appointed surgeon, &c., for Wadsworth's regiment, in the recruits (then) raised for Cambridge," and served some time in in that capacity. He died in 1820, in his 77th year.

Titus Hosmer, Esq., has been mentioned, and more must be said of him. While in Yale College, he was distinguished for the acquisition of science, excelled in the languages, and in fine writing. Being graduated in 1757, he probably settled here about 1760.

By nature he had the genius of a poet, and there is said to be a hymn in existence composed by him. He encouraged Barlow to write the Vision of Columbus, as Barlow gratefully acknowledges in an elegy addressed to his widow.

"Come to my soul, O shade of Hosmer, come,
Tho' doubting senates ask thy aid in vain;
Attend the drooping virtues round thy tomb,
And hear awhile the orphan'd muse complain.

The man which thy indulgence bade aspire,
And dare pursue thy distant steps to fame,
At thy command she first assumed the lyre,
And hop'd a future laurel from thy name.

How did thy smiles awake her infant song!
How did thy virtues animate the lay!
Still shall thy fate the dying strain prolong,
And bear her voice with thy lost form away."

In the subsequent part of the elegy, Barlow sympathizes with the large, and greatly afflicted family, and extols the excellencies of his friend.

The profession which Mr. Hosmer chose, led him to cultivate the powers of the understanding, rather than the imagination; and in this profession, faithfulness to his clients and strong powers of reasoning, soon raised him into esteem with the bar and the court; and secured him not only much professional business, but civil offices of honor and importance. Besides the common town offices and the commission of the peace which he held, he was elected a Representative to the General Assembly, from October, 1773, constantly until May 1778, when he was elected an assistant, and thus annually until 1780, the year of his death. In 1777, he was speaker of the house of representatives, and had great influence in prompting the Legislature to the adoption of vigorous measures against Great Britain. During a part of the war of the Revolution, he was a member of the Council of safety, and in 1778, besides being an assistant in the State Legislature, he was a member of the Continental Congress. In January, 1780, when the plan was matured by Congress, for establishing a Court of Appeals, principally for the revision of maritime and admiralty cases in the United States, he was elected one of the three judges. There seems to have been an understanding, that one of the judges should be elected from a southern, one from a middle, and one from an eastern section of the country. Seven men were put in nomination for election, and when the votes were cast, George Wythe of Virginia, William Paca of Maryland, and Titus Hosmer of Connecticut, were chosen. Mr. Wythe declined the appointment, Mr. Paca and Mr. Hosmer accepted. But on the duties of this appointment Mr. Hosmer was not permitted to enter, dying suddenly, August 4th, 1780, aged 44.

His person was above the common size, and his countenance expressive. His passions were naturally quick and strong, but kept under discipline. Fond of conversation, and extensively acquainted with men and books, he often entertained at his house a group of friends who courted his society. In deliberative bodies he was always heard with that attention and pleasure, which are secured by lucid and manly argumentation, connected with probity and patriotism. He was, in one word, a gentleman of correct moral habits, a thorough scholar, a learned and eloquent lawyer, and a sound practical statesman; deeply versed in national law and universal history. An obituary notice of him in the Connecticut Courant, says, that he was endowed with a natural genius and capacity of uncommon magnitude, which, cultivated by the best and most liberal education, and continually improving, shone with remarkable lustre, and made him eminently useful in every department of life. Such abilities and improvements, joined with the most polished and engaging manners, formed him, in a rare degree, for influence and service among mankind. He is also styled in this notice, "the gentleman, the scholar, the friend, the patriot, the judge, the benefactor."

The celebrated Dr. Noah Webster regarded him as one of the greatest men Connecticut ever produced. He numbered him among the three "*mighties*,": and these three he designated as William Samuel Johnson, L.L. D. of Stratford, Oliver Ellsworth of Windsor, Chief Justice of the United States, and the Hon. Titus Hosmer of Middletown.

Mr. Samuel Whittlesey Dana, son of Rev. James Dana, D.D. of Wallingford, afterwards of New Haven, was graduated at Yale College in 1775, and soon after came to this town. Having prepared himself for his profession, he opened a law office. He had popular talents, and his appearance at the bar was admired, and had he devoted himself entirely to his profession, he would probably have commanded a large amount of practice. By military promotions he was advanced to the command of a brigade. But his friends early sought to bring him forward into political employments, first by electing him a representative to the State Legislature, and then to the Councils of the nation, so that for a course of years he acted rather as a statesman than a lawyer, being either a representative or a senator in Congress through a part of the administration of Washington, through the whole of the administration of Adams, Jefferson and Madison, and a portion of that of Monroe. During this period, subjects of great difficulty and embarrassment came before the National Legislature, concerning which very different opinions were formed. General Dana, though frank in expressing his own views, conducted himself in such a manner that he retained the respect of both parties, as well as of his constituents. In the latter part of his life he was several years mayor of the city of Middletown: he also accepted the office of presiding Judge of the County Court, which he held until his death in July, 1830.

Mr. Asher Miller, a native of the parish of Middlefield, belonged to a class in Yale College, which was graduated in 1778, and has always been admired for the amount of talent which it contained. He ranked well in this class, and after he left college, made himself acquainted with geology, mineralogy and chemistry, much beyond scholars generally who lived at that time. He became a lawyer, and the people here esteemed and honored him. Though it is not likely that he began to practice law before 1780, yet in 1785 he was elected a representative to the Legislature and repeatedly afterwards, and the Legislature so esteemed him for his knowledge of law and integrity, that in 1793 they appointed him a judge of the Superior Court. He resigned his seat in 1795. Sometime after he went to the South, to survey a tract of wild land about the mouth of the Yazoo river, for a company who were hoping out of those lands to realize a fortune. He was again elected a representative to the Legislature, was long an assistant and many years presiding judge of the county court, and judge of probate. Upon the death of Col. Hamlin in 1791, he was elected mayor of the city, and held this office, with the two offices just mentioned, until his death, December 24th, 1821.

Two sons of the Hon. Titus Hosmer became lawyers, Stephen Titus Hosmer and Hezekiah Lord Hosmer. The former entered Yale College, and pursued his studies there, until the supension of the regular operations of the College in the Revolution, after which he completed his collegiate course under Dr. Dwight, and his name is enrolled in the class he entered, which was graduated in 1782. He studied law with the Hon. William Samuel Johnson, and the Hon. Oliver Ellsworth, his guardian, and about 1785 commenced practice in this place. Left without patrimony, he was thrown upon his own efforts for support and fame, and by the steady exertion of his talents he soon secured a very large practice ; larger it is believed than any lawyer who has lived in this county, and which he retained until he was appointed a judge of the Superior Court in 1815. His custom was to read the books connected with his profession with such fixed attention, and so repeatedly, page by page, that the contents became indelibly fixed upon his memory, and he could call up at will nearly all the reports of cases in support of any point, without referring to his books. By this means he acquired a wonderful memory, which was of great service in his judicial labors. His briefs were prepared with very great attention, the points clearly stated, and cases numerously cited. His habits were exceedingly regular, each week day being devoted to the study of law, interrupted only by the hour's walk which he daily took, and each evening devoted to general reading; for which enjoyment he had the means in a large library, containing among other books, many on theology, which he loved to peruse. He was also exceedingly fond of music, which he studied scientifically, and for many years in the earlier period of his life, he was a very skilful and acceptable leader of sacred music in the sanctuary of God. Among other honors conferred upon him by his fellow citizens, he was repeatedly elected into the Council of the State. In testimony of his great attainments and high standing, the Corporation of Yale College some years before his death, gave him the degree of Doctor of Laws.

In 1815, when he was first appointed judge, the Superior Court consisted of nine judges, a chief judge and eight associate judges, and thus remained until the adoption of the present constitution in 1819, though several changes occurred among the associate judges. The Court was then constituted of five judges; Mr. Hosmer was appointed chief justice, and three of the former judges and one new judge were appointed his associates. In this elevated situation he continued until January 10th, 1833, when arriving at the age of seventy, his term ceased by a provision of the constitution. He died in Middletown, August 6th, 1834, and the following obituary notice was issued the next week, in the New England Advocate then published in this city. This is given entire, with the exception of a few sentences, containing facts already stated.

"The observances at his interment by the public authorities and institutions of the place, and the citizens generally, evince the universal estimation of his worth."

A particular notice of the character of those who have become distinguished for superior talents, virtues or services, affords a rational gratification to their surviving relatives and friends—is just to their memory—and calculated to be useful by inciting to the performance of duty.

To none is such a tribute more especially due, than to

the subject of these remarks. The country at large, during the long course of years, which Judge Hosmer has occupied a seat upon the bench, have had a full opportunity to observe the exhibition of that extraordinary legal learning and purity which are evinced by his reported judgments and opinions; and it is not too much to say, that they have placed his name in the rank of our most distinguished and respected jurists. So far as the opinions of intelligent judicial tribunals and officers, are respected in other states than those in which they are pronounced, no judge has left higher claims than Judge Hosmer to the gratitude of those engaged in judicial pursuits or studies, out of this State. Following the example of several most illustrious judges of our country, particularly Parsons and Kent, it was not unfrequently the case that his opinion contained, not only the reasons for the judgment given in the particular case before him, but a collection of the leading cases on the subject generally, and a concise and lucid epitome of the law as involved in them. By this means, although a great portion of the opinion would not, perhaps, be deemed authoritative, the reader was furnished with an abstract of the leading principles applicable to the subject in one connection, and at the same time, the deliberate views of an able jurist, entertained after consultation with his fellow judges. What ever prejudice may exist in the minds of some against the expression of the opinions of Courts, on points other than those necessarily involved in the case before them, it is believed that on the whole, the benefits of that course far exceed its disadvantages. The opinions pronounced by Judge Hosmer, of this description, are most full and precise, prepared with much care—expressed with great perspicuity and force—and arranged with entire method; and they constitute so many valuable elementary treatises, so to speak, for the instruction of the judge, practitioner and student.

Such are some of the benefits, which the country at large have derived from the public services of Judge Hosmer. In addition to these, his native State has beheld in him for the eighteen years in which he has been a member of her highest judicial tribunal, and of which he was the Chief Justice for fourteen years, the model of that industry, punctuality, urbanity, impartiality, dignity and patience, which, united to extensive legal acquirements and sound judgment, constitute a perfect judge. The progress of public business was never checked by his absence, nor retarded by his remissness. He accorded to all the most punctilious courtesy, and was not only willing, but anxious to listen to all that could be suggested with propriety on the subject under discussion: while he ever maintained the dignity and honor of the Court, by exacting a proper regard to its honor and rights in the intercourse between the Court and its attendants, and of the members of the bar among each other. And it was always evident, that no personal, sinister, or calculating motive swayed his judgment.

His life was almost exclusively devoted to study. He preferred the pleasures of reading, to those of society. But his studies were by no means confined to his profession. His attainments in theology, history and general literature were very extensive, as his conversation and fugitive writings evinced. And it cannot be unknown to many, that he had a fine taste, and an enthusiastic fondness for music.

His habits of exercise and study, were most regular and exact, for a great many of the late years of his life; and even after his retirement from the bench, until reduced and enfeebled by his last illness, he devoted daily, stated portions of his time to exercise and to study. Until his last illness prevented him from taking his usual walks, we never felt the full force of that beautiful line of Gray,

> "One morn I miss'd him on th' accustom'd hill."

To his unvarying habit of morning, noon and evening exercise, he attributed the preservation of his health, which was never seriously, and but seldom slightly disordered.

His temperament was ardent, but his disposition most friendly and forgiving. Every object of philanthropy, and every case of suffering or want, immediately excited his sympathy and aid. And among the excellent traits of his character, one of the most striking was his readiness at all times to render service, by his advice and investigation, to the younger members of the legal profession, who applied to him for assistance. His eager thirst for the improvement of himself and others, led him at once to examine every subject on which he was consulted, and freely to communicate the result of his thoughts and enquiries. His personal appearance was commanding, his deportment dignified, his manners affable, and his elocution polished and graceful. At the age of forty-three, he publicly united himself to the church, and adorned his religious profession by the life and conversation of a christian."

Connecticut has gained celebrity from the number of literary and distinguished men, whom she has raised up and sent forth into different parts of the country, many of whom have held seats in the National Legislature, and others important offices under the General Government or in the States. In this good work Middletown has had a share. The Hon. Josiah Meigs has been mentioned. In the same class to which he and Judge

Miller belonged, were Ezekiel Gilbert of this town, and Ebenezer Sage of Portland. The former became a lawyer, settled in Hudson, N. Y., and was a member of Congress; the latter became a physician, settled in Sag Harbor, L. I., was a literary and political man, and also a member of Congress. Hezekiah Lord Hosmer was a lawyer in Hudson, and succeeded Mr. Gilbert in the National Councils. In the class of 1785, at Yale College, were John Dean Dickinson, son of Dr. John Dickinson, Return Jonathan Meigs, jr., and Phineas Miller, all natives of this town. Mr. Dickinson settled in Troy, N. Y., and was a member of Congress. Mr. Meigs was admitted to the bar in this place, and was a lawyer in Marietta, Ohio; chief justice of the Supreme Court in that State, and also governor; a senator in Congress, and besides other honors conferred upon him by the government of the country, post-master general of the United States.* Mr. Miller was a literary and polished man, a co-partner of Eli Whitney in the cotton-gin, a judge in one of the counties of Georgia, and a member of the State Senate.

Silas Stow, a native of this town, and a lawyer here about 1795, moved to Lowville, N. Y., and was a member of Congress. He died January 19th, 1827, aged 53. At a later period, Henry Randolph Storrs moved from this place to Utica, N. Y., practiced law, and was sent a Representative to the National Legislature.

Among the distinguished natives of Portland, besides Dr. Sage, Asahel Hooker Strong, son of Rev. Dr. Strong, and Rev. Dr. Samuel Shepherd, may be mentioned. Mr. Strong ranked among the very first scholars in his class, was a good special pleader at

---

* See Howe's Historical Collections of Ohio, p. 514.

the bar, and had he lived, would have been worthy of a seat on the bench of the Superior Court. Dr. Shepherd has recently died, and his talents, standing, influence and usefulness in the ministry are well known.

The Rev. James Brainerd Taylor, was a native of Chatham, and it may be stated in this connection, that one of the physicians of this town, though not a native of it, was some years since elected a Representative to Congress from another part of this State, the late Samuel Simons, M. D., of Bridgeport.

The younger Richard Alsop, Esq., has been incidentally mentioned as called upon by Mr. Barlow, to examine the manuscript of his Vision of Columbus. Though occasionally engaged in agricultural and commercial concerns, Mr. Alsop spent most of his days in the pursuit of elegant literature : for which he had an unusual fondness. He was an adept in the classical literature of England, and familiar with the French, Spanish and Italian languages. His love of poetry was enthusiastic, and was abundantly gratified by reading and composition. Numerous poetical pieces, published in newspapers and magazines, and others issued in different forms, were well received, and did honor to his genius. Other works gave him a respectable standing as a prose writer. These writings have been many years before the public, and his character is well known. They are all characterized by purity of expression, and indicate that delicacy of thought and feeling which appeared in his private life. He died suddenly at Flatbush, L. I., on the 16th of August, 1816, in the fifty-sixth year of his age.

John Alsop, the youngest brother of Richard, practiced law for a short time in New London, was then for a short time a bookseller in Hartford, and afterwards for a longer period in New York. The latter part of his life was spent in Middletown, where he died in 1841. He was a literary man, and wrote various pieces of poetry for his own gratification and not for the public eye. The editor of the work, styled "Poets of Connecticut," observes concerning him: "The writings of the younger Alsop, although less melodious than those of his brother, are yet characterized by so much vigor of thought and justness of taste, as to warrant the belief, that had he prepared them for publication, they would have proved fully competent to sustain undiminished the poetical honors of his name."

John G. C. Brainerd, who resided here as a lawyer, for a short time, was a universal favorite, so sweet was his temper, so correct his taste, and so interesting his conversation. His fame arose especially from his becoming afterwards the editor of the "Connecticut Mirror" at Hartford, and issuing in that periodical short pieces of prose and poetry. His conversion and his profession of religion were both remarkable, and when he came to die, faith in Christ turned the shadows of death into the light of the morning.

Arrangements were made in 1824, through the munificence of this town, for the removal of Capt. Partridge's American, Literary, Scientific and Military Academy, which had arisen in Norwich, Vt., to this city, more accessible and convenient for students from differerent parts of the country. A fine site for it was secured, and the foundation of a large substantial edifice laid, "according to the forms of masonic order by the fraternity," in the presence of numbers of the citizens. This and the Chapel being prepared, and the Institution opened, its fifth anniversary was celebrated in September, 1825. The Hon. Samuel W. Dana delivered the address, and besides the citizens, more than two hundred cadets from nineteen different States, and from the District of Columbia, were present to hear him. The occasion and the audience were adapted to enlist his feelings and call forth his talents, and he spoke ably in favor of the Institution. This was designed to answer to its name, to be appropriate to the wants of the American Republic, literary and scientific, exceedingly so in some branches, a part of the course being military science and instruction; to be "in organization and discipline" strictly military, the students to be called cadets, and dressed in uniform. It was intended to avoid the defects of other literary institutions, and to secure more than their advantages; to gratify different tastes and talents, predilections and attainments, by allowing students to enter from one to six years, and to advance as fast as possible, without detention from those who were less prepared or more sluggish, regard being had "to a thorough understanding of the branches" studied; to educate the mind and body together; to occupy leisure hours in agreeable, healthful and useful exercises, and to gratify detachments by tours to a distance, once a year, to interesting scenery, "battle grounds" and important places:—all which is an imperfect sketch of its objects.

Until 1828, "the exclusive control of the discipline" was in the hands of Capt. Partridge; its instruction by himself and teachers whom he employed: then a board of six trustees was appointed and the faculty increased. Ethical lectures, and other instructions were given by the chaplain, Rev. Walter Colton. An important one on duelling was given to the public. Others of the faculty attended to their assigned branches. The account of a tour to the city of Washington, occupies one hundred octavo pages.

One catalogue states the number of cadets belonging

to the Institution, to be two hundred and forty-three, though some twenty of them were in a primary school, taught elsewhere. Many students came from the southern States. Literary gentlemen present at an examination, in 1827, spoke very highly of the acquisitions of the students.

Some who were at the academy, have held seats in the National Councils, or otherwise have acquired distinction in the country or in the States, as writers on military tactics, as engineers, and officers in the Mexican war.

But the Institution was not continued here. In 1829 the buildings were vacated and reverted to the proprietors. They were for sale and at a reduced price. This occurred at an interesting period in the history of the Methodist Episcopal Church, when their leading men were contemplating the establishment of a College, somewhere in the north-eastern States. The proprietors were desirous of accommodating them. Some other places wished for the Institution. In these circumstances "the proprietors of the Academy offered their buildings as a gratuity, for the use of a college or university forever, on condition that there should be an additional endowment raised of $40,000. Citizens of Middletown and vicinity, with a commendable zeal, by a public grant and by private subscriptions, pledged about $18,000 of the endowment." Hence arose the Wesleyan University, which went into operation in 1830, though not chartered until the succeeding year. "The charter secures to it all the rights and immunities of a University." All persons are eligible as officers, and admissible as students without regard to sect or denomination.

The Institution could not have been more happy than it was, in the selection of its first President. Performing an astonishing amount of labor, for one so feeble in

WESLEYAN UNIVERSITY.

health, for the cause of religion and the advancement of the operations of benevolence, Dr. Fisk labored hard and successfully for the University. He loved it until death, offered prayers to God in its behalf, and sent entreaties to men, to exert themselves in its favor. His last interviews with the members of the Faculty and with the students, were adapted to accomplish more than the mere excitement of tender emotions.

The University has already conferred the Baccalaureate degree on four hundred and one students, and has now a greater number of undergraduates than ever. Of the graduated, seventeen were from this town, seventy-five or eighty from the State ; others from more distant parts of the country. A large proportion of the whole, probably would not have received a collegiate education, had not this Institution arisen. Of the graduates, some have entered the professions of law and medicine, some are holding offices in schools and seminaries of learning, and many have become preachers of the gospel. And here a fact exists, which deserves particular notice. It is this, that quite a number who had entered the ministry in the Methodist Church, have joined the University and secured a classical education, that they may more happily expound the scriptures, and more extensively advance the cause of Christ in the world.

The University is well established. Having teachers long experienced, some of whom have been here from nearly or quite the beginning, and sustained by the existing income ; with libraries, university and society, large for the time the institution has existed, with apparatus and cabinets suited to different professorships, with several conferences for its patrons, and graduates traversing the country, speaking good words in its behalf, it possesses the elements of increase and permanency.

A tribute of respect is due to the hero of Lake Champlain, on this occasion. Thomas McDonough was born in 1783, in New Castle County, Delaware, and at the age of seventeen entered the navy of the United States. He went with our fleet to the Mediterranean, where he was engaged in the destruction of the Philadelphia frigate, which the Tripolitans had taken, and the subsequent capture of a Tripolitan gunboat, by the side of the gallant Decatur. In these transactions particularly, he distinguished himself so much, that he was promoted to the rank of lieutenant. His alliance in the family of Mr. N. Shaler of this town, and his residence here as a citizen, neighbor and friend, are well remembered.

In Sept. 1812, then a captain, he took the command of the United States' naval force on Lake Champlain. To entertain anything like adequate ideas of what he did while in possession of that command, especially in the successful battle near its close, we need to read, or rather study, such an accurate and admirable account of the whole, as is given by J. Fennimore Cooper, and that spreads over twenty-five octavo pages. A sketch mostly from that account, is all that can now be attempted. Our force on the Lake in 1812 was small, but with that Capt. McDonough carried Gen. Dearborn's army into Canada, without opposition from the British force, which was then considered as inferior, and prevented all interruption of merchant vessels on the lake by the enemy, and molestation of our inhabitants on its shores. In the winter of 1812–13, when the vessels of the belligerent powers were laid up, both were busily employed in altering, repairing and fitting their respective squadrons for the ensuing campaign, when it was thought an action might take place that would determine the point, which of the powers should have the control of the Lake; but it passed off, and its various operations, without anything decisive. In the winter of 1813–14, preparations were more vigilantly made for the next campaign. Capt. McDonough, awake to his responsibilities, was all eye and activity, day and night. That campaign brought the anticipated result; but not until the summer had passed; not until the enemy had commenced and built that summer the frigate Confiance, a vessel of greater tonnage and force than any we possessed, nor until the Americans, aware of what the enemy was doing, built speedily by great exertion, the sloop Eagle, which joined our squadron at the lines, where that was blockading the enemy. About the last of August it was well known that the Confiance was nearly ready for service, and that the whole British force by water, consisting of that frigate, the brig Linnet, and two sloops of war, the Chubb and Finch, with eleven or twelve gallies, would soon be in the lake under the command of Commodore Downie, and that at the same time Sir George Provost would enter the United States with a formidable army. The immediate design of Sir George was to visit Plattsburgh, where Gen. McCombs was commanding with a handful of men in comparison, and where were a great amount of military stores, and other public property. The squadron carried ninety-five guns, and had about one thousand and fifty men.

In these circumstances our squadron sailed from its anchorage at the lines, and took a position in front of Plattsburgh, to cut off the co-operation of Commodore Downie with Sir George Provost, to prevent effectually Sir George from receiving any assistance from the British squadron in his contemplated attack, and to annoy at the same time the British army in its necessary passage over a ravine.

The American force consisted of the Saratoga, the Eagle, the Ticonderoga, the Preble and ten gallies, carrying eighty-six guns. The number of men was eight hundred and twenty. By the manner in which McDonough anchored his vessels, "with the shoal so near the rear of his line as to cover that extremity, and the land of Cumberland Head so near his broad side, as necessarily to bring the enemy within the reach of his short guns, he completely made all his force available."

Two or three days after, the British entered the lake and sailed for Plattsburgh, giving to Sir George Provost the preconcerted signal of readiness for attack.

On the morning of September 11th, the enemy were seen coming round Cumberland Head, and as they filled, the Americans sprung their broad sides to bear, and a few minutes passed in solemn and silent expectation. Suddenly the Eagle discharged in quick succession her four long eighteens in broadside at first without effect, and the enemies gallies opened. As soon as Capt. McDonough saw that the Eagle's shot told—he sighted himself a long twenty-four, and the gun was fired. This is said to have struck the Confiance, and to have passed the length of her deck, killing and wounding several men, and carrying away the wheel. This was a signal for all the American long guns to open, and it was soon seen that the English flag ship, in particular, was suffering heavily. The Linnet fired a broadside at the Saratoga. Commodore Downie had some difficulty in anchoring his vessel, and did not fire a gun till his ship was secured, "and then it appeared a sheet of flame, discharging all her guns at nearly the same time, principally at the Saratoga. The effect of a broad-side from sixteen long twenty-fours, double shotted, in perfect smooth water, with guns levelled to point blank range and coolly sighted, was terrible in the little ship that received it. About forty men in the Saratoga, near one fifth of her complement, it is supposed, were killed and wounded by this single discharge. The bodies so cumbered the deck that it was necessary to unfasten the hatches and pass them below, which was done in a moment, and the ship resumed her fire as gallantly as ever. Among the slain, however, was the first lieutenant, and only one officer of that rank was left in the vessel. All the guns on the side first engaged were soon rendered useless, and yet in these circumstances, Capt. McDonough found the means of winding her round and firing from the other side. His conduct throughout the battle, and particularly at this crisis, has been greatly extolled. "The personal deportment of Capt. McDonough in the engagement, like that of Capt. Perry in the battle of Lake Erie, was the subject of general admiration. His coolness was undisturbed throughout all the trying scenes on board his own ship, and although lying against a vessel of double the force and nearly twice the tunnage of the Saratoga, he met and resisted her attacks with a constancy that seemed to set defeat at defiance. The winding of the Saratoga, under such circumstance, exposed as she was to the raking broadsides of the Confiance and Linnet, especially the latter, was a bold, seamanlike and masterly measure, that required unusual decision and fortitude to imagine and execute. Most men would have believed that without a single gun on the side engaged, a fourth of the people cut down and their ship a wreck, enough injury had been received to justify submission; but Capt. McDonough found the means to secure a victory in the desperate situation of the Saratoga."

The battle lasted two hours and twenty minutes, and during the conflict the efforts of the parties were mainly against the ships of the commanders, though the Eagle suffered much in the loss of men. Commodore Downie fought as long as he could. He surrendered none too soon. Bad as was the situation of the Saratoga, the situation of the Confiance was worse. The former was hulled fifty-five times, principally by twenty-four pound shot, the latter one hundred and five times. Twenty-eight men were killed in the Saratoga and twenty-nine wounded, fifty-seven in all. A British officer, the day after the battle, reported the deaths in the Confiance to have been forty-one, and the English afterwards admitted the wounded to have been eighty-three, making a total of one hundred and twenty-four, but this number is supposed to be much below the truth. Taken in all its circumstances, the victory was great and triumphant. Capt. McDonough had been honored before, but he received a vast accession of renown from the transactions of this day. Besides the usual medal from Congress, and various compliments and gifts from different States and towns, he was promoted for his services. The Legislature of New York presented him also, with a small estate on Cumberland Head, which overlooked the scene of his triumph. "Albany granted him the freedom of the city. The officers and crews met with the customary acknowledgements, and the country generally placed the victory by the side of that of Lake Erie. In the navy, which is better qualified to enter into just estimates of force, and all the other circumstances that enhance the merits of nautical exploits, the battle of Plattsburgh Bay is justly placed among the very highest of its claims to glory." "The consequences of this victory were immediate and important. During the action, Sir George Prevost had skirmished in front of the American works, and was busy in making demonstrations for a more serious attack. As soon, however, as the fate of the British squadron was ascertained, he made a precipitate and unmilitary retreat, abandoning much of his heavy artillery, stores and supplies, and from that moment, to the end of the war, the northern frontier was cleared of the enemy."

Commodore McDonough was in the naval service till near the time of his death, and in command of the frigate Constitution, in the sea where he performed his earliest exploits. Forced by continual ill-health to give up the command of that ship, he embarked in a private vessel from Gibralter on the 24th of October 1825, and on the 10th of November following, died at sea. On the arrival of his remains at New York, the authorities of the city, in sympathy with the feelings of the nation, deeply mourned the loss of their country; the vessels in the harbor displayed their colors at half mast, and a detachment from the militia accompanied the hearse through the city. You know where his flesh rests in hope;—where the citizen lingers and the stranger stops to read and reflect. To the accomplishments of a gentleman and of an officer, he added the graces of a christian. "In a letter to a relative in his native State, written in June 1814, he expatiates upon the happiness which he derived from his reliance on the merits and atonement of Christ, and earnestly exhorted the friends of his youth to a religious life, as the only one which leads to happiness, and which good sense points out to those convinced of the reality of another world. To his brother's widow left in narrow circumstances, he tendered liberal pecuniary aid, declaring that his religion made him the widow's friend. On the morning of his great victory he prayed with his men, and as he saw the hostile fleet approaching, he remarked: "They are superior to us in force, but by the blessing of God we can beat them." During the battle he was obliged frequently to work his own guns, and three times he was driven across the deck by splinters &c., which flew around him. When asked how he escaped amid such carnage? he replied, pointing to heaven, "there is a power above which determines the fate of men."* In announcing his victory to the War Department, he said: "The Almighty has been pleased to grant us a signal victory on Lake Champlain, in the capture of one frigate, one brig and two sloops of war." Thus he did homage to the God of battles.†

In conclusion suffer me to say, the lines are fallen to you in a pleasant place, and you have a goodly heritage. There are many rivers in our country, longer and deeper than this, with larger cities on their banks than any of which we can boast, and the more beautiful and prosperous they are, so much the better. But the Connecticut has always been admired.

"Fair, noble, glorious river! in thy wave,
The sunniest slopes and sweetest pastures lave,
The mountain torrent, with its wintry roar,
Springs from its home and leaps upon thy shore:
The promontories love thee—and for this
Turn their rough cheeks and stay thee for thy kiss."

And on this river, or elsewhere it would be difficult to find a place, more delightfully situated than this where we are assembled, or scenery more charming than that which spreads itself around us. The elder President Adams in a journey in the month of June 1771 struck

* Religious Intelligencer, vol. 10, pp. 454.

† Allen's B. Dictionary.

the Connecticut river at Enfield, and passed down through Windsor and Hartford to Wethersfield, admiring the valley on the way, and saying when at the last place. "This is the finest ride in America, I believe: nothing can exceed the beauty and fertility of the country." But when he had proceeded on farther to Prospect Hill in Upper Middletown, and the river for miles opened before him, with the intervals and improvements on both sides; with the luxuriant crops ripening for harvest, the body of this town, and the mountains in the distance, he was enraptured, and said; "Middletown I think is the most beautiful of all." Spending two days here, he adds: "The more I see of this town, the more I admire it." Art and industry have added much to the beauty of the place since his visit; it has many more buildings, private and public, and many of superior architecture. The city and the scenery are seen to great advantage from the river eastward, and from slopes and elevations of land in different directions, from the dwellings of many of the inhabitants, particularly from those on High street, and from the University. By this scenery the most pleasing sensations are produced, when the sun throws his rays over the eastern hills, and when he sinks in the west.

Until the Valley of the Father of waters, and the regions beyond the Rocky Mountains, and the Sierra Nevada, shall be occupied; till the mines of California shall be ascertained and appropriated, there will be great emigrations from the East: and with the rapidly increasing influx of population from Europe, and recently from the Isles of the Pacific, and from Asia, these things may be accomplished sooner than we expect, and then the vallies of James river and of the Connecticut may come afresh into remembrance. In the meanwhile a healthful increase of population may be expected here. Manufactures may increase on the little, but valuable mill streams which come to the borders of the city on purpose to bless you. If the calls for the Portland stone multiply as they recently have done, there must be a dense population on the opposite side of the river; and if foreign commerce should not be revived with the West Indies, one, more foreign, may be carried on by them, through a ship channel across the Isthmus to the South Seas, and be the more productive by the enterprising and adventurous spirits who shall previously fly from us.

Yes, there are attractions enough now, to cause an increase of population here. And half a century hence, a century, two centuries, how many fine dwellings, country seats and charming cottages will appear on the surrounding slopes, and how will society be advanced by literature, by science and the arts, by kindness, and above all by Christianity. But who shall live at those periods? Our grave yards now are more numerous than our churches, and filled with larger congregations. The cemetery just laid out will soon be occupied, and how many now present, who shall go thither for a walk; to throw flowers on the graves of friends; to meditate, and to thank God for the glorious doctrine of the resurrection, will soon find there their own *narrow house?* But let us serve God and our generation faithfully, and then death will but unite us to our pious ancestry, and to the good of all past ages.

We copy as an appropriate Appendix to Dr. Field's Address, the following statistical account of "Middletown as it is," in 1850. It is from the pen of E. M. Gorham, Esq., and was originally published among the correspondence of the New York Journal of Commerce.

Publishers of Address.

Middletown---Its Manufactories.

As a place of residence and natural beauty, Middletown has few equals and still less superiors. Its numerous and well arranged shade trees, general healthfulness, clean and spacious streets, full complement of churches and schools,—stately private mansions, with ample grounds tastefully ornamented with delicate shrubbery and rare exotics, shedding forth, in the season, their genial influence—render it one of those quiet rural cities where wealth, satisfied with objects that impart refinement and rational enjoyment, must ever delight to dwell. Located on a gentle rise of ground gradually stretching up west from the river to an elevation of one hundred and fifty-five feet, (the height of the College grounds,) a profusion of beautiful landscape scenery is spread out to view, affording the lover of nature ample food for "a feast of reason, and a flow of soul." And not upon the city alone has nature made its bountiful bestowments. The surrounding country furnishes many fine pleasure drives, and is alike picturesque. Wealth it also has in no stinted measure, but like too many places possessing superior natural charms, the residence of capitalists, it experiences, to too great an extent, the need of their capital, without feeling its thrift-giving power.

The neat white dwelling-house, dotting in thick succession its central localities, speaking of the honesty and *true* citizenship of the journeyman mechanic and the factory operative, is most lamentably, and we might say, censurably deficient. There is in and around the city, a great surplus of eligible, yet unoccupied ground, which might be profitably laid out into suitable squares or plots, and thus afford at a cheap rate a spot upon which the steady and prudent mechanic might erect his "little castle," and at the same time instilin to his existence principles of frugality and a habit of husbanding his earnings, now too often worse than squandered, and, perhaps, simply because no such self-elevating and really tangible object offers itself as an incentive to sober industry and more ennobling action. It is for the capitalists and land-holders of Middletown, to offer these inducements to economy and frugality if they will, and at the same time not only enhance the value of their own property, but also add to the *real* wealth and business of the place.

Although centrally located, it has, nevertheless, in its connections with the business and traveling public, been almost isolated, like a cast-off member of a family, from the rest of the State, and as little sought by inquirers seeking to establish themselves in trade. With no means for the egress and ingress of trade, save by river navigation, and, during its close four or five months of the year, by means of teaming to some point of transportation, it is not strange that its business prosperity in times past should have failed to keep pace with that of sister towns. One advantage, it is true, it has possessed, and still possesses to much greater extent than formerly, over most other manufacturing districts of the State,—the cheapness of freight on heavier materials for home consumption. The large number of vessels employed by the Portland quarries, (now some seventy sail,) return in ballast after discharging their cargo, consequently bring freights of all kinds on return trips at a much less price than could otherwise be afforded, and as low, if not even lower, than the same tonnage can be had at New Haven, and at quite a deduction from the cost to places reached only by railroad communication. The vantage ground thus given manufacturers of Middletown, in connection with the "swift-winged" locomotive, which *now* comes in to supply, in part at least the deficiency heretofore experienced during the suspension of river navigation, makes it second to no other place in Connecticut as an available manufacturing locality,—a fact beginning to be understood as well as put to practical use.

Notwithstanding the limited facilities, especially in winter, for forwarding goods to market, against which manufacturers have had, until quite recently, to contend, the business of Middletown is much more extensive, taken as a whole, than is generally supposed, and no small item in making up the aggregate of the manufacturing interests of the State. Among those, who, despite of these minor difficulties, have profitably established themselves in various branches of *wholesale* manufacture; successfully competing with those elsewhere and more conveniently situated; some of whom have gained a well deserved reputation throughout the Union for the superior quality of their wares,—we find the following named; the statistics of whose business and the kinds of goods made, have been gathered during our peregrinations about the place, with no small degree of care in reference to their correctness, as well as entire completeness.

Commencing with the factories on the "Pameacha," a narrow stream which finds its way along the outskirts of the city, over a rocky bed deep buried between high and rugged banks, we find, first, in one factory, H. L. Baldwin, and F. Baldwin, the first making bank and store locks, and night latches, employing twelve hands; and the latter plate and closet locks, with eight hands, each turning out their appropriate quantum of work. Following up the stream, next comes the factory of Wm. Wilcox & Co., who make a superior article of plate lock, together with a more common lock of the same pattern, employ twenty hands, and turn off $10,000 worth of locks per year. In another part of the same building L. D. Vansands makes improved blind fasteners and saw-strainers, to the amount of $10,000 annually—and gives employment to fifteen hands. Further on stands the extensive sash and blind, flooring and planing mill," of I. W. Baldwin, who is driving a profitable business, and keeps employed some twenty-five hands; and again, the Tweed or Jean mill of the Pameacha Manufacturing Co., with its twenty operatives, and business of $20,000. Still further on, near the juncture of this and the Sanseer stream, are the works of Wm. Stroud, where machinery, castings, iron dirt scrapers, corn shellers, plows, &c., &c., are made, employing in the different branches twenty hands. In the same buildings, Nelson & Hubbard make rules, squares, and bevels; and employ fifteen hands; A. H. Derby also has his apartments for the manufacture of Britannia ware; and F. W. Atkins, for making blind fasteners—each and all of whom, judging by the prevailing activity in their several departments, find a ready sale for their labor.

Crossing from the last named works to "South Farms," a village about fifteen minutes walk from the Post Office, we find located on the "Sanseer Stream," the three Factories of the "Russell Manufacturing Company," who have an invested capital of $100,000, and employ about two hundred operatives in the manufacture of India Rubber Suspenders, cotton, and worsted webbing, of which they make at the present time the amount of from $150,000 to $200,000 a year. On the same stream stands the machine shop of the "Sanseer Manufacturing Company," where are made various kinds of machinery, by some sixteen workmen. This company have considerable repute for the excellence and cheapness of their work; more particularly is this true of their machinery for making fine ivory combs.

Leaving the more eastern suburbs, and retracing our steps back to the city, we are attracted when near its center by the commingled sounds of the ponderous machinery performing its part of the labor in the heavy establishment of W. & B. Douglas, who employ about eighty workmen, and are sending into all parts of the country their highly celebrated "Patent Metallic Pumps, and Hydraulic Rams"—articles that have gained a widely extended name for their superiority over any kind of pump, or water elevator now in use. In connection with these, they are making "Patent wrought iron Butts and Hinges" which, like their pumps and rams, are fast superseding in market other and less approved styles. These gentlemen use, of the raw material, of *iron* some *six hundred tons*, twenty tons of *brass*, and in working it up, three hundred tons of anthracite coal. Besides the articles above named, they also make of hardware, "wrought iron washers, well wheels, friction rolls, &c.," and a new article of "chain pump." Their entire machinery is driven by a powerful and skilfully perfected engine of their own manufacture.

The Messrs. Douglas have raised themselves, increasing year by year to their present business standing (now from $80,000 to $100,000 per year) entirely by their own inventive genius, artistical skill, and the aptness of their inventions to the wants of the public. And the demand for the labor of their heads and hands, is the best evidence that their calculations were based upon no visionary and unsound theory, as to what was really needed to supply the deficiency hitherto experienced in finding a successful, convenient, and cheap mode of forcing water for the various uses to which their Pumps, Rams, and other Hydraulic machines are applied.

Next comes Jesse G. Baldwin, who is largely engaged in the silver-plating business, such as tea, table and dessert spoons, forks, fish and butter knives, soup ladles, &c., together with the manufacture of patent wire, strengthened britannia, and common britannia spoons, wares, which, for beauty of finish, diversity of pattern, and favorable notoriety, will not suffer, we will venture to say, in comparison with anything of the kind made in the Union. It is the boast of Mr. B. that he has workmen equal in mechanical skill, in his line, to any in the country, and from the attractive appearance of the wares shown us at his packing and forwarding rooms, the boast is far from being an idle one. He employs thirty hands, and does a business of from $60,000 to $75,000 per year.

Continuing on through the city, we find Cooley & Danforth engaged in getting up the patent abdominal supporters and trusses, of Drs. Banning, Fitch, and Battle. Aside from the painful necessity of wearing these artificial props and supports, it would seem almost a pleasure to be braced up in so highly finished and beautifully wrought instruments. F. A. Hart & Co., employing about thirty operatives in making silk and cotton corset and shoe lacings, welting cord, shoulder braces, &c. Tewksbury & Tuttle, turning out bevels and squares. H. H. Graves & Co., making a very pretty and substantial article of britannia coffee and tea urns, sugar and cream cups, lamps and candle sticks, with twelve hands. Nathaniel Bacon, a gentleman quite extensively known as the maker of superior bank and safe locks. H. E. Boardman, manufacturer of gaiter boots to the amount of $12,000 per year, employing some fifteen hands. H. & W. Johnson, making the same style of boots to the amount of $5,000 or $7,000 per year. J. K. Penfield, turning out any quantity of patent grummets. Penfield & Camp, are doing a business of $6,000 per year in the manufacture of Judd's medicated liquid cuticle, a substitute for sticking and court plasters in surgical operations, and for dressing wounds, a remedial agent that has only to be tried to know its intrinsic value. H. Salisbury & Co., exclusively engaged in making gold spectacles to the amount of $20,000 yearly. Gleason & Dickinson, doing perhaps a less, but the same kind of business. C. F. Smith, who has recently commenced the manufacture of sand paper. This last named completes the list of wholesale manufacturers in the city.

Again leaving the city, we will spend a few moments among the factories in Upper Middletown. First in the list is that of J. & E. Stevens & Co., who are making wardrobe, coat and hat hooks, surplice pins, door buttons, shutter screws, toy and sad iron stands, axes, tack, shoe and other varieties of small hammers. We might thus go on in enumeration until we had reached the sum of about *seventy* different articles made at this establishment. Half a ton of iron wheels for children's toy waggons, is here made per week. This kind of wheel was, until a very short time since, wholly imported; now, however, those of homemake have, owing to their lesser price, and equal quality, driven the foreign make almost entirely out of the market. There is another interesting fact connected with the article of *tack* hammers here made, which is only another of the many instances where Yankee inventive ingenuity has triumphed over the slower movements and less fertile genius of manufacturers across the water. These miniature hammers are made of Scotch iron, which, of course, must first be imported, and duties paid. A large invoice of the same was, a short time since, exported and sold in Liverpool in competition with home make, or pauper labor, at a clear advance to the shipper of twenty-five per cent. The Messrs. Stevens & Co., employ at their works forty hands, and do a business of from $35,000 to $40,000 a year. William P. Allison makes hammers of the Allison, Browns, S. F. Claw, Warner, and cast steel stamps, said to be of very desirable styles and quality, to the worth of $10,000 a year, and keeps employed twelve hands. The Messrs. Norths are manufacturing brass knob chamber or shutter bolts, brass knob barrel, flat shutter, and improved tower bolts, also steel spring square bolts and japanned lifting handles, employ ten hands, and do a business of $8,000 to 10,000. Kelsey, Wright & Co., get up a fine article of suspender buckles, to the amount of $12,000 to $15,000, and employ some twenty hands. Still further up, or at Upper Houses, Warner & Noble manufacture hammers of the same styles as those made by W. P. Allison, and do about the same amount of business.

Once more taking our "note book," we will extend observations along the "Arrowmammett" River, which rises at Durham, flows through Middletown, (Middlefield Society) and empties into the Connnecticut, affording many excellent water privileges yet unoccupied, besides those already in use. Commencing at the Reservoir, some five miles out of the city, is the horn button factory of Alfred Bailey & Co., who are having a successful run of business. Turning our face towards the city, we successively meet in their order, the works of Mark Mildrum & Co., where are made brass and copper wash basins, coal shovels, sifters, &c.; bone grinding mill of Andrew Coe; the Falls Manufacturing Company, at Middlefield Falls, who, with thirty operatives, make suspender twist, to the amount of $20,000 per year. This company have just increased the size of their mill, and are otherwise extending business. H. Aston & Co., pistol factory, in the employ of the United States, have fifty hands, and make six thousand pistols a year, worth $35,000. Blasting powder mill of D. C. Rand, with six workmen—the powder here made is principally used at the Portland quarries. Paper mill of R. F. Brower —the style is light and heavy hardware wrapping. Carbine Factory of North & Savage, at work for the United States. This factory is not now under full blast, having just gone through thorough repairs, in anticipation of an enlarged business. Factory formerly known as Starr's Pistol Factory, now occupied by William Ashton, in the manufacture of pistols, and James Tidgewell & Son, try-squares, bevels and guages. Comb factory of Buckland, Stearns & Co., who employ sixteen hands, and turn off from $25,000 to $40,000 worth of ivory combs annually. It would seem hardly possible for human skill to invent machinery to work more precise, and we might say delicately, than that used at this establishment, or to find ivory combs possessing a more perfect completeness when finished, than those made by this firm. And last, though by no means least, the plane factory of Austin Baldwin. Mr. B. has been long and extensively known as a maker of joiner's planes, and by none better than those who have had occasion to experience the advantages of a good plane over a poor one. Planes of all patterns are here made to the amount of $25,000 a year, by twenty-eight workmen.

Again, in Westfield Society, a pleasant village some two miles west of the city, there is a never failing stream called "Willow Bridge Brook," having its rise in the mountains, and flowing into the Connecticut. There are several unimproved water privileges along its course, where a fall of twenty to thirty feet might be obtained with limited expense. Although it is but quite recently that attention has been turned to this stream for its manufacturing importance, there are already located here a factory owned by James O. Smith, extensively engaged in making Japan varnish, which has a large sale; the various articles in the line of tin and japanned ware, which, owing to its superior quality, has a successful competition in market with the foreign make. Mr. S. employs twenty hands, and supplies a demand for his goods to the amount of from $25,000 to $30,000 per year. A mill for weaving coach lace, with some six operatives, owned by J. B. Rose. And the factory of H. H. Graves & Co., where in addition to their works in the city, they make some $5,000 worth of Britannia ware.

As may be inferred from what we have already said, Middletown is evidently arousing herself, and shaking off the rust that has been allowed to gather and eat into her vitality for years past, and will soon have secured an honorable name beside the more noted manufacturing districts of the State. The factories herein named, located in Upper Middletown, have all risen up within five years, and other sections of the town give good evidence of newly infused business life. The Branch Railroad to Berlin, little as it meets the actual wants of the whole community, has unquestionably assisted to add new impetus to manufacturing, as well as to other branches of home industry. One manufacturer stated to us, that he saved by it in the transportation of his wares during the close of the river, at least one dollar per day; and, we presume, the same is true of others who have been compelled, at such time, to team their goods to a point from whence they could be taken to places of destination.

It is said that more building has been done during the past year, than in any previous year within recollection, while important projects have taken root which are calculated to add very materially to the prosperity as well as attractiveness of the place. Not among the least, is the purchase and appropriate laying out, by an association of gentlemen, of ground for a cemetery. This new place of sepulture is a vast and beautiful mound, rising to an elevation of some *two hundred and twenty-seven* feet above the river, about one mile from the centre of the city and bears the name of Indian Hill Cemetery, its name derived, it is said from traditionary story, which makes it the place where the Red men of the forest once lighted their council fires, and where are deposited the bones and hunting implements of several noted chiefs. The mound contains some forty-five or fifty acres, towers majestically above the surrounding country, and commands at once a most magnificent view far up the river, and overlooks the city with its busy life—ever standing like a faithful monitor to warn the thoughtless living of the fleetness of earthly existence, and to call their attention from worldly scenes to the solemn spot where sleep their kindred and friends. From this calm eminence, the grave side mourner may, from among the habitations of the dead, also catch the inspiration of full-lifed nature, and in holy adoration contemplate the goodness and greatness of God, as displayed in his mighty works, as well as in his no less instructive bereavments. We know of no cemetery in New England more pleasantly located, or susceptible of greater desirable improvements. Seven hundred lots, each containing six hundred and twenty-five square feet, have been staked off, leaving still ground enough for some seven or eight hundred more of like dimensions.

But to dwell on all that is indicative of the awakening of a correct public sentiment as to what is really needed to make Middletown what it should be, and what nature has designed it to be, would require too much time and space. It is enough to say that its course is, in all respects, if we can frame a conclusion from present evidences, henceforth to be onward and upward, and that a very few years at the most will place it by the side of the most important manufacturing towns of Connecticut.

E. M. Gorham.

Middletown, January 22, 1851.

NOTES,

Prepared by Dr. Field to follow his address ;

Indian Deed ; Origin of early settlers.

Sketches of the Towns and Societies within the original limits of Middletown, together with the Rise of different Denominations, their Churches and C. Officers ; Lists of Civil Officers, &c.

(NOTE A.)

Deed of the Indians to the Inhabitants of Middletown.

This writing made the twenty-fourth of January 1672, between Sepunnamoe, Joan, alias Weekpissick, Machize, Wesumpsha, Wamphaneh, Spunno, Sachamas, Taccomhuit, proprietors of Middletown, alias Mattabesett, of the one part, and Mr. Samuel Wyllys, Capt. John Talcott, Mr. James Richards, and John Allyn, in behalf of the inhabitants of Middletown, on the other part, witnesseth, that the said Sepunnamoe, Joan, alias, Weekpissick, Machize, Wesumpsha, Wamphaneh, Spunno, Sachamas, Taccomhuit, being privy to and well acquainted with Sowheag, the great Sachem of Mattabesett, his gift of great part of the township of Middletown to the Honorable Mr. Hanyes formerly, and for a further and full consideration to us now granted and paid, by the said Mr. Samuel Wyllys, Capt. John Talcott, Mr. James Richards and John Allyn, have given, granted, bargained, sold and confirmed, and by these presents do fully and absolutely give, grant and confirm unto the said gentlemen, all that tract of land within these following abutements, viz. on Wethersfield bounds on the north, on Haddam bounds on the south, and to run from the great river the whole breadth towards the east six miles, and from the great river towards the west so far as the General Court of Connecticut hath granted the bounds of Middletown shall extend; to have and to hold the aforementioned tract of land as it is bounded, with all the meadows, pastures, woods, underwood, stones, quarries, brooks, ponds, rivers, profits, commodities, and appurtenances whatsoever belonging thereunto, unto the said Mr. Samuel Wyllys, Capt. John Talcott, Mr. James Richards and John Allyn, in behalf and for the use of the inhabitants of the town of Middletown, their heirs and assigns forever; always provided, there be three hundred acres of land within the township of Middletown on the east side of Connecticut river, laid out, bounded, and recorded to be and remain the heirs of Sowheag and the Mattabesett Indians and their heirs forever; as also one parcel of land on the west side of Connecticut river, formerly laid out to Sawsean, shall be recorded and remain to the heirs of the said Sawsean forever, any thing in this deed to the contrary notwithstanding. And the foresaid Sepunnamoe, Joan, alias Weekpissick, Machize, Wesumpsha, Wamphaneh, Spunno, Sachamas, Taccomhuit, for themselves, do covenant to and with the said Mr. Wyllys, Capt. Talcott, Mr. Richards and John Allyn, in behalf of the inhabitants of Middletown, that they the said Sepunnamoe, Joan, Machize, Wesumpsha, &c., have only full power, good right and lawful authority, to grant, bargain, sell and convey all and singular the before hereby granted, or mentioned to be granted premises, with their and every of their appurtenances, according as is above expressed, unto the said Mr. Wyllys, Capt. Talcott, Mr. Richards and John Allyn, in behalf of the inhabitants of Middletown aforesaid, their heirs and assigns forever, and that they, the said inhabitants of Middletown, shall and may by force and virtue of these presents, from time to time and at all times forever, hereafter, lawfully, peaceably and quitely, have, hold, use, occupy and possess and enjoy the aforesaid parcel of land with all its rights, members and appurtenances, and have, receive and take the rents, issues and profits thereof to their own proper use and behoof forever, without any let, suit, trouble or disturbance whatsoever of the said Sepunnamoe, Joan alias Weekpissick, Machize, Wesumpsha, Wampaneh, Spunno, Sachamas, Taccomhuit, their heirs or assigns, or of any other person or persons, claiming right, by, from or under us, or any of us, or by the means, act consent, privity or procurement, and that free and clear, and freely and clearly acquitted, exhonerated and discharged, or otherwise well and sufficiently saved and kept harmless by the said Sepunnamoe, Joan, Machize, Wesumpsha, Wamphaneh, Spunno, Sachamas, Taccomhuit, their heirs, executors and administrators, of and from all former and other grants, gifts, bargains, sales, titles, troubles, demands, and incumbrances whatever, had, made, committed, suffered, or done, by the said Sepunnamoe, Joan, Machize, Wesumpsha, Wamphaneh, Spunno, Sachamas, Taccomhuit. In witness hereof they have signed, sealed and delivered this writing with their own hands the day and year first above written.

Signed, sealed and delivered in presence of us,
Joseph Nash,
George Graves,
Thomas Edwards,
Robert Sanford,
Nessehegen ⋈ his mark
Wannoae ⋈ his mark
Tarramuggus ⋈ his mark
Puccacun ⋈ his mark
Sachamas' mother ⋈ her mark

Sepunnamoe ⋈ his mark
Joan, alias Weekpissick, his mark
Mamachize, ⋈ his mark
Wesumpsha ⋈ his mark
Mamphaheh ⋈ his mark
Spunno ⋈ his mark
Sachamas ⋈ his mark
Tacumhuit his mark

The original is entered in the old Court Book of Records, fol 70, April 5th, 1673, per me, John Allyn, Secretary.

Middletown, April the eighth, one thousand, six hundred and three, Pashama, Rashiask, Massecumb, Robin, Pewamskin, with consent of the natives, who signed and sealed the deed above written, were acknowledged to be interested in this land reserved to them therein and for themselves, their heirs and assigns, did and by these presents do give grant and confirm unto the inhabitants of Middletown their heirs and assigns, forever all their right, title, interest, in all that tract of land granted by the above written deed unto the said inhabitants of Middletown fully and largely as is expressed in the above written deed, as witness our hands the day and year first above written.

Signed, sealed and delivered in the presence of us,
Nathaniel White,
John Hall,
Samuel Stocking,

Rachiask's ⋈ mark.
Pashunna's ⋈ mark.
Massakump's ⋈ mark.
Robin's ⋈ mark.
Pewampskin's ⋈ mark.

The above written is a true record of the deed of the land within the township of Middletown, from the Indian proprietors.

Per me, John Hall, Recorder.

In the copy of the Indian deed by Mr. Hall there is difficulty in reading the Indian names, and some of them are evidently written somewhat differently as they are repeated. Sachamas, (probably a title rather than a name,) is plainer than the names generally and the last syllable in it is written three ways. In the hope that the original in the Colony Records at Hartford, was better written, and knowing the great experience and skill of the clerk in reading ancient manuscripts, a request was made to him to give the names as written by the Secretary. The following is his answer :

"The names of the Indian grantors in the deed of 1672–3, as recorded, are Sepunnamoe, Joan, alias Weekpissick, Machize *, [in the *deed*, the signature Mamachiz,] Wesumpsha *, Wamphaneh *, Spunno, Sachamas, Taccomhuit, [*signature*, Tacumhuit *,] Witnesses (Indian,) Nessehegen, Wannoae, Tarramuggus *, Puccacun *, and Sachamus' mother *.

In the Coginchaug [Durham] purchase (24 Jan., 1672-3, the names of grantors marked (*) above, are spelled in the same way; besides these Wannoe, Tom alias Negannoe, Neseheag squaw, Spunno, Sarah Kemhosh squa, Marragan's mother, and Tahhows squa, [signature, Tubhous squa,] join in the grant. Witness Sepunnamoe, Nesehegen."

(NOTE B.)

Origin of early settlers, before and in 1670, those in the latter year being householders and acknowledged as proprietors.

While it is very evident that the early settlers or their parents were from the British Isle, and that they were nearly all of English extraction, there is not a little difficulty in ascertaining who came directly to this place, or almost immediately on landing this side of the Atlantic, and respecting others where they lived in Massachusetts and Connecticut before settling here. Dr. Trumbull in his History of Connecticut says, "that the principal planters were from England, Hartford and Wethersfield —that the greatest number were from Hartford, and that there was a considerable accession from Rowley, Chelmsford and Woburn in Massachusetts." There were also some planters from Windsor, and from some towns in Massachusetts, besides those which he names. Some had lived in several places. Various circumstances may have induced individuals to dwell here and there for a time with relatives, connections and acquaintances, and to have engaged in one employment and another, even where they did not themselves become possessors of houses and lands.

With respect to the settlers whose names do not appear among the householders and proprietors in 1670,

William Bloomfield was from Hartford, and it is said he returned thither: if he did, he afterwards removed to Long Island. Nathaniel Brown was from Hartford. He had five children born to him in Middletown, from 1661 to 1669, and it is probable that he died in the last mentioned year. His son, Nathaniel Brown, 2d, lived in this place after him. George Graves was from Hartford and returned to that place: while here he was elected twice a Representative to the General Court. William Markum removed to Hadley, Mass., and died there. What became of John Martin is not known. William Smith, who was from Wethersfield, removed to Farmington. Matthias Treat was also from Wethersfield and died before 1663, leaving a family which removed from this place. A man by the name of Joseph Smith died in Rocky Hill in Wethersfield in 1673, who may have been the same person who dwelt a while in the Upper Houses. Robert Webster was from Hartford, son of Gov. John Webster of Hartford, afterward, of Hadley, he was the ancestor of the late Noah Webster, L.L. D. While here he represented the town almost continually in the General Court.

Inquiries concerning the previous residence or residences, of *Thomas Allen*, have not been pursued to a satisfactory result.

Obadiah Allen, was recommended by the elders of the church in Windsor, which renders it probable that he at least resided in that town for a time. This name is not always spelt with an *e*, All*e*n; in a town record book it has been seen spelt, Al*y*n and All*y*n; on the old Church Records it is All*i*n.

Nathaniel Bacon, probably came directly from England. He was nephew of Andrew Bacon of Hartford.

The family were from Stretton in England, county of Rutland.

William Briggs, was from Wethersfield.

From whence *Alexander Bow* and *William Cheney* came, it is not ascertained. The latter was a representative to the General Court in several instances.

Jasper Clements, was born in England about 1614. He died here in 1678, aged 64, leaving property for support of schools in the town.

Henry Cole married in Hartford in 1646. He was not a landholder there, but may have been a resident. He moved from Middletown to Wallingford soon after 1670; Edward Higby purchased part of his property.

Nathaniel Collins, the first settled pastor in Middletown, and his brother *Samuel Collins*, were from Cambridge, Mass., sons of Dea. Edward Collins.

William Cornwall, was an early settler in Hartford, and had five sons; three of whom, John, Samuel and William, jr., accompanied him to Middletown. It is said that he died in 1677, an old man.

George Durant had lived in Malden, Mass., and probably came from that town to this place.

Samuel Eggleston, was from Windsor.

Edward Foster; of his previous history I have no information.

John Hall had been in a family state, many years before he left England, and was an early settler both in Hartford and Middletown. His three sons, *Richard*, *Samuel* and *John Hall, jr.*, probably came to Middletown, when he did. He died May 26, 1673, in the 89th year of his age. John Hall, jr., was the good deacon mentioned in the Address.

Giles Hamlin is generally considered as coming here immediately from England. He was born about 1612.

He was in the habit of crossing the Atlantic, and was engaged in foreign commerce, "partly by himself and partly with John Pynchon of Springfield, his brother-in-law John Crow, jr., who dwelt in Fairfield, and elder Goodwin of Hartford, afterwards of Farmington." He died in 1689.

William and Daniel Harris came to Middletown from Rowley, Mass.

George Hubbard was an early settler in Hartford, and had six sons, Joseph, Daniel, Samuel, George, Nathaniel and Richard. The two oldest sons settled in Middletown.

This George Hubbard, was a distinct person from the George Hubbard who resided in Wethersfield, Milford and Guilford. The genealogies of their families show this.

Thomas Hubbard, who became a settler and proprietor in Middletown, is supposed to have come from Wethersfield, as there was an inhabitant early there of that name. He died in 1671, and whether he was related or not to either of the George Hubbards just mentioned is not known.

John Hurlburt was from Wethersfield, son of Thomas Hurlburt of that town.

Isaac Johnson was from Roxbury and recommended from the church there to the church in Middletown.

John Kirby, one correspondent states, settled first in Boston, and it may be that he landed there and remained for a short time. Another correspondent says that his first child was born in Hartford, and a third that he had a child born or baptized in Hartford in 1646, but adds "that he lived in Wethersfield, and had children born there in 1649 and 1651. From this town he removed to Middletown. In 1654 he owned a house and land in Rowington, Warwickshire, Eng., and the presumption is that he emigrated first from that place.

Isaac Lane, I know not from what place he came.

William Lucas. There was a William Lucas at Marblehead in 1648, who may have been the same person that came here. He died in 1690.

Anthony Martin. There was an early settler in Wethersfield by the name of Samuel Martin; but the point has not been investigated, whether Anthony was from that town.

Thomas Miller was recommended to the church in Middletown, from the church in Rowley.

Thomas Ranney, is said to have been from Scotland. He was married to Mary Hubbard, the eldest child of George Hubbard of Middletown, in 1659, and had five children, Thomas, John, Joseph, Mary and Elizabeth. He died Jan. 25th, 1713, and was the first person buried in the oldest grave yard in the Upper Houses.

David Sage, is said to have been from Wales.

John Savage married in Hartford in 1653, and may have resided there, though not a proprietor in that place.

Samuel Stocking was from Hartford and a son of George Stocking.

Samuel Stow, who preached to the people in Middletown some years as a candidate for the ministry, I have very lately been informed by a friend, was not born in Concord, Mass., as represented on p. 48, but in Roxbury, and that he did not live in Concord, until after he became a candidate. The probability therefore is, that his brother *Thomas Stow*, if not his nephew, *John Stow*, were also born in Roxbury, Mass. Samuel Stow died May 8, 1704.

James Tappin. There was a man named James Tappan, married at Guilford to Hannah Garrett, March 5,

1656. But it is doubtful whether this was the same person that settled in Middletown.

Edward Turner was from Milford, and had two or three children baptized there. His wife was recommended to the church in Middletown, from the church in that place.

John and *William Ward* are supposed to have been both from Rowley. The former was recommended from the church in that town.

Andrew, *Robert* and *John Warner*, were sons of Andrew Warner, who emigrated from Hatfield, Eng., about 1630, who was at Cambridge in 1632, and at Hartford among the early settlers. He was a deacon in the Rev. Mr. Hooker's church and an influential man in that town. He removed to Hadley in 1659, where he died in 1684, at an advanced age. The three sons in Middletown were farmers. Andrew Warner died Jan. 26th, 1582. Robert repeatedly represented the town in the General Court; he died April 10th, 1690. John died in 1700. The Warners in Chester and Lyme, are descendants of Daniel Warner, one of their brothers.

Thomas Wetmore is said to have been from Wales. He married a daughter of John Hall in Hartford, in 1645 and had two or three children baptized there. He died in 1681, aged 66.

Nathaniel White was from Hartford, a son of John White of Hartford and Hadley.

John Wilcox was from Hartford.

Further investigation may show that some of those settlers whose origin we have not stated, were from Chelmsford and Woburn.

List of the Householders and Proprietors, as taken March 22d, 1670.

Name	£	s.	Name	£	s.
Thomas Allen,	£103	10	Joseph Hubbard,	38	00
Obadiah Allen,	30	00	Daniel Hubbard,	24	00
Nathaniel Bacon,	119	00	Thomas Hubbard,	61	00
William Briggs,	42	00	John Hurlburt,	26	00
Alexander Bow,	45	00	Isaac Johnson,	24	00
William Cheney,	101	00	John Kirby,	88	00
Jasper Clements,	98	10	Isaac Lane,	40	00
Henry Cole,	115	00	William Lucas,	42	00
Nathaniel Collins, this stock and person with £150 given him in land by the town,	225	00	Anthony Martin,	60	10
			Thomas Miller,	50	10
			Thomas Ranney,	105	00
			David Sage,	68	10
			John Savage,	129	00
Samuel Collins,	58	00	Samuel Stocking,	113	10
William Cornwall,	160	00	Samuel Stow,	194	00
John Cornwall,	41	00	Thomas Stow,	54	00
Samuel Cornwall,	45	00	John Stow,	24	00
William Cornwall, jr.,	45	00	James Tappin,	50	00
George Durant,	34	00	Edward Turner,	44	00
Samuel Eggleston,	55	00	John Ward,	44	00
Edward Foster,	26	00	William Ward,	110	00
John Hall,	99	00	Andrew Warner,	84	00
Richard Hall,	75	00	Robert Warner,	87	10
Samuel Hall,	130	00	John Warner,	96	10
John Hall, jr.,	26	00	Thomas Wetmore,	125	10
Giles Hamlin,	134	00	Nathaniel White,	169	10
William Harris,	200	00	John Wilcox,	140	00
Daniel Harris,	132	00			
George Hubbard,	90	10	Total,	£4,322	10

(NOTE C.)

Sketches of the Towns and Societies, within the original limits of Middletown, together with the rise of different Denominations, their Churches and E. Officers; Lists of Civil Officers, &c.

The territory of Middletown, which at first contained but one Ecclesiastical Society, the business of which was done by the town, as there was but one denomination of Christians in it, now contains four towns: Middletown and Cromwell on the west side of Connecticut river, and Portland and Chatham on the east; the first of which contains three local Ecclesiastical Societies, or which were so, until within a limited period, and which, in conformity with custom, it will be convenient to speak of as such still; the second and third contain one Society each, and the fourth one whole society, most of a second and a fraction of a third.

As the publication of the exercises in November, 1850, has been unexpectedly delayed until the beginning of 1852, an attempt will be made to bring down the statistics in this note to the present time.

We will begin with the First Society in Middletown, and then proceed to Middlefield and Westfield, the two other societies now belonging to Middletown.

The First Society is much the largest of the three and has the greatest variety of soil and surface. There is but little alluvial ground in it and yet the land is good with the exception of that on the range of the Strait Hills in the south east part, and that is valuable for wood. Beyond that in the district called Maromos, there are arable and productive lands near the river.—There is much rich soil in the society, and the arable lands here and in the vicinity are made more and more productive by increasingly skilful cultivation, helped onward by the proceedings and anniversaries of the Middlesex County Agricultural Society.

This Society includes the city, where a large part of the early settlers placed their habitations, and whence the population spread in different directions. Almost all the inhabitants here, as in the rest of the Society and in the other Societies, for a considerable period, were occupied in clearing and cultivating the ground.

In the profitable commerce which sprung up within the limits of the city and was carried on with the West Indies, about the middle of the last century, Richard Alsop was by far the most successful. The place afforded great advantages for carrying on this commerce, being situated on the largest river in New England, having a fine harbor, to which vessels could ascend drawing ten feet of water, with rich towns on its banks, where articles suitable for the West India market could be easily procured. Mr. Alsop knew well how to avail himself of these advantages. He was a son of John Alsop, Esq., of Newtown, L. I., afterwards of Esopus on Hudson river, an attorney at law. He was educated a merchant in the store af Philip Livingston, in the city of New York, and about 1750 came to this town and commenced business. He had his store, or rather stores, in the lower rooms of the old town-house, or court-house, as it was sometimes called, standing in Main street, a little above Washington street. He soon engaged in commerce, and prospered so much that he sometimes insured vessels for others on his private responsibility. He was a man of integrity, generosity and public spirit. His fellow citizens repeatedly elected him a representative to the Legislature. He died early in the Revolution, and the following summary of his estate, is from the Probate records. " Amount of inventory of Richard Alsop's estate,

£34,818:7:7," besides "a large amount of money lodged in Jamacia, stock in two partnership concerns, a large number of book debts due," and other property, the value of which could not be ascertained. The record of this inventory occupies fifty-one folio pages.

There were others who acquired much property by commerce, or concerns connected with it before the Revolution, though by the events of the war, or other causes, they did not all die rich. Philip Mortimer came here from Boston, sometime before the Revolution, and went largely into the rope-making business. The inventory of his estate was £6,177:7:8. Mr. Mortimer was a man of taste. He built a large and beautiful house for that day, on the bank of the river, now owned by Capt. William G. Hackstaff, ornamented a tract of several acres around it, planted lines of button-ball trees from it to Main Street, made a walk, placed seats by it under the trees and threw it open to the public, which became an object of attraction, not only to people of the town, old and young, but to strangers. When a portion of the French army in the Revolution were on their way from the east to Washington's encampment, stopping over the Sabbath in Middletown, the officers amused themselves by dancing in the evening under the shades. The names of Washington, Layfayette and other interesting characters, were cut in the trees.

The Revolution having come to a successful issue, commerce began to revive; and that this might be pursued to greater advantage, a petition, dated Jan. 15, 1784, was signed and presented to the Legislature the following May, that a part of Middletown, where commerce had been principally and almost wholly carried on before the war, might be invested with city privileges. The signers alledged that "many inconveniences were felt by them, as well as by strangers, for want of a due regulation of the police of the town;" and that keeping high ways in good repair, removing obstructions from the channel of the adjoining river and many other regulations for the commercial convenience and utility of the memorialists, were impossible to be accomplished without a separate and special jurisdiction. The petition was granted in May of the same year; and at the same session, Hartford and New Haven, New London and Norwich, were constituted cities.

The city is bounded as follows: "Beginning at the mouth of Little river, or Ferry river, thence in a north-east line, to the east side of Connecticut river, at high water mark, thence on the bank of the said Connecticut river, at high water mark, until it comes to a point due east from Sumner's Creek, thence in a west line to the mouth of Sumner's Creek, thence southerly and westrely as the said creek runs to Warwick's Bridge, thence west to the Little River, [or West River, as the stream is sometimes called,] thence northerly and easterly down the Little river, as the same runs to the first boundary, including the waters of the said Little river, Sumner's Creek and Connecticut river."

The medium length of the city may be a mile and a half, and its breadth, exclusively of the river, which varies here from 97 to 80 rods, is about the same. It is to be lamented that the petition does not state the number of inhabitants within the specified bounds, nor give any statistical information. But it is well known that the people then lived very generally on the streets running parallel, or nearly so, with the Connecticut, as far back as High street, and others crossing these streets at nearly right angles: the much greater part on the eastern half of the streets then existing: for since that time Broad street and some other streets have been opened. Since the incorporation of the city, more particularly, within the last thirty years, the western half has increased proportionally more than the eastern. And while the population has been increasing, many new buildings have been erected, some of large dimensions and improved style of architecture; some of more substantial materials. The general appearance of the city has been greatly improved within the memory of many persons now living, and not a little within a few years. The young can hardly believe, smooth as Main Street now is, that once there was such a depression in the road in front of the McDonough House, now building, that a person standing there could not see over a rise just below, so as to discern a load of hay passing a bridged ravine a little further onward.

In 1815, there were in the city two hundred and ninety-nine dwelling houses, and three hundred and fifty-three families; in 1850, there were six hundred and three dwelling-houses, and seven hundred and eighteen families. At the former period, there were in the city five churches, attended however, by people from all parts of the First Society, one Bank, a Court-house, Goal and Alms-house. There are now seven Churches, most of them attended in a similar manner, and one or two receiving many of their attendants from beyond the limits of said Society, four Banks, a Court-house, Custom-house, Goal and Alms-house; a number of them recently built: there are also the University buildings, and the house for the High-school.

The Church edifices, the University buildings, and the High-school House, will come into view hereafter. The first Bank edifice was erected after the bank was granted in 1795, and was so constructed that the stockholders might have a safe place for the deposit of their money and the officers for the transaction of their business. For the Banks of a later date, buildings were purchased and fitted for like purposes. These are, *Middlesex County Bank*, which occupies the building previously used by the Branch Bank of the United States; the *Middletown Savings Bank*, and the *Central Bank*.

The present *Court House*, the second building of the kind in Middletown, since the County of Middlesex was formed, was built in 1832: Its of brick, stuccoed in front, with a portico, 84 feet by 50. It cost $10,100, of which the County paid $2,600; the City $1,500; the Town $3,000, and individuals $3,000; it being all arranged at the time that the City and Town were to enjoy certain privileges in the building. Here the records of the City and Town and of Courts are kept, and here is the Town Clerk's Office.

The *Custom House* was not built until 1834, the customs being previously collected in buildings hired for the purpose. This is of hewn stone, 52 by 48, the first story rests on brick arches, the roof is zinc and fire-proof. It cost $17,500, all of which was appropriated by the United States, excepting $500, which individuals gave towards the purchase of the site.

Besides the conveniences which this building affords for the collector of customs, a room on the first floor is used for a Post Office.

The present *County Goal*, was built in 1848. It is of stone, forty-four feet by twenty-six, having twelve cells. This is the third building of the kind since 1784. Separately from the land which the town gave, it cost $3,300. The County paid $2,300, the Town $1,000. This is near the Alms-house in the southwest part of the city.

The *Alms-House*, was first occupied by the poor, in May, 1814. It is a brick building, sixty feet by forty, two stories in front and three in the rear, which, with the ground, two and a half acres, fences and furniture, cost $8,755.

For some years there have been three Taverns in the city—the *Central Hotel*, the *Mansion House*, and the *Farmers and Mechanics Hotel*. The Central Hotel is kept for the present, in a large private dwelling, and its former site has been purchased by the *McDonough Hotel Company*, formed in May, 1851. On this they are now building a Hotel, which already bears the honorable name of the "*McDonough House.*" It is fifty-six feet in front on Main street, and sixty-six in the rear; one hundred on Court street. It will cost about $30,000; it is expected to be completed soon, and opened in June, (1852.) The whole building will be devoted to the uses of the hotel, excepting two stores, in the first story on Main street. The large house first built for a hotel, corner of Main and Washington sts., belonging to the estate of the Rev. Dr. Jarvis, is soon to be opened as a private hotel.

Most of the mercantile business of Middletown has always been done in the city, the greater part on Main st., though considerable has been done on Water street. This has been fully doubled in thirty years, notwithstanding the rise of business in Meriden, whence many persons formerly came to trade, at stores here. If we include all the business done in the city, mercantile, mechanical and manufacturing, it has been much more than doubled. J. & D. Hinsdale did a very large business more than thirty years ago, and about the same period, some other merchants traded to a very respectable amount. But there is now a greater number of large stores.

The writer is indebted particularly to the kindness and examination of a friend, for the number of stores, shops, &c., at the present time (March 1852), in the city, which are: seven Dry Good stores, four Merchant Tailors', five stores dealing in Shoes, Clothing and other articles; and here it should be stated that several Dry Good stores and Clothing establishments carry on the tailoring business, twenty-nine Grocery stores, two Dry Good and Grocery, three Crockery, two Hardware, seven Shoe, four Hat, Shoe and Fur, one Hat and Shoe Store, one Hat Manufactory, three Apothecary stores, two Book stores, four Printing Offices, and two Book Binders: there are nine Milliners' shops, three Goldsmiths, two Saddle and Harness Makers, six Dentists, four Carriage and Wagon Makers, two Cabinet, four Tinners, and six Blacksmith shops, four Butcher Stalls, one Bakery, two Tallow Chandelery, four Lumber yards, and one Sail Loft. Besides the Stores in the city, there are three stores just beyond its limits, in which Dry Goods and Groceries are sold.

For an account of the manufacturing operations in and about the city, and also, in Middlefield and Westfield, the reader is referred to the preceding account of "Middletown—its Manufactories," by Mr. Gorham. It should be born in mind however, that since the facts in that account were collected, there have been changes in the establishments. The operations in them, generally, have been on the advance. This is true particularly in the establishment of W. & B. Douglas. In this, there were then *eighty* men employed; the number has since reached to *one hundred and twenty*, and their stock and whole business have been increased proportionally. The Carbine, or Gun Factory, of North & Savage, was then undergoing repairs. It has since been put in operation. About forty hands have been employed, and Carbines made at the rate of not far from two thousand per year. These are sold mostly to the Government of the United States, the residue at private sale, amounting in all to about $30,000.

We have said that city privileges were sought, that commerce might be pursued more advantageously from this port. Great things were anticipated, and commerce did flourish for a time, and some individuals thereby greatly increased their estates, though they had other sources of income. Among those who succeeded the most in the West India trade, after the Revolution, were Elijah Hubbard, Lemuel Storrs, Nehemiah Hubbard, and at a period considerably later, Joseph Wright Alsop. The inventory of Elijah Hubbard's estate was $144,971,91—the inventory of Lemuel Storrs' estate was $47,308, and he left a larger amount of property, not inventoried here, consisting of lands in the State of New York and Ohio—the inventory of Nehemiah Hubbard's estate was $79,374,34—and he possessed large tracts of Western lands—the inventory of Joseph W. Alsop was $47,002,87.

But commerce never reached the prosperity which it had before the Revolution. Successive adverse events injured it, and finally the trade with the West Indies, from Middletown was lost, and from the Connecticut river. Since then there has been but little foreign commerce from Middletown, and domestic commerce has been limited, though it is now increasing.

In consequence of the failure of Foreign Commerce, numerous enterprising men were under the necessity, either of removal to other places, or of resorting to manufactures. Many preferred the latter alternative, and the result is the rise and increase of the manufactures to which we have referred.

The factories generally are moved by water power, though the large establishment of W. & B. Douglas, and one or two others, are moved by steam. The water privileges of the town are very great, and as yet but partially improved. The streams which to a great extent bound the city and empty themselves into the Connecticut, immediately north and south of it, are invaluable for manufacturing purposes. Dams are built upon them at far less expense than on larger streams, and are not as liable to be carried away or injured by floods.

The effects of drouth on these streams is to a great degree prevented by two reservoirs of water, one of which is secured by a dam, directly on the outlet of Miller's pond, the rise of Miller's brook, which takes the name of Sumner's Creek before it enters the Connecticut. The other reservoir is on a tributary of West river, in Middlefield, which is called before it empties itself into Connecticut river, and in comparison with it, Little River.

On the north side of the Strait Hills, and near Butler's Creek, as it enters the Connecticut river, there is the mine usually called the Lead Mine, mentioned on p. 70, which excited a good deal of attention before the American Revolution, and on which foreigners had expended large sums of money. In May 1775, "Jabez Hamlin, Matthew Talcott and Titus Hosmer, were appointed a Committee to provide stores of lead as they should judge necessary for the use of the Colony, or to take the lead ore raised out of the mine at Middletown and refined and fitted for the use of the Colony." In July following, the Assembly ordered them to work the mine. They did so, and put up works for smelting and refining the ore, which were completed about the month of September; and at this time high expectations were raised of providing from it a large amount of lead. In March and July of the following year orders were given upon the committee to furnish quantities of lead for military purposes, and in November 5th one hundred and forty pounds were reported to be in the hands of the Committee, and Capt. Samuel Russell was added to the Committee to procure lead for the State and to work the mine. The vein ran northerly towards the river, was followed thirty or forty rods, and in some places was very rich. But the vein being enclosed in granitic rock it was very difficult to get the ore, and as it approached the river it sunk abruptly into the earth. The works, however, were continued until the beginning of 1778—but at a session of the Assembly begun in February of that year a report was made, that the manufacture of said ore was unprofitable to the State. The Committee were therefore ordered to discontinue the works, after having finished the ore then on hand. *

The ore was mineralized with sulphur, and a man from Pennsylvania, by the name of Thomas Bidwell, was allowed the privilege of using the sulphur ore without charge. It was partly steel-grained and this contained a portion of silver, and partly cubic lead ore, the ore also contained zinc.

The Committee having fulfilled their last direction, the mine was given up, and nothing has been done in it until the present time; but we are happy in adding that Dr. *Eugene A. Frankfort*, who came the last year to test the ore, which had been taken some months previous from the Cobalt mine in Middle Haddam, has examined this mine. The results he gives in a communication, recently published in the "Sentinel and Witness," in Middletown.

"Lead, he says, though present [in this mine], would never alone pay the expenses of mining here, as there is not enough of it. But there are several other metallic minerals abundantly found in the quartz veins of the Grauwacke Rock, which lying over the Gneiss here, on both sides of the creek, stretches as far as the river. These minerals are well worth mining, and the writer of these lines is just about erecting mining and smelting works here. These minerals are *Argentiferous Galena*, containing some twenty-five per cent of silver. The heavy deposits of Zincblende will be manufactured into white oxyd and sulphate of zinc—the former of which is now coming into extensive use, instead of white-lead, to which as a paint it is far superior. The latter is a well-known mordant in all dyeing and coloring operations. *Sulphuret of Bismuth* occurs here also, (along with the Galena and Zincblende,) in lead colored grains, and as this metals enters into the composition of the clinches for stereotypes, and is put into the best kinds of Britannia Ware, it will pay for refining. Copper Pyrites,

* See Hinman's American Revolution.

in gold yellow nodules and of great purity, is found here also, and the copper obtained from them. Silver, the preparations of Zinc and Bismuth, will form the basis of the mining operations which will be carried on here. Besides the above mentioned useful minerals, the Mineralogical collector may find here, Iron Pyrites, Mispickel, or Arsenical Pyrites, and fine drusy crystals of common quartz." The vein of the metals runs in quartz rock.

The old works, which were carried on near by in the Revolution, until 1778, as just mentioned, would have been profitable, had the operators been searching for minerals more generally, and had they known how to turn the Zincblend into use, but zinc then being but little employed for technical purposes, they could not separate it with advantage and their object was lead for use in the existing war with Great Britain.

The Feldspar Quarries, nigh the Middlesex Turnpike, three miles south-easterly from the city, may be properly mentioned in this connection. Concerning these, Dr. Franckfort observes, in the communication from which a quotation has just been made as follows.

"The Granite is here partly composed out of a very fine white or pinkish white Feldspar, which has been quarried considerably, and with profit, as I have been told; but at present, quarrying operations have been suspended. The Feldspar, when not mixed with Quartz or Mica, is the material from which the greatest part of China Ware and Porcelain is manufactured. Feldspar is a Silicate of Alumnia and Potash. Besides the common Feldspar found here, a white, shining, crystalized variety of it, called *Albite*, has been often observed also. The *Mica* occurs here, as in the above mentioned Columbite locality, in large foliated layers and crystals, some half a foot in thickness, and is often of pitch black color. *Columbite* has also been found here, and it is said, in crystals of greater beauty and larger size, than those which we obtain from Haddam. This Mineral is, however, now very rare here. The Mica, and a pinkish variety of it called *Lepidolite*, of this locality, contain some very fine specimens of transparent green *Tourmalines*. Red Tourmalines have also been found, though not often. *Apatite*, a lime containing mineral, is frequent in green colored nodules and crystals, imbedded in the Feldspar. *Rutile*, an almost pure oxyd of the metal called Titanium, has been obtained here of such beauty, that, according to Dana, it formed, when cut and polished, a gem of rare brilliancy of lustre. Its color is a splendid brownish red. Amongst other Minerals, I collected here a few specimens of *Uranite*, in small, almost microscopic scales, of a lemon yellow color. Large rough Beryls are commmon here.

From the above, it is evident that these Quarries will pay well a visit to them; and it is to be hoped that they will be worked again, when many more beautiful minerals will be brought to light, that rest now imbedded in the Feldspar."

The city of Middletown enjoys advantages for the erection of buildings. Free stone, or rather a dark sand-stone abounds in the town, and as early as 1726, the selectmen were directed take care of the quarries on the West side of the river, as well as on the east side, in what is now Portland. The first quarry opened on the west side is within the limits of the city and at different times has been improved to a considerable extent. Some of the stone have been used in the city and some have been carried to other places. Recently the Portland stone have been principally used; they are within sight of the city and can be brought to it without much difficulty or expense. A large brick yard until within a short period, has been improved within the city limits; a better one is now improved a mile or two beyond them. As for lumber so far as the town cannot furnish it, it can be brought from other parts of the country, by vessels or by cars.

Besides, the facilities for intercourse which this place has with other parts of the country, by the river and by railroad, it has others by turnpikes and public roads to neighboring towns, and through them to others beyond them.

From the Post Office mails are sent twice, daily, to

New York, Hartford and Boston, and are received twice. A daily mail passes to and from New Haven, Saybrook, East Haddam, and Wethersfield, and intermediate places, and also to and from Portland. A mail passes to and from Lyme, and to and from East Hampton on the east side of the Connecticut river, thrice weekly and through the intermediate places. By these and other mails the inhabitants are enabled to maintain perpetual intercourse with all parts of the country.

But the great object of the Colonists, who settled in Middletown, as well as in other parts of New England, was, to enjoy unmolested the right of worshipping God according to the dictates of their own consciences. Let us then advert to their ecclesiastical proceedings, to the formation of the First Congregational Church; also to the rise of other denominations and the formation of their churches, in what is now the First Society.

In the address, a few words were said in regard to the religious character of the early settlers, and of their employment of Mr. Samuel Stow, graduate of Harvard College, 1645, as a candidate for the ministry, and of his preaching to them a number of years. For some time they may have hardly felt themselves able to settle a pastor, but in August, 1657, they voted to continue him on trial, and appear afterwards to have made some further advances towards his settlement. But some difficulties arising in the town respecting him, a vote was passed in 1659, that they did not wish to continue him, but to look elsewhere. In 1661, the difficulties came before the General Court, which declared the town to be free from Mr. Stow, as their engaged minister; and the Court appointed a committee to further a settled ministry in the place. The following is a copy of the report of the committee.

"Whereas upon divers agitations before the General Court between Mr. Stow and the inhabitants of Middletown, the Court did declare that the Town of Middletown, are free from Mr. Stow as their engaged minister, and the Court appointing a Committee to further a settled ministry in that place—and after long endeavors by the people there, to procure them a minister, there appears a probability of their obtaining of Mr. Collins for that purpose—the Committee doth approve of their proceedings therein and of his acceptance of their motion, and according to the mind of the Court, do advise both Mr. Stow and all the inhabitants of Middletown, to a loving carriage to Mr. Collins and friendly compliance with each other—that the memory of all former differences may be wholly buried, and that Mr. Collins may have all due encouragement in the work of the ministry, that he is called unto in that place—and that the long desired, comfortable and peaceable settlement of Middletown may be obtained, which is the desire of the Committee appointed by the General Court to promote the settlement of the ministry there.

MATTHEW ALLEN, *in the name of the Committee.*

Hartford, December 6, 1661."

The action of the General Court appears to have finished the business respecting the settlement of Mr. Stow in the ministry in Middletown, and the people went forward according to advice, and at length with entire unanimity settled Mr. Collins. But in 1681, application was made to him to preach in Simsbury, and he supplied the desk four years. In May, 1682, a "Humble Motion of Simsbury men" was made to the General Assembly for countenance to settle themselves in gospel order, and at that time it was expected Mr. Stow would become their pastor. But as his term of service for four years drew towards a close, he desired of the inhabitants an "answer whether they would continue him in the work of the ministry and settle him in office amongst them." They did not see cause to settle him in office, but seem to have referred the matter to him, whether he would continue any longer in the work of a teaching minister. That he did not choose to do, any farther than to fulfil his existing engagement.* He then gave up his designs of the ministry, and lived in Middletown as a private citizen.

But we proposed to give an account of the formation

* History of Simsbury, Granby and Canton, by Noah A. Phelps.

of the First Congregational Church in Middletown, which had been contemplated from the beginning of the settlement. Numbers of the settlers were members of churches in the place from which they came, and must have greatly desired it, but the matter was long delayed by circumstances. The people of the town as a body wished for it, and manifested by a vote, "that they were willing to lay out themselves in all regular endeavors that they might enjoy God in all his ordinances among them. "The desires of all were gratified" on the 4th of the 9th month, (the 4th of November,) 1668, when the fathers of the Church, ten in number, owned a confession of faith and entered into covenant with God and with one another," with the approbation and concurrence of the honored messengers then present, sent from the respective churches. These were from the Church of Christ at Windsor, Hartford, Farmington, and] Northampton, by name, the Rev. Mr. Hooker, Mr. Mather, Mr. Whiting, Mr. Nathaniel Chauncey, Deacon Moore, Deacon Hart, Deacon Judd, Deacon Hancket, John Stanley, John Wadsworth. Other members of Churches, came forward afterwards and united with this church; some of them the wives of these ten.

The ordination of the pastor, Rev. Nathaniel Collins, who had preached to the people some years, followed, and the desires of the Town and the call of the Church are both mentioned in the brief account of the transaction as follows: "The 4th of the 9th [month] 1668, being the day of our ecclesiastical embodying, (the town having formerly jointly invited to and desired it,) the Church elected and called Nathaniel Collins, to the office of pastor among them, promising that, if desired by him, and themselves [should be] in capacity, they would provide a fellow laborer in the word and doctrine: whereupon he accepted, and at the request of the church was ordained by the Reverend Mr. Mather and Mr. Whiting."

The views of the Church were in accordance with the Cambridge Platform.

January 20th, 1669, "the Church concluded upon a monthly conference to be kept by the whole body, and occasionally the conference day to be improved as a day of fasting and prayer."

March 20th, 1670, Thomas Allen, Samuel Stocking, and John Hall, jr., having been duly elected, "were ordained in the office of deacons in this particular church of Christ, and commended to the grace of God therein, by prayers with the imposition of hands."

This Church has had seven pastors. The first four are dead, Rev. Nathaniel Collins, Noadiah and William Russell, father and son, and Enoch Huntington. Mr. Collins, graduate of Harvard College, 1660, died December 28th, 1684, aged 42. Mr. Noadiah Russell, a native of New Haven, was graduated at Harvard, 1681, and ordained Oct. 24th, 1688. He died December 3d, 1713, aged 54. Mr. William Russell, born in Middletown and graduated at Yale College, 1709; succeeded his father as pastor of the church, June 1st, 1715, and died June 1, 1761, aged 70. Mr. Huntington, native of Windham, graduated at Yale, 1759, was ordained Jan. 6, 1762, and died June 12th, 1809, aged 69. Sketches of these ministers are given in the address.

The three pastors living are Rev. Dan Huntington, Chauncey Allen Goodrich, D. D., and John R. Crane, D. D.

Mr. D. Huntington is a native of Lebanon, was graduate of Yale, 1794, tutor there and at Williams College. He was pastor of the Congregational Church in Litchfield several years before coming to Middletown, where he was installed September 10th, 1809, and dismissed February 6th, 1816. He has since lived in Hadley, Massachusetts.

Dr. Goodrich is a native of New Haven, graduate of Yale, 1810, and tutor. He was ordained in Middletown July 24th, 1816, and dismissed December 23d, 1817. Immediately after, he became Professor of Rhetoric at Yale College, where he is now professor of Pastoral Charge.

Dr. Crane, native of Newark, N. J., graduate of Princeton College, 1805, was ordained November 4th, 1818, and is the present pastor.

Mr. Collins admitted to the Church,	- 76	persons.
" N. Russell, " "	- 180	"
" W. Russell, " "	- 305	"
" E. Huntington, " "	- 346	"
" D. Huntington, " "	- 98	"
Dr. Goodrich, " "	- 32	"
Dr. Crane, " "	- 539	"

These, with ten at the organization make a total of 1586

The number of communicants January 1st, 1852, was 309.

DEACONS OF THE CHURCH.

	Elected.	*Died.*	*Ages.*
Thomas Allen,	March 16, 1670.	—— ——	——
Samuel Stocking,	" "	—— ——	——
John Hall, jr.,	" "	Jan. 22. 1694.	75
Daniel Markum,	About 1690.	—— ——	——
William Sumner,	Aug. 11, 1695.	May 31, 1706.	——
Obadiah Allen,	May 31, 1704.	—— ——	——
Joseph Rockwell,	" "	Oct. 27, 1742	74
Boriah Wetmore,	May 5, 1713.	—— ——	——
Solomon Atkins,	Jan. 8, 1735.	Oct. 5, 1748.	70
John Hubbard,	May 26, 1743.	March 12, 1753.	60
Jonathan Allen,	" "	Dec. 23, 1783	80
William Rockwell,	April 6, 1749.	July 28, 1765.	63
Hon. Jabez Hamlin,	Feb. 7, 1754.	April 25, 1791.	82
Joseph Clark, Esq.,	Aug. 16, 1765.	April 21, 1778.	58
John Earl Hubbard,	" "	July 27, 1782.	59
Chauncey Whittlesey,	Sept. 17, 1778.	March 14, 1812.	65
Jacob Wetmore,	March 7, 1782.	Sept. 25, 1825.	90 *
Oliver Wetmore,	March 4, 1784.	Dec. 1, 1798.	46
Timothy Boardman,	April 1, 1784.	May 5, 1792.	64
Matthew T. Russell, Esq.	May 3, 1798.	Nov. 13, 1828.	68
Thomas Hubbard,	—— 1812.	Aug. 27, 1828.	42
Joseph Boardman,	May 16, 1812.	Sept. 25, 1846.	79
Samuel Eells, 2d.,	" "	Moved to N. Y. City.	
Henry S. Ward,	Oct. 27, 1825.	Resigned Oct. 9, 1844.	
Richard Rand,	Dec. 27, 1828.	June 9, 1844.	52
Cyprian Galpin,	July 22, 1840.	Moved to N. Haven.	
John B. Woodford,	July 2, 1844.	Moved to Windsor.	
Evan Davis,	Nov. 26, 1844.		
John H. Sumner,	Nov. 18, 1846.		
Robert P. Rand,	May 22, 1850.		
Selah Goodrich,	June 19, 1850.		

* Did not act as deacon for sometime before his death.

The first Society formerly had very considerable funds, the yearly income of which was devoted to the support of the gospel among them, but has none at the present time; and it is very well able to sustain religious institutions without them. This is evident from contributions which the people make to the American Bible Society, Missionary Societies, foreign and domestic, and other institutions of a similar character. These have been condsiderably more in some years than in others, but are calculated to have been, for twenty years, $1,500 annually.

Sketch of the Strict Congregational Church, now the South Congregational Church of Middletown.

About the time of the great revival of religion in New England, and in other parts of the English American Colonies, in 1741 and '42, a few individuals in the towns of Wethersfield and Middletown, embraced the principles of the Strict Congregationalists. These were formed into a Church in Wethersfield, Oct. 28th, 1747, and Rev. Ebenezer Frothingham, a native of Cambridge, Mass., was ordained their pastor. But as the principal members in Wethersfield, within a few years, emigrated into the State of New York, Mr. Frothingham came to Middletown and was installed over the Strict Congregationalists living here, about 1754. These resided in the First and Fourth Societies. They were few in number, but increased considerably under his ministry. In 1788 they were divided into two churches, those in the First Society constituting one church, and those in the Fourth or Westfield Society constituting the other church. Mr. Frothingham was dismissed about the time of this division, but remained in Middletown until his death, Nov. 30th, 1798, at the age of 81.

Some idea of the strength which the Congregation gathered under the ministry of Mr. Frothingham, may be formed from the fact, that eighty persons under date of Oct. 13, 1788, signed the following agreement:

"We the subscribers of the Second Strict Congregational Church and Society in this town, believing it to be our duty to attend the public worship of God, and support a gospel minister, do agree according to our several abilities, to raise such supplies as shall be necessary to render the life of a gospel minister comfortable in order for his usefullness among us, and that we will attend a society meeting, annually, on the last Monday in September, in order for raising such supplies as shall be necessary for the comfortable support of a gospel minister. And we further agree that we will be accountable to this church and society for any neglect of fulfilling this our agreement—provided always that no force of civil law is to be used, in collecting support for the gospel ministry among us."

The names appended, placing them alphabetically, are these: Anthony Ames, Joshua Arnold, Thamer Atkins, Ebenezer Pierpont, and Benjamin Bacon; Daniel, George, Caleb, Giles and Reuben Barnes; Solomon and John Bill; Solomon, Samuel, and John Edward Blake; Amos Bow, Michael Braddock, Noah Brooks, Daniel and Samuel Clark; Jesse, Joseph, and Ezra Coe, and Jesse Coe, jr.; Cornelius Cornwall, John Cotton, 2d; John, Daniel and Samuel Crowell, and John Crowell, jr.; Joseph and Israel Driggs, and Joseph Driggs, jr.; John Gilbert, Enoch Green, John and Jonathan A. Hall, and John Hall, jr.; David Harris; Jacob, Elias, Oliver, Manoah and Enoch Hubbard; Trustam Hull, John and James Johnson, Samuel Lee, Moses Lucas, jr., Ezekiel Lyman, Ebenezer Markham; Joshua, Caleb and Peter Miller; Robert and George Paddock; Aaron Plumbe, Oliver Prior, Samuel Redden, Collins Roberts; Collins S., Hinchman, Aaron, Noyce and Edward Roberts; John Rogers, jr., Samuel Savage, Elias and Nathan Sears, Daniel Sizer, Nathan Strong, Jesse Tryon, Jonathan Turner, Joseph Ward and Joseph Ward, jr., John Wetmore, Daniel and Stephen Whitmore, and Abel and Giles Wilcox.

On the 3d of January, 1788, the Church invited Stephen Parsons, a native of Middletown to be their pastor. He accepted their invitation, and was ordained on the 31st of the same month. He was dismissed on the 9th of August, 1795, having changed his sentiments on the mode and subjects of baptism.

Rev. David Huntington, a native of Lebanon, and graduate of Dartmouth College 1773, who had been previously settled in Marlborough, was installed the pastor of this people, Nov. 8, 1797. He labored among them until Oct. 1800, and was afterwards settled in North Lyme. He was a man of ardent piety.

Rev. Horatio Thomas McGeorge, preached to the people from Oct. 27th, 1801, until Jan. 14th, 1802.

Rev. Benjamin Graves, a native of East Haddam, was ordained their pastor, Oct. 3d, 1803, and labored among them until the close of 1811, or beginning of 1812.

Not far from the time of his dismission, the church was dissolved "by consent of the brethren," and the prospects of this denomination were very gloomy. But on the 11th of January 1816, four males and nine females, who had belonged to the old church, were formed into a new church, and the congregation was in some measure collected.

Soon after this, the Rev. Ahab Jinks was procured to preach to them, and on the 7th of August, 1816, was ordained by the Presbytery of Hudson, with which he was connected, with a view to his becoming their pastor. Under his ministry the church received large accessions. But having been appointed by the Connecticut Missionary Society, to labor in the States of Ohio and Indiana, he requested a dismission, November, 10th, 1819. The church consented to his fulfilling his appointment, and in case he should then "desire a dismission," they voted, "it shall be granted." He renewed his request May 17th, 1820, and was dismissed accordingly. He has since labored at the West.

On the 31st of May 1822, Rev. Thomas T. DeVerell, from North Stonington, became their pastor and remained with them about a year.

Between his dismission and the settlement of the next pastor, Rev. Messrs. ——— Dickinson, George Carrington and others preached to the congregation. Rev. Horace Hooker of Hartford, supplied them regularly in 1826, and until September, 1827.

In the month last mentioned, Rev. Edward R. Tyler, native of Guilford, Ver., and graduate of Yale College, 1825, commenced preaching among them, and was ordained and constituted their pastor on the 27th of December following. His influence as a candidate and pastor was very great among them. Many old members were gathered into the church, some united with it by letter, and more in consequence of a revival in 1831. Young and enterprising men joined the Society. But in consequence of ill health, he asked for a dismission, and was dismissed in April, 1832. He was afterwads pastor of the church in Colebrook, an agent, of the American Antislavery Society, editor of the Connecticut Observer, and editor, proprietor and principal conductor of the New Englander. He died at New Haven, September 28th, 1848, aged 48, and his associates in the last mentioned work, in the last number for that year, inserted a very interesting obituary notice of him.

Rev. William H. Beecher, son of Rev. Lyman Beecher, D. D., was installed pastor, March 13th, 1833, and dismissed on the 16th of the succeeding September. He was afterwards pastor or stated supply for a time, of a church in Trumbull, Ohio, and is now preaching in some part of that State.

Rev. Robert McEwen, native of New London, graduate of Yale, 1827, Tutor, studied theology at New Haven, succeeded Mr. Beecher, May 7, 1835, and was dismissed August 8th, 1838. He is now pastor of the church in Enfield, Mass., where he was installed Feb. 16th 1842.

Rev. Arthur Granger, native of Suffield, who studied theology at Princeton, and who had been pastor of the First Congregational Church in Meriden, followed Mr. McEwen, April 24th, 1839. He was dismissed in May, 1844, and immediately after became pastor of "High

Street Church," in Providence, R. I., where he died Aug. 2, 1845, aged 42.

Rev. Andrew L. Stone, native of Oxford, graduate of Yale, 1837, was installed Sept. 3d, 1844, and dismissed in Jan., 1849, being then under a call to the Park Street Church in Boston, where he was installed soon after.

Rev. John N. Dudley, native of Andover, N. H., graduate of Amherst College, who studied theology in Newport, R. I. and in Andover, Mass., was engaged to preach to the Congregation in Sept., 1849, and still supplies them.

The number of members of the Church, admitted by each of the successive pastors, cannot now probably be found, particularly those admitted by the earlier pastors.

Mr. Jinks admitted, - - - - - -	84	members.
Mr. Tyler gathered in 43 old members, of the church, and by letter and profession 125 more, total, - -	168	"
Mr. Beecher, - - - - - - - -	4	"
In the 18 months following, when there was no settled minister, there were admitted, - - - - - - - - -	16	"
Mr. McEwen admitted, - - - - -	62	"
Mr. Granger, - - - - - - - - -	173	"
Mr. Stone, - - - - - - - - - -	82	"
Since Mr. Stone's dismission, there have been admitted, - - - - - -	11	"
Total from the commencement of Mr. Jinks' services, - - - - - -	600	

Of those admitted since the beginning of Mr. Tyler's services, the following number are now resident members, viz:

Of the old ones gathered by Mr. Tyler, 9, and of the others admitted by him, 19, total, -	28	members.
Of those admitted by Mr. Beecher, -	1	"
Of those admitted between his dismission and the settlement of Mr. McEwen,	4	"
Of those admitted by Mr. McEwen, -	10	"
" " by Mr. Granger, -	58	"
" " by Mr. Stone, - -	36	"

All admitted since Mr. Stone's dismission, 11 "

Total of resident members, Jan. 1, 1852, 148 "

The number of absent members is not ascertained. The number of families connected with the Society, is 118.

The records do not show who were the earliest deacons. John Johnson and Ebenezer Bacon were deacons, Oct. 13, 1788. The following deacons have been elected at the times specified.

Samuel Spaulding, April 15, 1818.
Joseph Lewis, April, 9, 1825.
William Woodward, March, 19, 1829.
Josiah Danforth, } Aug. 28, 1839.
Joseph W. McKee, }

When the Strict Congregationalists first arose, they held meetings in the dwelling house of their minister, Mr. Frothingham, on the north side of Mill Street. In 1774, they built a meeting house on the east side of Main Street, 56 feet by 46, now changed into dwellings for two families. The present church edifice was dedicated June, 1830. It is 72 feet by 55, the audience room 52 feet square, and cost $6,000. In 1839 a cupola and bell were added at an expense of $750 and in 1845, the galleries were lowered at an expense of $350 more; the expense in the first instance being borne by subscription. In 1851, the interior of the house was painted in fresco by subscription, at an expense of $500, and $1400 were paid on an old debt.

No accurate accounts have been kept of the contributions for public benevolent objects. They may have been annually for some time $150. The debt of the Society may have diminished them.

Only one mode of worship was statedly observed in Middletown for about a century after the settlement was commenced. Now, besides the Congregationalists, several denominations have houses for their worship. We shall give sketches of them in the order in which they have arisen.

Sketch of the Episcopal Church.

That there was occasionally Episcopal worship before 1750 is altogether probable, aside from tradition. Rev. James Wetmore, a native of the town, the first Congregational minister of North Haven, became an Episcopal minister about 1724, and it is very likely performed service sometimes in the dwellings of his friends. Jeremiah Leaming, a native of the town at a later period, an Episcopal clergyman, may have done the same before 1750. Before that time some of the inhabitants had become so much attached to Episcopal forms, that they took some steps to secure a site on which to erect a house for public worship; to the building of which Mr. Wetmore most earnestly advised them. Hence the town voted, April 29th, 1749, "that the professors of the Church of England, have liberty to erect their church in the highway, between Jaffries' corner, (so called,) John Foster's corner, and the dwelling house of Mr. Ephraim Doane, and the selectmen, or any three of them, are hereby empowered to stake out the place for the said building."

Many years since the writer was assured, that at the close of 1749, there were sixteen Episcopal families in the town, though measures in due form do not appear to have been taken to organize a parish till Easter Monday, April 16th, 1750. A church was erected on the site, designated in the vote of the town in 1752, fifty feet long and thirty-six wide, with a towering steeple, though not finished for two or three years. This was used as a sanctuary more than eighty years; when the proffer of a thousand dollars from the Ladies of the Assistant Society, prompted the gentlemen to the work of erecting their present church edifice. This was completed in 1834. It is of Portland stone, seventy-eight feet by sixty, twelve feet porch, and cost $14,000.

A bell for the first Episcopal Church was procured in 1759, and a second was given by Mr. John Alsop, a wealthy merchant of New York, brother of Richard Alsop of this place, in 1785. This is now in use in the present church.

For many years the people were aided in the support of their ministers, by the Society in England for the propagation of the gospel in Foreign Parts. Rev. Dr. Leaming, already spoken of, and Dr. Richard Mansfield, performed at least occasional services for them.

Rev. Ichabod Camp, a native of Durham, graduate of Yale 1743, divided his labors between the Episcopalians here and in Wallingford, from 1752 until 1760. He removed to Louisburgh, Vir., where he was murdered by a son-in-law. In the triennial catalogue, his death is represented as having occurred in the last mentioned year, but it has been supposed that it occurred at a later period.

Rev. Abraham Jarvis, native of Norwalk, and graduate of Yale, 1761, was reader for the congregation from 1761, until he sailed to England, for orders, in the autumn of 1763. His people advanced forty pounds sterling to pay the expense of his voyage. Upon his return he entered on the duties of his ministry, on a salary of ninety pounds, twenty of it being given by the Society for propagating the gospel. He continued rector until 1799, two years after he was elected Bishop of Connecticut, and then removed to Cheshire, afterwards to New Haven, where he died May 3d, 1813, aged 75.

Rev. Calvin White, a native of this town, graduate of Yale 1786, was invited in Sept., 1799, to become rector, and performed services until July 27th, 1800. A like invitation was given to *Rev. Joseph Warren*, in Oct., 1800, who was rector until Aug., 1803. *Rev. Clement Merriam*, was rector from April, 1804, till April, 1806. For some six months afterwards, *Mr. Samuel Birge* was employed as a lay-reader, and then the church was supplied by preachers employed from sabbath to sabbath, or by visiting clergymen.

On the 3d of April, 1109, *Rev. John Kewley, M. D.*, an Englishman, educated at Eton College, Cambridge, who had practised medicine in the West Indies, and in Pennsylvania, but who had taken orders and been minister in Chester, in Maryland, was called to the rectorship and soon after instituted. His ministry was both very acceptable and very profitable to his parishioners. But unhappily for the parties, though with their consent, the connection was dissolved by the Bishop in March, 1813. In the same year he was duly installed rector, in St. George's Church, in the city of New York, and the Rev. John Brady assistant rector. Both resigned their charge in 1816, and Dr. Kewley soon after returned to England. It is generally understood that he afterward went to Rome and became connected with the Catholic Church. A curious fact, confirmatory of this is given in the "Life of Dr. Milnor," * his successor in St. George's Church.

Birdsey Glover Noble, native of New Milford, graduate of Yale 1810, succeeded Dr. Kewley, in 1813, though *then* in deacon's orders, and officiated until Sept., 1828, when he resigned. He was elected rector of the church in Elizabethtown, N. J. in, March, 1829, and resigned in 1833. He engaged subsequently in teaching in Bridgeport, and then in Brooklyn, N. Y., where he was assistant minister in the church of the Holy Trinity. In 1849, he died in Bridgeport, aged, it is believed, about 58.

Rev. Smith Pyne, who had been rector in Elizabethtown from June 1st, 1826, till December, 1828, was in the course of the month or year last mentioned, elected rector in Middletown, and entered upon his services the following month, but in August, 1830 resigned; though in the autumn of 1831, he resumed services here and continued them until August, 1836. He is now settled in Washington, D. C.

In the interval between the two periods of Mr. Pyne's services, *Rev. George Jones* was invited to become rector, and consented to serve the congregation a few months. He had been chaplain in the United States Navy several years, and then two years tutor in Yale College, where he was graduated in 1823. His services in Middletown were highly valuable and productive of much good. But his health not allowing him to discharge steadily the duties of a parish, he again accepted a chaplaincy in the Navy, in which service he is now acting.

---

* P.

Rev. Dr. Samuel Farmer Jarvis, son of Bishop Jarvis, born in Middletown and graduated at Yale 1805, was elected rector April 11th, 1837, and the *Rev. Dr. John Williams*, native of Deerfield, Mass., and graduate of Trinity College, assistant rector; but Dr. Williams was afterwards called to the rectorship of the Episcopal church in Schenectady, where he officiated until called in 1849, to the Presidency of Trinity College; which office he still holds, though recently elected and consecrated assistant Bishop of Connecticut.

Dr. Jarvis resided in Middletown until his death, March 29th, 1851, aged 64. He was rector of the church in Bloomingdale, near New York city, and of St. Paul's in Boston, before settling in Middletown, and also a professor in Trinity College. Dr. Williams preached at his funeral, and it is understood, is preparing a memoir of him, which will of course give an account of his writings.

Rev. H. B. Sherman, supplied the congregation in Middletown for a time after the call of Dr. Williams to Schenectady, but was not rector. He has now the charge of the church in Bellevue, N. J.

Rev. Edson Wilson Wiltbank, began to officiate in Middletown, April 11th, 1842, and was succeeded by *Rev. Horace Hills*, February 11th, 1844.

The present incumbent, *Rev. F. J. Goodwin*, is a native of South Berwick, Maine, graduate of Bowdoin College 1832. He entered upon his services here, August 17th, 1845.

This church has passed through various scenes. It was generally on the advance until the Revolutionary war, when it was involved in difficulties, as Episcopal churches were elsewhere, by the connection of such churches with the state in England. The rectors generally held that they were bound to pray in public assemblies, for the king and royal family, as they had done aforetime, in a manner, which the great body of the Americans deemed to be wrong under existing circumstances, and which after the declaration of independence, was deemed an act of hostility to the government of the

United States. Most rectors in the northern and middle States, after this declaration, closed their churches. The venerable Dr. William White of Philadelphia, did not follow their example, and in his Memoirs of the Protestant Episcopal Churches in the United States, (p. 77) he undertakes to show that the obligation then, to pray openly, and by name for the king and royal family, was not as strong as most of the rectors thought it to be. Whether right in his reasoning or not, it is certain Episcopal churches were in great trouble in the Revolution. But after the war was over the Episcopal church in Middletown revived. The people connected with it had not been confirmed, there being no bishop in America to perform that service, until Rev. Samuel Seabury was consecrated Bishop of Connecticut, in Scotland in 1784. On the 17th of September, 1786, this Bishop confirmed one hundred and twenty-seven persons in this town, a few of whom, were perhaps from neighboring places.

The number of communicants in the Church, in 1799, was 47; in 1810, 50; in 1812, 84; in 1814, 85; in 1831, 90. The present number of communicants is about 180.

Within the last four years, Mrs. Martha Mortimer Starr, now deceased, gave $3,000 to Domestic Missions and $3,000 more to Foreign. Within the same period, the congregation separately from her, have given $972-87 to the first of these objects, and $463 50 to the second; to other public benevolent objects, $3,685 78: total $5,122 15.

Sketch of the Baptist Church.

Individuals had been attached to the sentiments of the Baptists for some time. The First Church was formed in the city, Oct. 19th, 1795, consisting of eleven members, five males and six females. This has enjoyed the instruction of the following elders:

Joshua Bradley, a native of Kingston, Mass., graduate of Brown University, preached to them for a time.

George Phippen, native of Salem, Mass., and graduate of the same institution, preached to them more or less, from June 11th, 1812, to July 1816.

Jeremiah F. Bridges, a native of Colchester, succeeded Mr. Phippen, and preached to them till Oct. 3d, 1818.

Eli Ball, preached to them from Nov. 6th, 1818, to May 4th, 1823; *James A. Boswell*, from June 25th, 1823, to the close of the year; *Daniel Wildman*, from sometime in 1824, till April 1st, 1825; *John R. Dodge*, from May 1825, to Nov. 1827.

John Cookson, an Englishman, preached to them from some time in the winter of 1828–9, until 1839; *Thomas Wilks*, from 1839, to sometime in 1840, and *D. C. Haynes* from May 1840, till Nov. 1841.

William G. Howard, a native of Newburyport, Mass., preached to them from some time in 1843, to Feb. 28th, 1847. He has since been pastor of the Baptist Church in Essex, and of a Baptist Church in the city of Albany. He is now preaching in Rochester.

Beriah N. Leach, a native of Middletown, Ver., educated at Madison University, N. Y., commenced services in Middletown, September 1st, 1848, became pastor March 2d, 1849, and ministered to the congregation until Aug., 1851, when he resigned.

Meriwether Winston, accepted the pastoral charge in October, 1851.

How many communicants were admitted to the Church by the first two of the foregoing elders, is not ascertained.

Elder	Bridges,	admitted	31
"	Ball,	"	11
"	Boswell,	"	2
"	Wildman,	"	8
"	Dodge,	"	22
"	Cookson,	"	168
"	Wilks,	"	15
"	Haynes,	"	33
"	Howard,	"	39
"	Leach,	"	74

The number of Members Jan. 1st, 1852, was 339.

The Baptists built their first meeting-house in 1809, fifty-three by thirty-eight feet. Their present house was built in 1842. It is of brick, seventy-six feet by fifty-six, and cost $12,500. Towards this, Mr. Robert Paddock, a brother in the Church, and his wife, Mrs. Martha Paddock, paid more than five thousand dollars. Since her husbands death in May, 1845, she has also given $1,000 for a permanent fund, the interest of which is to be applied towards the support of the ministry.

Regular contributions are made by the people to the American and Foreign Bible Society, to Foreign and Home Missions, and for Ministerial Education. Contributions too are occasionally taken up for other public benevolent objects.

Sketch of the Methodist E. Church.

Although Methodist preaching was begun in Middletown in 1789, it is understood first in Middlefield; although a circuit, to be called Middletown circuit, was in contemplation in 1790, and two preachers were sent to form and travel the circuit, yet the Society in the city takes its date from December, 1791. The circuit was formed, and continued a circuit until 1816, when Middletown became a station, or separate charge. It has been attached to several Districts, as New York, New London, Rhinebeck, New Haven and Hartford, which has made the change of presiding elders greater in proportion to the time allowed for services, than the circuit and stationed preachers.

The Congregation increased rather rapidly before the establishment of the Wesleyan University in the city. It has increased more rapidly since, not only as the Faculty, their families and the students generally are connected with it, but as families in a considerable number of instances have moved into the city for the sake of helping their sons the more conveniently through their classical course. This is evident among other proofs, from the increase of communicants in the church. In 1816, the number was 112; in 1826, 172; in 1846, when the University had become quite prosperous 515. It should be stated, however, that at the last mentioned date, the number was unusually large, and that members in Middlefield then belonged to the Church, as well as members from the families of officers in the University and such students as had joined the church by letter and profession. Ever since 1840, about sixty students have been communicants, rather more than half being professors of religion. The number of communicants, Jan. 1 1852 was 430.

The following account of the preachers to this church and of the presiding elders, has been kindly furnished by Rev. Mr. Reid, the present officiating minister.

Rev. Jesse Lee first preached in Middletown, 1789.

1790. He sent two preachers to form and travel the circuit, and Daniel Smith formed the first class in Middletown.

1791.	John Allen & Dan'l Smith travelled the circuit,		Jesse Lee, P. Elder
1792.	Richard Swain, Aaron Hunt, circuit preacher,		Jacob Brush, "
1793.	Joshua Taylor, Benj. Frisbe,	"	Geo. Roberts, "
1794.	Menzes Raynor, Daniel Ostrander,	"	" "
1795.	Evans Rogers, Joel Ketchum,	"	Jesse Lee, P. Elder.
1796.	Joshua Tayler, Lawrence McCombs,	"	S. Hutchinson, "
1797.	Michael Coats, Peter Jayne,	"	" "
1798.	Augustus Jocelyn,	"	" "
1798.	Ebenezer Stevens,	"	" "
1800.	James Coleman, Roger Searles,	"	F. Garretson, "
1801.	Elijah Batchelor, Luman Andrews,	"	" "
1802.	Abner Wood, James Annis,	"	" "
1803.	Abner Wood, Nathan Emory,	"	D. Ostrander, "
1804.	Ebenezer Washburn, N. Emory,	"	" "
1805.	Ebe. Washburn, Luman Andrus,	"	" "
1806.	Luman Andrus, Zalmon Lyon,	"	Wm. Thatcher, "
1807.	W. Thatcher, R. Harris, O Sykes,	"	Jos. Crawford, "
1808.	James M. Smith, Phineas Rice,	"	" "
1809.	Nobel W. Thomas, Coles Carpenter,	"	" "
1810.	Oliver Sykes, Johnathan Lyon,	"	" "
1811.	Zalmon Lyon, Jesse Hunt,	"	Wm. Anson, "
1812.	Aaron Hunt, Arnold Scholfields,	"	Elijah Woolsey, "
1813.	Elijah Woolsey, Arnold Scholfields,	"	Nathan Bangs, "
1814.	Wm. Jewett, Peter Bussing,	"	" "
1815.	Wm. Jewett, Jonathan Lyon,	"	" "
1816.	Middletown a Station, Tho's Thorpe, S. Prea.		" "
1817–18	Marvin Richardson,	"	E. Washburn, "
1819–20.	William Jewett,	"	" "
1821–22.	Phinehas Cook,	"	Sam'l Merwin, "

1823.	Josiah Bowen,	"	Sam'l Merwin,	"
1824.	"	"	Sam'l Lucky,	"
1825-26.	Ebenezer Washburn,	"	"	"
1827.	Heman Bangs,	"	D. Ostrander,	"
1828.	"	"	Laban Clark,	"
1829-30.	Thomas Burch,	"	"	"
1831.	Fitch Read,	"	"	"
1832.	"	"	Heman Bangs,	"
1833-34.	Bartholomew Creagh,	"	S. Martindale,	"
1835.	John C. Green,	"	"	"
1836.	Charles K. True,	"	"	"
1837.	Elisha Andrews,	"	John Lindsey,	"
1838.	"	"	Fitch Read,	"
1839.	Francis Hodgson,	"	H. Bangs,	"
1840.	"	"	C. W. Carpenter,	"
1841.	Abiather M. Osbon,	"	"	"
1842.	"	"	S. D. Furgerson,	"
1843-44.	Edwin E. Griswold,	"	Barth. Creagh,	"
1845.	John L. Gilder,	"	"	"
1846.	James Floy,	"	"	"
1847.	"	"	E. E. Griswold,	"
1848.	Zepheniah N. Lewis,	"	S. Landon,	"
1849-50.	Moses L. Scudder,	"	"	"
1851.	John M. Reid,	"	J. B. Stratton,	"

The late excellent President Olin, was in the habit of giving $100 annually for Foreign Missions, and the Society, separately from him, were in the habit of giving about $200 more. Collections are taken up for the Colonization and Seamen's Friend Societies, and for general educational purposes.

The society built their first Church edifice of brick, in 1805, 42 feet by 32, on the north side of the South Green. They built their second church on the same site, and of the same material in 1828, 75 feet by 55, height of wall 30; audience room 63 by 52: cost, including steeple, $7,500. A lecture room in the rear of this, also of brick was built in 1851, 56 feet by 40, audience room 38 by 34 feet, cost $1600. Immediately by these buildings the Society have a parsonage.

African Methodist Episcopal Church.

This church was organized by Rev. James Anderson, a colored clergyman of New Haven in 1828. The first trustees were Asa Jeffrey, Joseph Gilbud, E. Deforest, G. W. Jeffrey and John Hambleton; all of whom, excepting E. Deforest, are now dead.

Their church edifice, 39 feet by 31, was built and dedicated in 1829. It stands a short distance west of the University. It was built by subscription and involved the trustees in a debt for some years, from which they are now free.

The average congregation consists of about 100 persons, 30 of whom are communicants. They are supplied with preaching by Conference, and have had a very efficient Sabbath School, and Temperance Society. The superintendant of the school, has been many years, if not uniformly, one of their own people—the greater proportion of the teachers, 12 in number, have been whites. The scholars on an average are about 50. The Library contains 281 volumes.

Universalist Church.

The Universalists in Middletown held a meeting Nov. 29th, 1829, for the purpose of forming themselves into a legal society, and to raise funds for the support of preaching. The Lancasterian School house was hired by them, and preaching supported in it for about ten years. In the autumn of 1838 committees were appointed to procure a site for a church, and to contract for the building: the succeeding year, a site was secured, and a church raised and completed on the south-west corner of Main and Parsonage street. This is 70 feet by 52; the front of the basement is used for stores, and in the rear there is a conference room with desk and seats. The building, with the site, cost about $12,000. Several individuals united and gave a bell, which weighs 1831 pounds.

The house was dedicated in October, 1839, and at

the same time *Rev. L. S. Everett* of Baltimore installed pastor.

Mr. Everett was called to Salem, Massachusetts in April 1841, and the *Rev. Merritt Sanford* of Vermont, was installed his successor the same season. Mr. Sanford becoming unable to preach by a bronchitic affection, an arrangement was made to hire a supply until he should recover his health, but some dissatisfaction growing out of the arrangement, he asked for a dismission which was granted.

September 15th, 1844, *Rev. T. P. Abell* from Haverhill, Massachusetts, was settled as their pastor, and still ministers to the congregation.

About 80 families are connected with ths Society, and from 25 to 30 persons are members of the church.

Contributions have been taken up for the Bible cause, and for Sabbath Schools among their own denomination.

Roman Catholic Church.

The oppressed and suffering Catholics of Ireland for some years past, have been coming to this place and vicinity, as they have to other centres of business in the State and country, seeking employment and the means of support for themselves and their families.—While many females have gained their objects, in the dwellings of inhabitants here, and many males on the farms of the owners and cultivators of the soil, no where within a considerable distance have so many men found employment as in the Portland Quarries, opposite the north end of the city. They needed a house of worship. Accordingly under the guidance and control of Rev. John Brady, their pastor at the time, they began in Oct. 1843, to build them a brick church of respectable size, fronting the North Green. This was soon found insufficient to accommodate their growing numbers. They therefore under the guidance and control of their present pastor, Rev. John Brady Jun., a relative of his predecessor, began in June 1850 to build a much larger church of Portland stone, of Gothic architecture, on the site of the previous building, which is now very nearly ready for consecration. The audience room contains 224 slips, and though there are no side galleries, it has an Organ gallery sufficient for a very large choir. This exceeds in size any other audience room in the city, and in beauty none can be compared with it. The cost of the church we cannot state.

SKETCH OF MIDDLEFIELD.

The settlement in this Society was begun about 1700. The earliest settlers were Samuel Allen, Benjamin Miller and Samuel Wetmore from the First Society. With these, others soon united from the same society, by the name of Bacon, Hubbard, Stow, Turner and Ward; from Durham by the name of Camp, Coe and Lyman; from Stratford by the name of Birdsey; from Guilford by the name of Bartlett: persons also were there by the name of Chilson and Hale. When the Society was incorporated in Oct. 1744, there were more than fifty families living within its limits. The names of the heads of these families were, Samuel Allen, Sen., Samuel Allen, Jr., Ephraim and Obadiah Allyn, Thomas Alvord, Nathaniel and Joseph Bacon, John Bartlett, John Birdsey and John Brown, Abraham and Edward Camp, John Chilson and John Chilson, Jr., Joseph, David and Robert Coe, Gideon and Thomas Cooke, John and Isaac Doud, and Daniel Driggs, Jeremiah Guild, Ebenezer and Joseph Hale, Eliakim Hall, Samuel Stow, Hawley and Ebenezer Hubbard, Jeremiah Leaming, Benjamin Miller and Benjamin Miller Jr., Joseph Miller, Sen., Ichabod, Amos and David Miller, Moses Parsons, John Rockwell and Daniel Stow, David Strickland and David Strickland, Jr., Stephen Turner, Sen., and Samuel Warner, Samuel Wetmore, Sen., Benjamin Wetmore and Benjamin Wetmore, Jr., Beriah, Joseph, Thomas, Daniel, Caleb and Prosper Wetmore, and Josiah Wetmore, jr., and Titus John Whitmore. The aggregate list of all these persons exceeded £3,000.

Almost all these persons were farmers, and soon after the incorporation of the Society, the population reached a point from which it did not greatly vary for many years. But the important water privileges on West river, in its passage through the Society; particularly those on the tributary of this stream, issuing from the mountains on its western border, rendered much more valuable by a large reservoir secured by a dam erected in 1848, have induced numbers to engage in manufactures. Hence the population has been increasing for some years, and *more*, recently, and a village is springing up on this tributary. The number of families in Middlefield in 1815 was ninety-two, and the number of dwelling houses about eighty-one. The families in the beginning of the current year, (1852,) were one hundred and thirty-five, and the dwelling houses one hundred and seventeen. The people built their first meeting-house, in 1745, forty feet square. But at what time the church was organized does not certainly appear, as the ancient records of the church are lost. It was *probably* organized by the same Council that ordained the first pastor, *Rev. Ebenezer Gould*, Oct. 10th, 1747.

With this pastor some individuals became dissatisfied, for reasons which do not now fully appear, and considerable disturbance was occasioned. Still he remained pastor until about 1756, when he was dismissed. He afterwards removed to East Granville, Mass., where he died in 1779. The senior pastor in that place, Rev. Dr. Cooley, has a faint recollection of having seen him in the last hours of his life, when he was too much exhausted to speak distinctly. He never heard of Mr. Gould's preaching in Granville, in a single instance. The probability is that his ministry ceased when he was dismissed, unless in some rare instances he preached an occasional sermon.

After his dismission the people in Middlefield made several attempts to settle a minister and failed; but on the 28th of February, 1765, they settled *Rev. Joseph Denison*, a native of Windham and graduate of Yale College, 1763. He died Feb. 12th, 1770, aged 31.

Rev. Abner Benedict, native of North Salem, N. Y., and graduate of Yale, 1769, succeeded Mr. Denison, Nov. 20th, 1771, but was dismissed 1785, that he might remove to New Lebanon in the State of New York, that a feeble daughter might enjoy the benefits of the medicinal waters of that town, where he was installed, and labored in the ministry six years. He afterwards preached in various places; but died at Roxbury, in the county of Delaware, Nov. 19th, 1818, aged 78.

Mr. Benedict was a son of Dea. Peter Benedict, and brother of Rev. Joel Benedict, D. D., of Lisbon, afterwards of Plainfield; and of Lieut. Peter Benedict, an officer in the Revolutionary war. He was a man of strong affections and an able divine. While in Middlefield he accomplished by his address and efforts, the fredom of all the slaves held by his people.

He left several manuscripts, on which he had bestowed much labor, particularly a dissertaion on the book of Revelation, but whether any of these have been published is not known.

This dismission was exceedingly unfavorable to the interests of religion in Middlefield. Had he remained there, the church would probably have been greatly strengthened, and the society united and prosperous. But after he was gone the Society remained vacant more than twenty years. No minister of Christ was statedly in the desk on the sabbath, enlightening and establishing the minds of the people in the great truths of the gospel, and telling them on week days from house to house, words whereby they and their children might be saved. The old professors of religion died or removed, until the church was almost extinct.

But the Lord having revived his work in the neighboring town of Durham, and this having spread somewhat in this place, the church was reorganized, or rather a new church was formed in Dec., 1808, and 29 persons solemnly entered into covenant with God, and with one another. A few of these had been members of the old church, the others were those who had recently entertained hope of a saving interest in Christ.

But the members of this church, and those disposed to attend worship with them, had no meeting-house of their own, and difficulties existed in the way of their occupying the old meeting-house. In this situation they met for a time in private dwellings, and then assembled for worship in a conference-house, which they erected, until they found means to build a sanctuary. This they raised on the site of the old meeting-house in 1841, and dedicated it June 8, 1842. This, separately from the foundation, cost about $2,000. It is 46 feet by 38, and for this a bell has since been procured at an expense of $150.

"For a number of years they were without a permanent ministry. Sometimes they enjoyed the labors of a minister for several months together; occasionally they were supplied by neighboring ministers; and frequently were destitute of the preaching of the gospel on the sabbath."*

On the 24th of May, 1820, *Rev. Stephen Hayes*, of Newark, N. J., was installed their pastor, with the understanding, that he should preach for them one third of the time, and two-thirds of the time in Westfield. Thus he labored until June 6, 1827, when he was dismissed.

Rev. James Noyes, of Wallingford, graduate of Union College, 1821, was constituted pastor of the church July 23d, 1829, and devoted his whole time to their service; but in Jan. 1839, was dismissed. Since then he has been settled in Burlington, but has spent most of the period in Haddam, where he has instructed youth part of the time; sometimes he has helped his brethren in the ministry, and sometimes has supplied vacant congregations.

After the dismission of Mr. Noyes, the people were supplied for two or three years by *Rev. Dwight Seward*, who had previously been settled in New Britain, and has since been settled in West Hartford. He is a native of Durham, graduate of Yale College, 1831, and graduate of the Theological Depart; is now pastor of a Dutch Reformed Church in Yonkers.

Rev. James T. Dickinson, native of Lowville, N. Y., graduate of Yale, 1826, succeeded Mr. Seward, and supplied the people a year and a half. He was for a time pastor of the church in Norwich city, and then a Foreign Missionary.

December 30th, 1846, *Rev. James D. More*, native of Gorsham, in Wiltshire, Eng., took the charge of the church. He was dismissed April 18, 1850, and installed in Clinton on the 2d of July following.

Rev. A. V. H. Powell, commenced serving here in May, 1851, and is the present supply.

There were three Deacons in the church before its re-organization, and there have been four since, viz:

	Elected.	*Died.*	*Ages.*
Ichabod Miller,		Aug. 22, 1788.	87.
Joseph Coe,		June 10, 1784.	71.
Giles Miller,	About 1774.	March 1, 1804.	77.
Prosper Auger,	Jan. 10, 1809.	Dec. 16, 1836.	81.
William Lyman,	April 28, 1838.		
Horace Skinner,	" "	Oct. 1848.	56.
Phinehas Auger,	April 5, 1850.		

While the church has been blessed at times by the special influences of the spirit, so many have been removed by death and dismission, that it has never had at one time more than eighteen male members, nor an aggregate of members exceeding sixty-eight. This was the number at the commencement of the current year, 1852.

The church and their associates, (for they have no distinct ecclesiastical society,) are free from all pecuniary embarrassment, and besides their conference and meeting-house, have a parsonage, which cost $1507 57; and funds for the support of the gospel, amounting to $1457. Of the latter sums, $200 were given by Mrs. Eunice Stow. They of course are in much better circumstances than heretofore for sustaining religious institutions.

As their circumstances have improved, the contributions of the congregation to benevolent objects have increased. A collection has recently been taken up of nearly $100, mostly for the American Missionary Association. Some small contributions have been made for the Bible Society; and the Sabbath School the last year raised a few dollars for the Tract Society.

The Methodist Church.

This was commenced in 1791, and from that time onward enjoyed more or less preaching. In 1815, the members were reckoned with the members of the M. E. Church in the city, and perhaps at other times. The denomination gathered so much strength, that in 1834 they built a church edifice, 38 by 28 feet, which cost from fifteen to eighteen hundred dollars. They have since remodeled it at an expense of four hundred dollars more. From the time of the erection of this building, they have generally had preaching on the Sabbath. For the last fifteen years the communicants on an average have been about fifty-five ; which is the present number.

There are now six school districts in Middlefield. One formed in 1832, has recently taken the name of Falls District, because it includes the new village already mentioned. The number of children in the Society, between the ages of four and sixteen, is 160.

There are two grave yards in Middlefield. The North yard, about a mile above the churches, was laid out in 1737, and is nearly filled with graves. The Central Grave-yard is on elevated ground very near the Methodist church. It was purchased by the Society and laid out in 1828, and enlarged in 1849. It is laid out in lots, separated by narrow walks.

This Society is regarded as very healthy, and the proportion of deaths is small compared with the population. The average annually for the last few years is reported as six.

SKETCH OF WESTFIELD.

This Society lies directly north of Middlefield and is inhabited generally by a farming population, though some have turned their attention to manufactures. The first settler was Edward Higby, who lived at the foot of the bluff, which from him is called Higby Mountain. He settled there about 1720, perhaps a little earlier, and died in November, 1775, aged about 90. The other early settlers were, Benjamin Atkins, Benjamin, Nathaniel, John and Joseph Bacon, Joseph Cornwell, Joseph Doolittle, Samuel Plumb and Daniel Roberts, from the First Society of Middletown; John Warner, Israel, John and Jeremiah Wilcox, from Cromwell; Joseph Clarke, a native of West Haven, Nathaniel Churchell, from Wethersfield; Edward and Josiah Boardman, from Glastenbury; David and Richard Doud, Asahel Dudley and Joseph Graves, from Guilford.

The people were incorporated as a parish in 1766, but did not build them a house for public worship until 1773. In this year they built one 48 by 38 feet, which they used as a sanctuary more than three fourths of a century. On the 29th of December, the same year, the church was organized, consisting of twenty-six members, twenty-one of whom were received from the church in the First Society, and five from the church in Cromwell. At this time *Rev. Thomas Minor*, a native of Woodbury, graduate of Yale College, 1769, was ordained their pastor. He sustained this relation until death, April 28, 1826, aged 88; but was so enfeebled in the latter part of his life, that *Rev. Stephen Hayes*, mentioned in the account of Middlefield, was installed May 24, 1820, as a colleague pastor with him.

Mr. Hayes preached in Westfield two-thirds of the time, and more than a year after the death of Mr. Minor, being dismissed June 6, 1827. He afterwards preached in North Madison, and Exeter.

Rev. Stephen Topliff, a native of Willington, graduate of Yale in 1825, and of the Theological Department in that institution, having preached sometime in Westfield, was installed May 27, 1829, and dismissed September 25th, 1838. He has been pastor, since September 1st, 1841, of the church in Oxford.

Rev. James Hanmer Francis, native of Wethersfield, graduate of Yale 1826, and of the Theological Department of that college, who had been pastor of the church in Dudley, Mass., was installed in Westfield, December 2d, 1840, and dismissed, June 11th, 1845.

Rev. Lent S. Hough, native of Wallingford, educated classically at Bangor, Maine, and theologically at Bangor and New Haven, was pastor in Chaplin and in North Woodstock, and stated supply in North Madison, and in Bethel in Danbury, before he came to Westfield, sometime in 1846, where he was stated supply until his installation, February 10th, 1847. He is the present pastor.

There have been two hundred and ninety-four members in this church from the beginning; twenty-six at the organization, ninety-two admitted by Mr. Minor, when sole pastor, twenty-one admitted while Mr. Hayes was colleague, and while sole pastor after Mr. Minor's death; ninety-two while Mr. Topliff was supply and pastor; thirty-three by Mr. Francis, and thirty-eight by Mr. Hough. The number of members January 1st, 1852, was one hundred and eighteen.

Deacons.	*Elected.*	*Died or moved from Soc.*	*Age.*
Nathaniel Boardman,	About 1779.	April 9th, 1807.	64
Amos Churchill,	do.	Became a Baptist & left.	
Samuel Galpin,	" 1794.	Sept. 21, 1842.	82
Jedediah Wilcox,	Ap'l 30,1830.		
Selah Galpin,	Ap'l 14,1843.		

The people built a new house for public worship, in 1849, which was dedicated in December of that year. This is 64 feet by 40, and exclusive of the foundation, cost $4,500. This sum however covers the expense of the bell, clock and furniture.

The Society had a fund, raised by subscription in 1818, about half of which was lost by the failure of the

Eagle Bank, in New Haven. The present funds of the Society are:

The residue of that fund, about	$1,000 00.
Appropriation money,	27 79.
Money lent, secured by mortguage,	250 00.
Money lent, not thus secured,	200 00.
Lands given by the late Thomas Minor, M: D., estimated at	570 00.
Parsonage, estimated at	1,000 00.
Total,	$3,047 79.

The contributions made by the people to benevolent objects for the last four years, have been, for the Bible cause $100 54; for Foreign Missions, through the American Board, 199 51; for Home Missions, $105 04; for the Tract Cause, $93 48—to which may be added $10, given to the Sabbath School Union—total, $508-57.

The Baptists in Westfield.

The Strict Congregationalists in this place, spoken of in the sketch of the First Society, professed themselves Baptists in 1804, and were formed into a church, which then consisted of 12 members. Elder Josiah Graves was their pastor. He died July 24, 1825, and after his death they had preachers by the name of Higby, Judd, Goodwin, Wakeman, Ballard and Baty.

A meeting-house which they built in the west part of Westfield in 1812, 36 feet by 26, in 1840 was moved to near the site of the Congregational church, and repaired. For two or three years the Baptists have not held meetings by themselves.

In 1815 there were 93 families in Westfield, and about 81 dwelling houses. In the beginning of 1852, there were 120 families and 104 dwelling houses. There are four school-houses in the Society, but the children of some families attend school without the bounds of the Society, while the children of some other families come from beyond the bounds and attend school here.

There have been four Cemeteries in the Society. One is wholly abandoned on account of the wetness of the ground, another is nearly abandoned. Of the other two one is not far from the churches; the other is on West Street, belongs to families and is much used.

The deaths in the Society for the last ten years, have been eighty-four. In some years the mortality has been much greater than in others, as the following statement shows: In 1842, there were 7 deaths; in 1843, 9; in 1844, 3; in 1845, 8; in 1846, 8; in 1847, 9; in 1848, 4; in 1849, 17; in 1850, 7; in 1851, 14.

PHYSICIANS IN MIDDLETOWN.

In the Address mention is made of *Drs. John Cooper, John Arnold, Abijah Moore, Eliot Rawson, John Osborn and John Osborn, 2d,* father and son, and *John Dickinson,* as physicians in Middletown. All these are believed to have lived in the first Society, and within the limits of the city. Besides these, many other physicians have resided in the city, of whom a few particulars will presently be given. Some of the earlier and some of the later physicians obtained their education in literature and medical science, in private, and others at public institutions. A greater proportion of the later physicians have had their medical education at institutions of a public character. Most who have been in practice since the existence of the Medical Society of the County, have been members of it, and through that members of the Medical Society of the State. A part of those hereafter named are dead, some live here, and some in other parts of the country. Those whose birth-places are not spoken of are regarded as natives of the First Society of this town.

Ebenezer Gilbert, was for a time a member of Yale College, but by sickness was obliged to suspend study and leave the institution before the time for taking his degree. He afterwards studied medicine with Drs. Ives and Hubbard, in New Haven, but completed them with Dr. John Dickinson of this city. During a part of the Revolution he was surgeon in one of our vessels of war. He afterwards went to the West Indies for his health, settled at St. Pierre, in the island of Martinique, where he remained twenty-five years, practising his profession during most, if not the whole of that period. He returned to this place in 1813, and though advanced in years, practised considerably here. He died January 17th, 1833, in his 78th year.

Ebenezer Tracy, native of Norwich, studied medicine and surgery with Dr. Turner of that town: has practised medicine and surgery in Middletown, since 1785.

William Brenton Hall, native of Wallingfied, grauate of Yale, 1786, studied medicine, and probably began practice here, about 1790, of which he had a respectable share. He was Treasurer of the Medical Society of the State from 1801, until his death in 1809.

Dr. Bennet, an Englishman, practised in Middletown a few years.

Thomas Minor, native of Westfield Society. See onward.

William Tully, native of Saybrook, graduate of Yale, 1806, M. D., studied medicine with Dr. Mason Fitch Coggswell, of Hartford, and spent two winters with Dr. Nathan Smith, at Dartmouth College. He began practice in Milford, practised a short time in Cromwell, and a number of years in Middletown—practised also a number of years in Albany, in partnership with Dr. Alden March, and then resided in New Haven twenty-one years. He was Professor in the Vermont Academy of Medicine, for fourteen years, where his department for about half the time was the principles and practice of medicine solely, which required one lecture a day, and for the other half, he taught in addition, Materia Medica and Therapeutics, giving two lectures a day. In New Haven was professor of Materia Medica and Therapeutics in the Medical Department of Yale College, fourteen years. He is now practising in Springfield, Massachusetts.

Henry Woodward, native of Torringford. See onward.

Isaac Conkling, native of East Hampton, L. I., student of Dr. Ebenezer Sage, of Sag Harbor, L. I., attended lectures in Columbia College, New York City, practised three or four years in Portland, about as many in Oneida County, N. Y., and nine years in Middletown. Died in Portland February 24, 1824, aged 44.

Edward S. Cone, son of Rev. Salmon Cone, of Colchester, graduate of Middlebury College, 1815, student of Dr. William Tully, attended lectures in New Haven, had good share of practice; died February 13, 1831, aged nearly 36 years.

Frederic Morgan. See Physicians in Middle Haddam.

David Harrison, native of North Branford, student of Dr. Parker, of Wallingford, graduated M. D., at Yale College, 1825, began practice in Durham, moved to Middletown, in 1829; in 1837, went to the Spanish West Indies for his health and practised there, returning to Middletown in 1842.

Joseph Barratt, an Englishman by birth, professor of Botany, Chemistry and Mineralogy, in the Military Academy, was graduated M. D., at Yale College, in 1834. Besides performing professional duties, he has paid much attention to the language of the American Indians, and various branches of natural science.

Gurdon H. Parkis, attended lectures at Pittsfield, and was graduated M. D., at Williams College, in 1829. About this time he came to Middletown and practised, left in 1833; at an after period he practised dentistry in Norwich.

Chester Parkis, brother of Gurdon, came to Middletown a few months after him, and left about the same time. He afterwards practised dentistry, in Salem, Mass.

Charles Woodward, M. D., son of Dr. Samuel Woodward of Torringford, studied medicine with his father, and with his brother, Dr. Samuel B. Woodward, in Wethersfield, where he practised in 1821, then ten years in Windsor; in 1832, he came to Middletown, where he has since practised.

Samuel Gray Southmayd, M. D. graduate of Yale, 1834. After practising for a time in Middletown, he settled and practised in New York. He has since given up his profession, as a principal concern, and engaged in other business.

Thomas Miner, M. D., native of Stonington, attended lectures in Pittsfield, practised medicine some years in West Stockbridge, and then in Middletown; is now practising in Hartford.

William B. Casey, *M. D.*, graduate of Columbia College, N. Y., 1833, studied medicine and was graduated at the University of Pennsylvania, began practice in New York in 1836, and in Middletown, 1839; was mayor of the city in '51.

Elisha B. Nye, native of Sandwich, Mass., graduate of Wesleyan University in 1835, studied medicine with Dr. Thomas Miner, 2d, of Middletown, and in New Haven, where he was graduated M. D., in 1837; practised in Moodus, a village in East Haddam, from 1837 till nearly the close of 1851; is now settled in Middletown.

Hamilton Brewer, native of East Hartford, graduate of Wesleyan University, 1838, graduated M. D., at New Haven, in 1841, practised in Middletown several years, moved to Brooklyn in '51; is now engaged in insurance.

Franklin Woodruff, native of Burlington, studied medicine with Dr. William Brown of Collinsville, and his brother Dr. Lucius Woodruff of New Britain. The degree of M. D., was conferred upon him at the New York University in 1844, and in the same year he settled in Middletown.

George W. Burke, native of New Haven, graduate of the Wesleyan University, 1839, studied medicine with Dr. A. Brigham of Hartford, and in New Haven, where he was graduated Doctor of Medicine in '43; practised in Palmer, Mass., has come to Middletown since the commencement of the current year.

Ellsworth Burr, native of Haddam, Botanic Physician, who studied with Dr. Isaac G. Sperry of Hartford, has practised in Middletown and vicinity since 1837.

William C. Bell, Homœpathic physician, studied medicine one year under Horace Ballard, M. D., of Chester, Mass., and then mostly under Professor Child, of Pittsfield, where he was graduated M. D., in 1833. He afterwards practised in Austerlitz, N. Y., and in Great Barrington, Mass., till, '49, when he came to Middletown, where he has since practised.

Physicians in Middlefield and Westfield.

The people in Middlefield and Westfield have depended principally for medical aid upon the physicians in the First Society, and in other adjoining places. About the few physicians who have resided and practised in these places, a few words will be added to what is said in the address, (pp. 95 and 6.) Dr. A. Ward practised in Middlefield a few years only, dying August 12th, 1788, aged 32. Dr. J. Hoadley, native of Branford, graduate of Yale, 1768, practised a longer period, had the reputation of being very skilful in curing the cholic. He died March 2d, 1810, aged 66*. Dr. Hatch who practised in Westfield for a short time, and then moved to New Hartford, and afterwards to Granville, Mass., though a very respectable man, engaged only in part in his profession in New Hartford, and very little in Granville. A Dr. Morris is said to have practised for a short time in Westfield, about 1830, who moved to Meriden, and thence to Ohio.

Thomas Minor, M. D.

There are published accounts, in Williams' American Medical Biography, of two of the deceased physicians in the foregoing list, which in an abridged form will now be given.

The first is an account of Dr. Thomas Minor, son of Rev. Thomas Minor, of the parish of Westfield. This is mostly autobiographical; the rest is from the pen of Dr. S. B. Woodward, who well knew him. The whole is much too long for insertion. But it is due to the standing of Dr. Minor, that some facts should be here given concerning him. He was born Oct. 15th, 1777, and in childhood and early youth suffered much from feebleness and disease, but entered Yale College in 1792,

* Phineas Miller, a native of Middlefield, and brother of the Hon. Asher Miller, who studied medicine with the 2d Dr. John Osbone, settled in Norwalk, and had a large practice. He has been dead more than twenty years.

when he was about fifteen years of age, and was graduated in 1796. He speaks very modestly of his attainments in College, and though the four years "were far from being trifled away or lost," he declares they were spent under very great and permanent disadvantages, and expresses the opinion that he "did not acquire half the solid learning" he might have done "had he been two years older and proportionally better prepared." During the five or six years following, it is believed that his scholarship was greatly improved in accuracy and amount, by teaching, and at the same time studying himself. During this period he taught an academy for about three years in Goshen, N. Y., and then another about two years in Berlin, though in the meanwhile he was visited once and again by disease in some of its forms. When about twenty-five, he commenced the study of medicine under Dr. John Osborne, engaging also in the instruction of youth, and in the beginning of 1807 he entered upon his profession. From some time in 1808 into '10, he was in full practice in the town of Lynn, Mass., whence he removed to Lyme, in this State and thence to the city of Middletown, where and in the vicinity he had for a number of years, "as much professional business as he could attend to, and more than his health would bear." In Feb. 1819, "he was seized with an affection of the lungs and heart, which suddenly ended in a great degree," his "professional career, and left him a confirmed valetudinarian at the premature age of forty-one," though for several years after he "practised some in consultation, and amused "himself in reading two or three foreign languages, besides writing occasional medical and literary essays," which appeared in the columns of different publications. In fact, in various ways he did much for the advancement of medical science and the relief and benefit of his fellow men. In 1823, in connection with Dr. Tulley, he published essays on fevers and other medical subjects; and in 1825, an account of Typhus Syncopalis [the sinking typhus.] This work Dr. S. B. Woodward speaks of as *one* which caused a great deal of controversy; one which was most severely criticised; but one about which, although the public were divided as to its real worth, they were generally satisfied that it evinced great erudition and research. "At any rate," he says, "it was one which gave the author great notoriety as a writer and great fame as a practitioner." Dr. Minor himself declares it was published several times entire, or abridged in other works."

After the organization of the Medical School of Yale College, he was perhaps three-tenths of the time, one of the censors or members of the committee. He was a member of the committee for devising ways and means and forming the plan for the Retreat for the Insane, at Hartford, as a colleague with Doctors Todd, Woodward, Tulley, Ives and others, and with the assistance of Dr. Tulley, wrote the committee's address to the public, which preceded their solicitation of donations.

He corresponded with many distinguished physicians in different parts of the country, and with some distinguished men who did not pursue the medical profession. The late venerable Noah Webster, LL. D., was one of his correspondents. To that eminent lexicographer he wrote letters on criticism, etymology and other philosophical subjects. Dr. Webster did him the honor occasionally, to send him manuscripts, soliciting his remarks previously to their publication.

Having been afflicted twenty years and more, with a disease of the heart, early in March, 1841, he went to Worcester to visit his friend Dr. S. B. Woodward, to see what could be done to alleviate his sufferings, and as he said himself, "if he could not be relieved, to die with his friend." With that friend he did die, on the morning of April 23d, 1841, in the 64th year of his age.

It is surprising that one so feeble from his early days, and suffering so much from disease, should have lived so long and accomplished so much.

In communicating his death to Dr. Smith, editor of the Boston Medical and Surgical Journal, Dr. Woodward observes, "Dr. Minor was a remarkable man. He has left behind him few as ripe scholars, profound philosophers and philanthropists in the medical profession. Ill health having for some years prevented active engagement in professional duties, he has devoted his whole time to study and reflection. His mind was very active to the last. He was, perhaps, one of the most learned physicians in New England, not only in professional attainments, but in foreign languages and theology. He was acquainted with the French, Italian, Spanish and German languages, and was often employed by publishers in the country to translate them. He was particularly fond of the German, and read works on medicine, theology and philosophy in that language with great pleasure. You well know his estimable and moral qualities. His heart was benevolent, his feelings kind. In his life he exemplified the christian character; in sickness and death he bore testimony of unbroken confidence in the christian hope of a joyful resurrection."

Henry Woodward, M. D.

The second person referred to as being the subject of a memoir, in Williams' Medical Biography, is Dr. Henry Woodward, and brother of Drs. S. B. and Charles Woodward. The memoir is from the pen of the elder of these brothers, with whom after having studied awhile with the father he pursued the studies preparatory to his profession. With this brother too, while resident in Wethersfield he was associated about four years after admission to practice. From that town, he came to Middletown, where he spent his remaining life.

From the memoir and from other evidence it is apparent that he possessed naturally a very vigorous mind, that he was exceedingly apt to learn, and that he examined subjects philosophically; also that he had a kind and social temper, polished manners, and was active and faithful in the discharge of his public duties. He possessed that discretion in the use of these attributes and acquisitions which made him acceptable as well as useful. He had the requisites for being popular with the people, securing the esteem of his patients and the respect of his medical brethren. Accordingly he soon gained extensive practice, and for years "his business was equal to that of any other physician in the State, both for respectability and extent. He received the honorary degree of Doctor of Medicine from the Connecticut Medical Society at an earlier age than any other gentleman in the State; and no young man was more esteemed by the faculty in an extensive circle of acquaintance."

"He was twice chosen to represent the town of Middletown in the Legislature of the State, and was at the time a candidate for higher advancement. In the public stations he filled he always sustained himself with dignity and ability, and was considered one of the ablest members of the House of Representatives."

Investigating thoroughly the causes of disease and applying remedies skillfully; felicitous and happy in his intercourse with the sick, he gained their affections. "He loved society and society loved him."

"His moral character was above reproach. He was a man of active benevolence, gave much in charity, and took hold of the great moral enterprises of the day with true zeal. He was a regular member of the Episcopal Church, of which he was for some time vestryman and warden."

But "in the midst of his activity and usefulness he was cut down by a disease of the chest, which in a few months terminated his life by a rapid consumption. He died October 10th, 1832, at the early age of 37 years."

LAWYERS IN MIDDLETOWN.

These are understood to have lived universally in the city. In the Address *Titus Hosmer*, *Samuel Holden Parsons*, *Samuel W. Dana*, *Asher Miller*, and *Stephen Titus Hosmer*, are noticed somewhat particularly, and *Silas Stow*, and *John G. C. Brainerd*, in few words. The list about to be given contains the names of all the other lawyers, or nearly all, who have ever lived and practised in this place.

Notwithstanding the numbers admitted to the bar, it is generally acknowledged that the amount of law business now, is less than it was thirty-five or forty years ago. The litigations arising from failures and change of property from the restrictive system and the second war with Great Britain, have years since been adjusted; the fisheries on the river, formerly the source of much controversy, have nearly ceased; human rights and the proper modes of doing business are better understood and more respected; the temperance reformation, preventing wild speculation and wasteful expenditures, has prompted to productive industry and frugal economy—these and other causes have lent a peaceful influence. This may be a reason why some lawyers have given up their profession: another may be that they find business enough of other kinds to occupy them.

List of Lawyers with a few Items.

William Plumbe, a native of the Society of Westfield, graduate of Yale College, 1769, practised law a short time, became a preacher and chaplain in the army in the Revolution, afterwards a merchant. He died June 2d, 1843, leaving a few thousand dollars worth of property for Foreign Missions, under the care of the American Board. The exact sum cannot be given, as the estate is not entirely settled.

Ezekiel Woodruff, said to be a native of Farmington or Southington, graduate of Yale, 1779, practised here a few years. He was City Clerk from 1786 to 1789 inclusive, resigned this office and probably soon after moved away, to what place is not known.

Matthew Talcott Russell. See close of this list.

William Brown, native of Guilford, graduate of Yale 1784, practised law some years here, was City Clerk after Mr. Woodruff, three years. He afterwards practised in Madison a few years, and then in the city of Hartford, where he died in the close of 1803. He was a man of good abilities and much respected.

Joshua Henshaw, native of Middletown, and graduate of Yale, 1785. He moved to Vermont, and thence, it is understood, to Montreal, in Canada.

Enoch Huntington, son of Rev. Enoch Huntington, graduate of Yale, 1785, had superior natural talents, was a Dean scholar, spoke with great fluency at the bar, and was Colonel of militia. He died March 7th, 1826, aged 58.

Silas Stow, was a native of the Society of Middlefield. See p. 106.

George W. Stanley, born in Wallingford, graduated at Yale, 1793, practised law many years in his native town, came to Middletown in 1819, and was State's Attorney; moved to Cleveland, Ohio, about 1837.

Alexander Collins, son of General Augustus Collins, of North Guilford, graduate of Yale, 1795, studied law in the office of the late Judge Hosmer. He died while on a journey, Sept. 14th, 1815, aged 41, at Brattleboro, Ver., where his body is interred. The enterprising men, from whom Collinsville derives its name, are his sons.

Elijah Hubbard, graduate of Yale, 1795, studied at the Law School in Litchfield, practised law some years in New London, returned to Middletown upon the death of his father, Elijah Hubbard, Esq., in 1808, was many years President of Middletown Bank, and repeatedly mayor of the city. He died Dec. 4th, 1846, aged 69.

Chauncey Whittlesey, son of Chauncey Whittlesey, Esq., graduate of Yale, 1800, and a Dean scholar, read law with the Hon. Charles Chauncey of New Haven, and was admitted to the bar in November, 1804. See onward.

John L. Lewis, native of Philadelphia, studied with Judge Hosmer, and was admitted to the bar in March, 1805. In May, 1818, he was appointed Sheriff of Middlesex County. He afterwards moved to Florida, where he died.

William Van Deusen, graduate of Yale, 1801, studied law in Middletown and Litchfield, was admitted to the bar as early as 1807, received a captain's commission from the General Government, and for a time had command of the fort at New London. He died in Middletown Sept. 26th, 1833, aged 49.

Levi H. Clark, a native of Sunderland, Mass., and graduate of Yale, 1802, studied law with the Hon. Charles Chauncey of New Haven, and with Asa Bacon, Esq., in Canterbury. He commenced practice in Haddam in the Spring of 1805. See onward.

Noah A. Phelps, native of Simsbury, studied law with Hon. Elisha Phelps, was admitted to the bar in Hartford in 1811, and practised in that city—was sheriff of Hartford county from 1819 to 1828. He came to Middletown in 1829, being appointed collector of customs; he has since been judge of the County Court, mayor of the city of Middletown, judge of Probate, State Senator, and Secretary of Connecticut.

Jonathan Barnes,, son of Jonathan Barnes, Esq., of Tolland, (attorney in Tolland county,) graduate of Yale, 1810, studied law with his father, and after he came to Middletown, for a time with Chauncey Whittlesey, Esq., began practice in Middletown, in 1813, and has ever since confined himself closely and unusually to the appropriate duties of his profession.

Major Andre Andrews, native of Cornwall, studied law, for a time at least, with his brother, Benajah Andrews, in Wallingford, began to practice in Middletown, as early as 1815—was appointed State's Attorney in Sept., 1818, moved to Buffalo in 1819, where he died during the second prevalence of the cholera in the place Aug. 17, 1834, aged 42.

Minor Hotchkiss, born in New Haven, graduate of

Yale, 1813, studied law in Litchfield and New Haven, was admitted to the bar in New Haven in the close of 1815, and came immediately to Middletown. See onward.

Abiel L. Loomis, began to practice law in Middle Haddam, as early as 1816; in two or three years he moved to Killingworth, now Clinton, where he remained about ten years, he then came to Middletown, but afterwards removed to Hartford where he died.

William L. Storrs, graduated at Yale, 1814, read law with his brother, Henry R. Storrs, Esq., at Whitestown, N. Y., was admitted to the bar in New York, in 1817, and in Connecticut soon after. He was Representative to the Legislature of Connecticut, in 1827 and '28, and to Congress from March, 1829 to 1823—was speaker of the House of Representatives in Connecticut in 1834. He was elected member of Congress again for two years, from March 4, 1839, but in 1840, became a judge of the Superior Court. He has also been professor in the New Haven Law School. The Western Reserve College has conferred upon him the degree of LL. D.

Ebenezer Force, studied law with the Hon. Sylvester Gilbert of Hebron, practised in Middle Haddam, in 1819, '20, and '21, came to Middletown and practised a short time, enlisted into the army of the United States. Has been dead some years.

John G. C. Brainerd, native of New London, and graduate of Yale, 1815, son of Hon Jeremiah G. Brainerd. See p. 108.

Enoch Thomas Parsons, graduate of Union College, 1818, was admitted to the bar in 1822, practised a short time, lost his health, died April 15th, 1830, aged 30.

Asahel Utley. See list of lawyers in Middle Haddam.

Samuel Holden Parsons, graduate of Yale, 1819, admitted to the bar in 1822, practised for a time in Middletown, and then in Hartford; is now travelling in Europe.

Samuel Dickinson Hubbard, graduate of Yale, 1819, studied at the New Haven Law School, practised law some years, has been mayor of the city, and Member of Congress.

John Hiram Lathrop, graduate of Yale, 1819. Tutor, LL. D., practised law here a short time, has since been professor in Hamilton College, and in the University of Missouri; and is now president of the University of Wisconsin.

Ezekiel L. Hosmer, son of the late Judge Hosmer, was admitted to the bar in 1823, and died Nov. 14th, 1826, aged 24.

Charles Richard Alsop, graduate of Yale, 1821, studied law in the office of Jonathan Barnes, Esq., and was admitted to the bar in this State. He then attended the lectures of the late Chancellor Kent in New York, studied in the office of Daniel Lord, Esq., an attorney in the city, and was admitted to the bar there. He remained in that city until 1832, when he returned to Middletown. Upon the resignation of Noah A. Phelps, Esq., he was elected mayor of the city of Middletown, April 25th, 1843, for the residue of the term. He was then re-elected for two years, after which he declined a re-election. While mayor he first started the movement for the New York and Boston Railroad, usually spoken of as the Air Line Railroad. He also obtained the charter for the Middletown Railroad (now the Branch to the Hartford and New Haven Railroad.) Of this road he was the President until it was merged with the Hart. ford, New Haven and Springfield Railroad Company. He was one of the original corporators of the New York and Boston Railroad Company, and in Nov., 1850, was elected the President of it.

Isaac Webb, born in Chester, graduate of Yale, 1822, and tutor; studied law in New Haven, began to practice here in 1827 or '28; afterwards established a school for the instruction of lads; died September 29th, 1842, aged 45.

Stillman K. Wightman, graduate of Yale, 1825, studied law with Jonathan Barnes, Esq., and at the Law School in New Haven, and was admitted to the bar in 1827—was State's Attorney, Speaker of the house of representatives, and State Senator. He moved to the city of New York about 1844, where he now practises.

Ebenezer Jackson, native of Savannah, Ga., educated at the college of St. Mary's in Baltimore, studied law in Litchfield, was admitted to the bar in 1827—has been a Member of Congress.

Charles C. Tyler, native of Haddam, studied law with Judge Storrs, was admitted to the bar in 1828, has been State's Attorney and Judge of the County Court.

Thomas Griswold Mather, graduate of Yale, 1826, studied law with Judge Storrs, was admitted to the bar in 1829, has been town clerk.

Samuel W. *Griswold*, was born in the Society of Westfield, studied law with Abiel A. Loomis and Jonathan Barnes, was admitted to the bar in Oct. 1832, died Feb. 16th, 1844, aged nearly 36.

Alfred Hall, native of Portland, graduate of Trinity College, 1828, studied law in Middletown, New Haven, and Cambridge, began to practice in Middletown, about 1833 or '34, but soon returned to Portland and is a merchant in that town—has been Representative to the General Assembly from that town for two or three years past.

Elihu Spencer, native of Warren, Ohio, graduated at the Wesleyan University, 1838, studied with Judge Storrs, was admitted to the bar in Oct. 1841—has been Town Clerk, Clerk of the County and Superior Courts, and Treasurer, and Representative to the General Assembly of the State.

Dennis Sage, graduate of Wesleyan University, 1839, studied law with Judge Storrs, admitted to the bar in 1842—practised a short time, then went into other business; has been to California, but recently returned.

Charles W*hittlesey*, born in Salisbury, graduate of Williams College, 1840, studied law in Litchfield county, where he was admitted to the bar in 1844—came the same year to Middletown, has been State's Attorney.

Norman L. Brainerd, born in Portland, studied law in Cambridge and N. Y. city, was in a law office and practised in that city, has been a year or two in Middletown.

A few words in addition, in regard to M. T. Russell, Chauncey Whittlesey, Levi H. Clark, and Minor Hotchkiss.

Matthew Talcott Russell, was named after Col. Matthew Talcott, who had married his aunt, and had no children of his own. He was educated at his expense at Yale College, where he was tutor four years. He studied law with the Hon. Oliver Ellsworth, and commenced practice in this city. Though of a slender constitution and delicate health, he was able through great care and prudence to attend continually to his professional concerns. He was accurate and methodical in every thing, and therefore well fitted to transact the large amount of collecting business which was entrusted to his hands. For some time he was State's attorney. The community respected him for his integrity and faithfulness and the church honored him for his consistent christian conduct. He died Nov. 13, 1828, aged nearly 68 years.

From the close of 1804 until 1819, *Chauncey Whittlesey, Esq.*, practised in this county and though able lawyers from Middlesex and adjoining counties, attended the courts, he acquired an elevated rank among his brethren. He was also advanced in military life to the command of a brigade. In the last mentioned year he removed to Louisville, Kentucky, where he practised about four years, and afterwards to New Orleans, where he practised about four years more. His health having been seriously injured while in the latter city, he returned to his native town in 1827, and attended in a degree to official business until the autumn of 1829, when his illness became distressing. His sight and other bodily powers were affected, so that for the residue of his life he was almost helpless, and often racked with severe pain. He died Dec. 24th, 1834, aged 51.

Gen. Whittlesey's earthly disappointments and sufferings served to render the grace of God, in which he trusted, the more conspicuous. Those who visited him in his afflictions were surprised in view of his weak and disordered body, and at the continued vigor of his mind; were instructed by his conversation, and improved by his resignation to God and his benevolence to men, and prospects of blessedness in the life to come.

An able writer in the Philadelphian for Jan. 8, 1835, declares concerning him: "When almost every earthly comfort was withdrawn, he was not cast down, for he looked to his inheritance among the saints in light. When blindness and darkness came over his bodily sense, the eye of his mind remained strong and unclouded, and the light of Heaven still penetrated to his soul and kept up a constant warmth in his heart. While he was in a condition which would have made some men forget all but self and suffering, his expansive benevolence, worthy of its celestial origin, constantly flowed out to his fellow beings. His intellect was still firm and vigorous after years of severe disease had taken from his body almost all power but that of endurance, and his feelings, instead of being souered by disappointment and calamity, grew more tender and affectionate while one faculty and enjoyment after another, in melancholy succession departed from him." "Thus through long years of trial he acted out the faith and patience of the saints."

Levi H. Clarke, removed from Haddam to Middletown, in 1807 or 8. In both towns he had considerable practice. About 1816, he removed to Carthage, N. Y., invested property in that village and engaged in the building of the famous "Carthage Bridge," which was the wonder of western tourists. In the fall of that bridge he lost much property, and resorted afterwards mainly, to the use of his pen for support. In 1821, he was appointed an associate judge of the County Court, for the new county of Munroe, and that year he reported the proceedings of the Convention which formed a constitution for the Empire State. His reports were subsequently published in an octavo volume, styled, "Clarke's Reports." From that time until 1835, he was generally connected in some way with papers and publications in New York city, as owner, partner, editor or correspondent, and from 1835 until June, 1839, was a justice of the 7th, 10th and 15th wards. He died at Feeding Hills in West Springfield, Feb. 6th, 1840, aged

57. There is much evidence that before his death he became a sincere christian.

Minor Hotchkiss, Esq., is remembered by many. Upon his appearance in this county he was marked as a young man of talents and promise. He soon became distinguished in his profession, and his prospects of business and usefulness in the world were as great as those of any man of his age in the State. With a mind well stored with knowledge were associated dispositions, manners and habits adapted to secure affection and confidence. In the two last years of his life he represented the town in the Legislature of the State, with credit to himself and satisfaction to his constituents. A long and distressing sickness "he bore with patience and resignation, and gave the strongest evidence of personal piety." He died Oct. 21st, 1825, aged 34.

MEANS OF COMMON AND HIGHER EDUCATION.

The Common Schools of Middletown, First Society, and also of Middlefield and Westfield, have corresponded in character generally with the common schools in other societies throughout the State; and these have furnished to the great body of children the rudiments of an English education, which have been variously improved in after life. Different circumstances have conspired to render the terms in these schools longer in some districts than in others, and to the securing of teachers of higher qualifications. The schools of this description are generally considered as being on the advance; some unquestionably are. The number of common schools in the First Society, and out of the city limits, are now ten, and the number of children, reported as being in the district where these schools are situated, and between the ages of four and sixteen, in 1851, was five hundred and two. The number of such children reported in 1851, as being in the city was nine hundred and nine. Here provision was made for them, as in other parts of the Society, until 1840, when the citizens, desirous of placing all the children, before reaching sixteen, in circumstances in which they might attain a higher education, than was expected at the common schools, obtained from the Legislature a special act, in virtue of which all the children, entitled to the benefit of the great school fund of the State, might be instructed after reaching the age of nine years and so onward until sixteen, in a High School, while other children from four to nine, might be instructed in four Primary Schools. Rooms for the High School were hired until a suitable edifice was prepared in the summer of 1841. This is sixty-six feet by forty-eight, two stories, in which there are rooms for study and recitation. There is a basement in which a family resides, having care of the building, and a large arched attic for lectures, or any other purpose for which it is needed.

The Institution is under the instruction and government of a male principal, having male and female assistants. The older children occupy the upper story and the younger the lower.

The average number of children has been about two hundred and thirty. More girls have generally attended than boys, about one hundred and twenty-five girls, and about one hundred and five or one hundred and ten boys. Of both, in some seasons, there have been two hundred and eighty. The attendance in the primary schools has been about the same.

The benefits of the High School have been vast, by bringing the higher English branches and the elementary branches of Latin and Greek, within the means of all. Several scholars have been fitted for college. None are required to pay more than four dollars a year, and the tuition of the poor is abated.

But invaluable as the Common Schools have been from the beginning to children generally, there have been all along some parents who wished to secure for their children higher advantages than the common schools afforded, especially where they were designed for the learned professions, or the more important branches of business. For a long time, parents in such cases placed their children under the tuition of settled clergymen. The important and long continued efforts of Rev. Enoch Huntington, in the instruction of youth, were mentioned in the Address; and yet in his time highly qualified teachers were employed in keeping school in Middletown. Chauncey Whittlesey, graduate of Yale College, 1764, when he came to this town was employed in the instruction of youth. So was Jonathan Ingersoll, graduate of the same college in 1766, and while teaching youth he was a student of law under Hon. Titus Hosmer. Others of like qualifications, probably followed them. Before the commencement of this century, Rev. William Woodbridge opened a school for young ladies, which was continued several years. At a subsequent time, Mr.

Elijah Garfield from Lee, Mass., opened a school for the instruction of youth of both sexes; though in the latter part of the time in which he instructed here, he taught lads only, who were seeking qualifications for doing business or entrance into colleges. Isaac Webb, a graduate and tutor of Yale College, who settled in Middletown as a lawyer, instructed a school of lads a number of years before his death, in 1842.

THE PREPARATORY SCHOOL of *D. H. Chase, A. M.*, has been in successful operation sixteen years. Two courses of study are pursued, the first embracing "all that is necessary to prepare youth for any college or university—the second, besides common English, includes book-keeping, algebra, geometry, surveying, astronomy, geology, philosophy of natural history, rhetoric, logic, mental, moral and political philosophy, &c. Exercises in composition and declamation, alternate weekly, lectures and experiments are given on interesting and useful subjects. The School is supplied with Chemical and Philosophical apparatus, and a select Library."

"Moral and religious education receives an attention due to its extreme importance. Students attend the churches designated by their parents. A portion of each Sabbath is devoted to a bible lesson, and to sacred music."

Some years a School for Young Ladies was kept in the city, by *Miss Mary Ann Bartlett*, which was followed by another, kept also some years by *Mr. Sidera Chase.*

THE MIDDLETOWN FEMALE SEMINARY, under the instruction of *Rev. Josiah Brewer and Lady*, who have had much experience in instruction, has been in operation two years, and attended by more than one hundred young ladies on an average. They have a competent supply of able assistants, native teachers of the modern languages, and skilful professors of music, drawing, &c.

"There are two sessions of eleven and thirty-three weeks, beginning on the second Monday in May, and the first Monday in September, divided into quarters, each eleven weeks. The principal vacations are in the months of August and April, with a week from Christmas to New Years."

"The pupils are mainly arranged into two departments, viz: the Preparatory and the Principal. A full course in each requires two or three years, but may be modified to meet the wants of individuals. Those of mature age, or advanced in their studies, are admitted for a part of a year."

"Among the studies of the Preparatory Classes are mental and practical arithemtic, geography, first lessons in grammar, elements of botany, physiology and natural philosophy, general history, and history of the United States; manual of morals and youths book of natural theology."

"In the Principal Department, are taught arithmetic, algebra and geometry, antient geography and mythology; histories of Greece, Rome, France and England; English grammar and rhetoric; natural history, physiology, natural philosophy, chemistry, geology, botany, astronomy and meteorology; science of government, mental and moral science; geography of the bible, natural theology and evidences of christianity."

Composition forms a prominent object of attention. Latin and Greek Languages are taught to all who wish for them. Instructions in Instrumental Music, Drawing, Painting and Modern Languages, are furnished at the usual city prices.

The health, manners, morals and religious welfare of pupils, especially of those who become members of the family of the Principals, are watched over with parental care. They attend public worship at such places as meet the wishes of their friends.

The WESLEYAN UNIVERSITY, is spoken of in the Address, pp. 110, 111. Since that was delivered, the institution has been afflicted by the death of another revered President, *Rev. Stephen Olin, S.T. D.*, who died Aug. 16th, 1851, aged 55. Although a memoir of him is expected, it may be well to state that he was born in Leicester, Ver. and graduated at Middlebury College, in 1820, where he held a very high standing as a scholar. Soon after leaving college he went to South Carolina and had the charge of an academy. While there he experienced religion, connected himself with the South Carolina Methodist Episcopal Conference and became a circuit preacher. He was stationed sometime in Charleston, but was interrupted in his self-denying and arduous labors by ill health. He was afterwards professor of Moral Philosophy and Rhetoric, in the University of Georgia, and then President of Randolph and Macon College. This presidency he resigned, took a voyage to Europe, and thence passed into Egypt, Arabia Petraea and the Holy Land. An account of his travels in these countries, published in 1843, has had a wide circulation; and it is altogether probable that he will long be remembered and respected as a writer; for an edition of other works of his pen has just been issued. These compose two volumes. The first containing sermons and sketches; the second, Lectures on Education, Baccalaureate Discourses, and various occasional Addresses and Essays."

As a drawing of the University building and chapel accompanies this work, it is not necessary to say much about them and other buildings belonging to the Corporation. The university building is of the Portland stone, 150 feet by 50, four stories, containing sixty-four rooms. The Chapel of the same material, 54 feet by 44, is also four stories, and has projection in front, in which beside the room appropriated to devotion, there are rooms for the Library, Philosophical Apparatus, the Cabinet of Minerals, and for recitations. Connected with these there is a Laboratory with a lecture room, and a large three-story brick building, designed at first for a public boarding house; in which now there is one room, called the Missionary Lyceum, in which various and interesting articles received from Missionary stations in different parts of the world, are already collected; where meetings are held to hear information concerning Missionary operations and prospects, and to pray for the conversion of the world. In this also, are rooms for the students.

The grounds on which these buildings stand are 160 feet above the level of the Connecticut river and five-eights of a mile distant from it.

Graduates of Colleges, natives or inhabitants of Middletown, not particularly mentioned in the Address, among the settled Clergymen, nor in the lists of Physicians and Lawyers; with a notice of a very few others who without going through a collegiate course have entered the sacred office.

GRADUATES FROM MIDDLETOWN,

FIRST SOCIETY.

Harvard College.

Nathaniel Collins, 1697. He was son of the first settled pastor in Middletown, and became himself the first pastor of the church in Enfield, where he labored more than twenty years. He then resigned his ministry in that place, but preached in other places; he died in Enfield in 1757, aged 79.

Yale College.

Seth Wetmore, 1714. Was the first Congregational minister in North Haven, embraced episcopacy about 1722, went to England for orders, in 1723, was rector of the Episcopal Church in Rye, N. Y., where he died May 14th, 1760. He published a defence of Waterland's discourse on Regeneration and two or three other controversial pieces.

Joseph Clark, 1745. Was town clerk, justice of the peace, and deacon in the First Congregational Church.

Jeremiah Leaming, S. T. D., 1745. He became an Episcopal minister, preached eight years in Newport, R. I., twenty-one in Norwalk, and eight or nine at Stratford. He died in New Haven, in Sept., 1804, aged 86. Besides two controversial pieces, he published Evidences of the Truth of Christianity, and dissertations on various subjects. His writings indicate a strong and well informed mind.

Israkiah Wetmore, 1748. Was pastor of the First Church in Stratford, preached the election sermon before the Legislature in Connecticut in 1773, died in 1798.

Jabez Hamlin, 1769. Son of Col. J. Hamlin, went to Boston, as ensign in the company commanded by Return J. Meigs, in 1775, afterwards received a captain's commission, and died of sickness, while in the service of his country, at East Chester, N. Y., Sept. 20th, 1776, aged 24.

Robert Hubbard, 1769. Entered the ministry, settled in Shelburne, Mass., became consumptive, was brought to Middletown, after his sickness commenced, where he died Nov. 2d, 1788, in the 45th year of his age. His body rests with those of his friends, in Tomb-lane Yard.

George Phillips, 1769. Was a merchant in the city, and the first collector of customs for the District of Middletown. He died in New Orleans, in 1802.

Elisha Atkins, 1773. Chaplain in the Revolutionary army, and pastor of the Congregational Church in Killingly, where he died in 1839.

Alexander Wolcott, 1778. Practised law in Hartford County, possessed a strong mind and superior legal attainments. He was collector of customs in the district of Middletown, from Aug., 1801, until his death June 26th, 1828, when he was in the 70th year of his age.

Wait Cornwell, 1782. Preached occasionally, but never had the charge of a parish—moved late in life to some part of the State of Ohio, where he died in March, 1816.

Samuel Mather, 1792. Native of Lyme, merchant in Albany, N. Y., has resided in Middletown many years.

Joseph Washburn, 1793. While fitting for college and while studying theology, he was under the instruction of Rev. Enoch Huntington. By talents, education and grace, he was well prepared for the sacred ministry. He was pastor of the First Congregational Church in Farmington, between ten and eleven years and discharged the duties of his office to the great acceptance and benefit of his people. Being in declining health he commenced a journey to the south, near the close of 1805, and undertook to pass from Norfolk to Charleston by by water, but died at sea Dec. 25th.

A question has been raised whether he was born in Middletown as here represented, or in what is now the town of Portland. In a funeral sermon preached in Farmington by Rev. Asahel Hooker, he is said to have been born at Middletown, May 13th, 1766. But at that time Portland was one of the parishes of Middletown. His parents lived in Portland a number of years, and some persons who knew the family well, have a strong impression that they lived there at the time of his birth.

Samuel Gray Huntington, 1800. Was a Dean scholar, studied law probably with his brother Enoch Huntington, was admitted to the bar and practised three years in East Haddam, then moved to Waterford, and thence to Troy. Has been judge of the Court of Common Pleas for Rensselaer County.

Alexander Wolcott, 1809. Was born in Windsor, before his father, just named, moved from that town. He studied medicine with Dr. Nathan Smith, at Hanover, N. H. In the second war with Great Britain he was an assistant surgeon, and stationed at Fort Moultrie, S. C., and afterwards on Governor's Island, N. Y. He established himself as a physician, in Vincennes, In.; but in 1819, was appointed Indian Agent at Detroit, and after spending a year or more there, was transfered to Chicago, where he held his post until his death, Oct. 23, 1830, aged 40.

Richard Hubbard, 1813. Son of Nehemiah Hubbard, Esq., was elected mayor of the city of Middletown in 1838 and died in office, Sept. 1st, 1839, aged 47.

Henry Dana Artemas Ward, 1819. Settled as a planter in South Carolina; lived in Columbia, (near which his plantation lay,) where he died April 3d, 1827, in his 27th year.

Seth Birdsey Paddock, 1820. Studied theology in the Episcopal Theological Seminary, about the time of its temporary establishment at New Haven, preached for a time in St. John's Church in Essex; was afterward colleague with Rev. John Tyler, in Christ Church in Norwich city, and after his death, rector, laboring there, in both capacities, more than twenty years. He was then preceptor of the Episcopal Academy in Cheshire, about six years and a half, where he died June 24th, 1851. His body was brought to his native place for interment.

Enoch Huntington, 1821. Studied theology in Norwalk in 1822 and '23, and preached in Pennsylvania and Connecticut from 1823 to 1826, was rector of the Episcopal Church in New Milford, from 1827 to 1846, and is now living in Bridgeport.

Phineas Bacon Wilcox, 1821, studied law in Columbus, Ohio, in 1822 and 23, where he has practised law since that time.

Timothy Rogers, 1823. Was afflicted with feeble health, did not study a profession; died in 1829.

William Edward Hurlbut, 1824. Was clerk in Middletown Bank; died Sept. 19th, 1845 aged 42.

Jabez Brooks Hubbard, 1825. Was merchant in New York; is now occupied in a counting room.

Simeon North, 1825. Tutor, LL. D. S. T. D., studied theology in New Haven, professor in Hamilton College, N. Y., now president of that institution.

Charles Bezaleel Fisk, 1826. Son of John Fisk, Esq., an engineer, much employed and greatly esteemed, in his profession, living in the city of Washington.

Samuel Gaylord, 1826. A young man of much promise, died on the 14th of November following his graduation.

Samuel Lee, 1827. Studied theology in New Haven, is stated supply at Mantua, Ohio.

Thomas Robinson Hubbard, 1829. Studied law at Dayton, Ohio, and settled as a lawyer, firm of Ballistier & Hubbard, Chicago, Ill.; is now corresponding clerk in the Bank of Commerce, N. Y. city.

Phineas Timothy Miller, 1833, M. D. Kept an apothecary store in New Haven, where he died in 1850.

William Huntington Russell, 1833, M. D., Tutor. He and Mr. Stiles French, are the principals of a very important school in New Haven, styled the "Collegiate and Commercial Institute," in which the design is "to secure to boys, at as early an age as possible a thorough English education, and upon this as a basis, to give a critically accurate preparation for any year in College, or for commercial business."

James Burnet Crane, 1838. Studied law with Johnson & Kent in New York city, where he practised some time. He has given up the profession of law, and is now studying theology at Princeton.

Charles Chauncey Whittlesey, 1838. Studied law with Jonathan Barnes, Esq., went to St. Louis, Missouri, in 1840, where he is now practising law.

John Smith Kelley, 1840. Was a teacher, and for a time preceptor of Brainerd Academy in Haddam. Died while a student of Union Theological Seminary, in the city of New York, Dec. 29th 1844, aged 24.

Henry Dana Artemas Ward, 1842. Son of H. D. A. Ward, before mentioned, studied law with Jonathan Barnes, Esq., and at the Law School in Cambridge, Mass., and also in Detroit, where he is now settled as a lawyer.

George Walter Crane, 1850. Died one week after graduation, Aug 22d, 1850, aged 22.

Middlebury College, Ver.

John P. H. Henshaw, 1808. Studied theology, was rector of an Episcopal Church in the city of Baltimore. Is now Bishop of the Episcopal Church in Rhode Island. Died in Maryland, while officiating for Bishop Whittingham, July 20th, 1852.

Wesleyan University.

Samuel Livingston Mather, 1835. Was a merchant for a time in New York; has since studied law, and is now practising in Cleveland, Ohio.

Theodore Hinsdale, 1836. Studied law and is practising in the city of New York.

Loudon B. Ward, 1842. Taught school in Virginia several years; now resides in Middletown.

Ebenezer Tracy Whittlesey, 1843. Studied law for a time, but has relinquished the study and is now pursuing mercantile business in San Francisco, California.

Abram J. Wright, 1843. Is a merchant in New York city.

Jonathan Kelsey Burr, 1845. Studied theology at the Union Theological Seminary in New York; is now a member of the New Jersey Methodist Episcopal Conference, and preaches in that State.

Silas W. Robbins, 1847. Studied theology at Yale College, is a Congregational minister and now preaches in Meriden.

Perry Child Smith, 1847. Studied law in the city of New York, where he was admitted to the bar in 1851. He is now in Albany.

Jonathan E. Barnes, 1848. Is studying theology at Yale College.

Joseph A. Bailey, 1849. Studied theology at the Baptist Theological Seminary in Newton, and is now pastor of the Baptist Church in Essex.

Theophilus Bradbury Chandler, 1850. Is a preacher, labored a while in Plymouth, is now stationed at Haddam.

Ira E. Chase, 1850. Present residence and employment not ascertained.

Graduate from Middlefield, not mentioned in the Address, &c.

Brown University.

Curtis Coe, 1776. Studied theology, was settled over the Congregational Church in Durham, N. H., Nov. 1st, 1780, and dismissed May 1st, 1805. He died at Newmarket, June 7th 1829, aged 79.

Oliver Wetmore, born in Middletown and for a time a merchant in the city, moved to Western New York, when that part of the State was very new, and entered the ministry. He died at Utica, Jan. 1st, 1852, aged 77. An obituary notice of him declares him to have been an eminent Presbyterian clergyman; a descendant of Rev. Timothy Edwards, father of President Edwards, and in a direct line from Elder William Brewster of the Mayflower.

All the graduates from Westfield Society are noticed elsewhere.

NEWSPAPERS IN MIDDLETOWN.

In 1785, the same year in which Middlesex county was formed a printing office was established in the city by William Woodward & ——— Green. This published the Middlesex Gazette. Sometime after, Mr. Green withdrew from the concern, and Mr. Woodward continued it until about 1797, when he sold it to Tertius Dunning, who published it until his decease in Oct. 1823. His son Charles Dunning continued it until it was sold by the administrator of his father's estate, to Epaphras & Horace Clark, in 1824. They sold it to Theodore N. Parmelee and Edwin T. Greenfield, in July, 1828. About a year after this, Mr. Parmelee sold his interest in it to Mr. Greenfield, who continued it until the year 1830, when Mr. Parmelee took it again and published it two years. It was then sold to Edwin Hunt, and the late Samuel W. Griswold, Esq., was its editor. Mr. Hunt continued it but a short time and then it passed into the hands of Joseph Longking, jr. The publication of this paper, having been in the hands of so many partners and individuals, publishers or editors, sometimes circulating more and sometimes less within Middlesex county and beyond it, ceased in 1834.

Soon after the cessation of this paper, George F. Olmsted commenced a paper, called the New England Advocate, using the same apparatus with which the Gazette had been published. The Advocate ceased in 1836, but the presses are now owned by Charles H. Pelton, and are used by him in book and job printing.

In Jan., 1814, Loomis & Richards started a paper in Middletown, styled the "Connecticut Spectator." In Feb. or March, 1815, Loomis disposed of his interest in the paper to Richards, who continued it a year or two longer.

The American Sentinel was established in the city, and the first number of the paper issued Jan. 1, 1823, by

William D. Starr and William H. Niles, under the firm of Starr & Niles. Mr. Niles retired from the concern in 1827, and Mr. Starr became the sole proprietor. Mr. H. W. Green established the "Witness," in Jan., 1832, and after publishing thirty-two numbers, discontinued it as a separate paper and it was united with the Sentinel on the 14th of August, in the same year; the title being changed to that of Sentinel and Witness; Mr. Starr continuing the sole proprietor until March 25th, 1851, when he took his son, William J. Starr and William H. Dunham, into company with him, the latter however leaving in October following. The Sentinel & Witness is now published by the original founder, W. D. Starr, and his oldest son, W. J. Starr, under the firm of W. D. Starr & Co.

The Constitution, a weekly newspaper, was commenced by Abner Newton, jr., on the first Wednesday of Jan. 1838, and is still continued by him. Mr. Newton issued a daily newspaper from the Constitution office, July 1st, 1847, the first paper of the kind published in the city, but he continued it no longer than until the 10th of July following.

The Daily News. This was the first serious attempt at the establishment of a Daily paper in Middletown, and was commenced by J. N. Phelps & Co., in Oct., 1850. In March, 1851, it passed into the hands of W. B. Casey & Co., who continued its publication until Oct., 1851, when its circulation being limited, and the Editor's time taken up with his other professional duties, it was discontinued.

The News and Advertiser, a weekly paper published at the same office, was started, Jan., 1851, and continued as a Neutral or independent paper, until July, 1852. when it was enrolled in the Whig ranks and advocated the election of Gen'l Scott to the Presidency.

LISTS OF OFFICERS OF THE TOWN AND CITY OF MIDDLETOWN—JUDGES OF MIDDLETOWN PROBATE DISTRICT—POSTMASTERS—COLLECTORS OF CUSTOMS.

Town Clerks.

These Officers in Middletown were first called Recorders, afterwards Registers, or Town Clerks.

The following table contains the names of such as have held the office in succession, together with the year of their first appointment.

Robert Webster,	appointed	in	1653.
William Smith,	"	"	1656.
John Hall,	"	"	1665.
Nathaniel White,	"	"	1695.
John Hamlin,	"	"	1696.
Joseph Rockwell,	"	"	1708.
Jabez Hamlin,	"	"	1734.
William Rockwell,	"	"	1735.
Joseph Clark,	"	"	1765.
Bezaliel Fisk,	"	"	1777.
John Fisk,	"	"	1797.
Thomas G. Mather,	"	"	1847.
Elihu Spencer,	"	"	1849.
E. W. N. Starr,	"	"	1851.

Justices of the Peace in Middletown.

Justices of the Peace in Middletown, appointed before the adoption of the present constitution of the State. Lists of later justices have not been collected. Those to whom U. H. are attached, lived in the Upper Houses, now Cromwell; those to whom M. is attached lived in Middlefield, those to whom W., in Westfield.

Names.	*Died or moved from town.*	*Ages.*
Robert Webster, U. H.,	Moved to Hartford 1659.	
Hon. Giles Hamlin,	Sept. 1, 1689.	67.
Nathaniel White, U. H.,	Aug. 27, 1711,	82.
Thomas Ward,		
Hon. John Hamlin,	Jan. 2, 1733,	74.
Israhiah Wetmore,		
Giles Hall,	Feb. 11, 1750,	69.
Joseph Southmayd,	June 8, 1772,	75.
Seth Wetmore,	April 12, 1778.	78.
George Phillips,	Feb. 1778,	67.
Joseph Clark,	April 21, 1778,	58.
Hon. Titus Hosmer,	April 4, 1780,	43.
Thomas Johnson, U. H.,	Dec. 26, 1774,	56.
Hon. Jabez Hamlin,	April 25, 1791,	82.
Col. Matthew Talcott,	Aug. 29, 1802,	89.
Gen. Samuel Holden Parsons,	Moved to Marietta, Ohio,	
Doct. John Dickinson,	Oct. 3, 1811,	82.
Nathaniel Chauncey, U.H.,	Sept. 3, 1798,	77.
Philip Mortimer,	March 15, 1794,	84.
Elijah Treadway,	June 10, 1792,	75.
Isaac Miller, M.,	July 20, 1817,	80.
Gen. Comfort Sage,	March 14, 1799,	67.
Hon. Asher Miller,	Dec. 24, 1821,	68
Benjamin Williams,	June 15, 1812,	45.
Nathaniel Gilbert, W.,	Moved from town.	
Chauncey Whittlesey,	March 14, 1812,	65.
Hon. Samuel W. Dana,	July 21, 1830,	70.
Hon. S. Titus Hosmer,	Aug. 6, 1834,	71.
Matthew T. Russell,	Nov. 13, 1828,	68.
Elijah Hubbard,	May 30, 1808,	63.
Nehemiah Hubbard,	Feb. 6, 1836,	85.
Ebenezer Sage,	Dec. 19, 1834,	81.
Isaac Gridley, U. H.,	Nov. 15, 1836,	82.
Amos Sage,	Feb. 15, 1820.	73.
Amos Churchell, W.,	Moved from town.	
Col. Lemuel Storrs,	Nov. 29, 1816,	63.
Ebenezer Roberts, 2d, W.,	Aug. 29, 1840,	82.
Capt. John Pratt,	Dec. 27, 1824,	71.
William Plumbe,	June 2, 1843,	94.
Elijah Hubbard, 2d,	Dec. 4, 1846,	69.
Alexander Collins,	Sept. 14, 1815,	41.
Richard Alsop,	Aug. 20, 1815,	55.
Samuel Eells, U. H.,	Moved from town.	
Eli Coe, M.,	March 27, 1835,	---
Samuel Wetmore,	Moved from town.	

Jozeb Stocking, U. H.,	June 29, 1841,	87.
Josiah Sage, U. H.,	Sept. 15, 1839,	67.
Gen. Chauncey Whittlesey,	Dec. 24, 1834,	51.
Levi H. Clark,	Moved from town.	
Samuel Gill,	Oct. 4, 1826,	46.
Daniel J. Griswold, W.,	July 10, 1847,	65.
Alexander Wolcott,	June 26, 1828,	69.
Elisha Coe, M.,	Dec. 1, 1831,	68.
Seth Paddock,	May 13, 1839,	83.
Arthur W. Magill,	Moved from town.	
Major A. Andrews,	Moved from town.	

OFFICERS OF THE CITY OF MIDDLETOWN.

Mayors.

Hon. Jabez Hamlin, from July 13, 1784, till his death April 25, 1791.*
" Asher Miller, " 1792, till his death Dec. 24, 1821.
" Samuel W. Dana, " 1822, till 1830.
Elijah Hubbard, Esq., " 1830, till 1838.
Richard Hubbard, Esq., " 1838, till his death, 1839.
Hon. S. D. Hubbard, " 1840, till 1842.
" Noah A. Phelps, ", 1842, till he resigned in Ap'l 1843.
Charles R. Alsop, Esq., " April 25, 1843, till 1846.
Horace Clark, Esq., " 1846, till 1850.
Dr. William B. Casey, " 1850, till he resigned in Nov. 1850.
Benjamin Douglas, Esq., " Nov. 22, 1850, till

City Clerks.

Bezaleel Fisk, from July 13, 1784, till 'released from office,' Jan., 1785.
Benj. Henshaw, " Jan. 1785, till 1786.
Ezekiel Woodruff, " 1786, till 1790.
William Brown, " 1790, till 1793.
John Fisk, " 1793, till 1818.
Henry Wolcott, " 1818, till 1819.
John Fisk, " 1819, till his death February 22, 1847.
E. B. Tompkins, " Feb. 22, 1847,

* At the first city meeting, July 13, 1784, Jabez Hamlin was elected Mayor, and he continued in office without the formality of a re-election, till 1788, when he tendered his resignation. He was however persuaded to retain the dignity of the office, and appears to have done so until his death, while the duties were performed by Asher Miller, the senior alderman. After Mr. Miller's election, Elijah Hubbard, father of the mayor above mentioned, then senior alderman, presided a part of the time in the meetings of the city authorities. This was doubtless the fact while Mr. M. was absent surveying lands about Yazoo river.

Treasurers.

Nehemiah Hubbard,	from	1795 to 1800 inclusive.
Matthew T. Russell,	"	1801 to 1816.
John Fisk,	"	1817 till his death.
Elihu B. Tompkins,	"	1847.

It will be perceived that in 1817, and again in 1819, and thence forward the offices of clerk and treasurer were united in Mr. Fisk, and that they have been thus united since in Mr. Tompkins.

OFFICERS OF BANKS.

Middletown Bank, was incorporated in Oct., 1795, but for some reason did not go into operation until the Spring of 1801. Perhaps the reason lay in the embarrassments which befel the trade of the place about the close of the last century. This has now (March 1852,) a capital of $369,300.

Presidents of this Bank.

Elijah Hubbard, from May 13, 1801 till his death May 30, 1808.

Nehemiah Hubbard, jr., from Oct. 24, 1808, till Jan. 3, 1822, when he declined a re-election.

Elijah Hubbard, (son of the first President) from Jan. 3, 1822, till his death Dec. 4, 1846.

John H. Watkinson, from Feb. 12, 1847.

Cashiers.

Timothy Southmayd,	from	May 13, 1801, till his death,	Dec. 13, 1821.
Thomas Hubbard.	"	Jan. 3, 1822, till his death,	Aug. 27, 1828.
Henry Carrington,	"	Sept. 2, 1828, till his resignation,	May, 1836.
Dyer Ames, jr.,	"	June 13, 1836, till his resignation,	Oct., 1844.
John H. Watkinson,	"	Oct. 12, 1844, till his resignation,	Feb. 1847.
Frederick L. Gleason,	"	Feb. 12, 1847.	

Middlesex County Bank, incorporated May, 1830, has now a capital of $327,300.

Presidents.

Henry L. De Koven,	from	Sept. 1, 1830, till he resigned	April 11, 1832.
Joseph W. Alsop,	"	May 3, 1831, "	April 19, 1832.

Henry L. De Koven,	" April 19, 1832, "	Dec. 19, 1835.
Samuel Russell,	" Dec. 19, 1835, "	July 3, 1839.
William C. Bowers,	" July 3, 1839, "	July 7, 1841.
Samuel Russell,	" July 7, 1841, "	July 1, 1846.
Charles R. Sebor,	" July 6, 1846.	

Cashiers.

Samuel Cooper, from Sept. 10, 1830, till his resignation, Nov, 2, 1830.
Charles Foote, " Nov. 2, 1830, till his resignation, Sept. 13, 1831
Eleazer Lacey, " Oct. 8, 1831, " " Jan. 4, 1847
William S. Camp, " Jan. 4, 1847.*

MIDDLETOWN SAVINGS BANK, was incorporated in May, 1825, and organized in June following.

Presidents.

Nehemiah Hubbard, from June, 1825, till his death in 1837.
Richard Rand, " 1837, till his death in 1844.
Joseph Taylor, " 1844.

Secretaries and Treasurers.

Ebenezer G. Southmayd, from June 1825, till 1832.
Samuel Southmayd, " 1832, till 1837.
Henry S. Ward, " 1837, till 1843.
Henry Carrington, " 1843.

THE CENTRAL BANK, incorporated in May 1851, has a capital of $150,000, and began operations in November of the same year.

President, Charles Woodward.
Cashier, Henry D. Smith.

---

* The Branch Bank of the United States, kept in the same building, now occupied by the M. C. Bank, began its operations in Sept., 1817, and was moved to Hartford in 1824 or '25. Samuel W. Dana, was president of this bank, from 1817 until about 1819, when Enoch Parsons was appointed president, and held the office till its operations were closed about 1835. Arthur W. Magill, was cashier from 1817, till about 1822, when Joshua P. Burnham was appointed, and held the office till the bank was closed.

MIDDLESEX MUTUAL ASSURANCE COMPANY, Middletown, Conn. Charter granted, May 1836, commenced business, June 1836.

Presidents.

Richard Hubbard,	June 1836.
Samuel Cooper,	Sept. 1839.

Secretaries and Treasurers.

John L. Smith,	June, 1836.
William Woodward,	June, 1838.
Stephen Taylor,	June, 1849.

MIDDLETOWN PROBATE DISTRICT.

This District was formed in 1752, and included Chatham, with the exception of that part lying south of Salmon river, the part of Berlin which at first belonged to Middletown, Haddam and Durham. The parts of this District east of the Connecticut were detached from it in 1824, upon the formation of Chatham District; and at the same time the part of Berlin, just named, was detached from it, upon the formation of Berlin District. Haddam, west of the Connecticut, was detached from it in 1830, and made a separate district, in connection with Haddam Neck. Middletown District now embraces the present towns of Middletown, Durham and Cromwell.

Successive Judges.

Hon. Jabez Hamlin,	of Middletown,	appointed	May,	1752.
Hon. Asher Miller,	"	"	"	1789.
Dr. John Dickinson,	"	"	"	1793.
Hon. Asher Miller,	"	"	"	1807.
John Alsop,	"	"	"	1822.
Stillman K. Wightman·	"	"	'	1832.
Augustus Cook,	"	"	"	1834.
Stillman K. Wightman,	"	"	"	1835.
Samuel Cooper,	"	"	"	1838.
Linus Coe,	"	"	"	1842.
Samuel Cooper,	"	"	"	1844,

Linus Coe,	of Middletown,	appointed	May,	1846.
Samuel Cooper,	"	"	"	1847.
Elihu Spencer,	"	"	"	1849.
Noah A. Phelps,*	"	"	"	1850.

MIDDLETOWN POST-OFFICE ESTABLISHED IN 1775.

Post Masters.

Winslow Hobby,	from	1775 to Oct.	1807.
Thaddeus Nichols,	" Oct.	1807 to April	1815.
Joshua Stow,	" April,	1815 to April,	1818.
Samuel Williams,	" April,	1818 to Nov. 11,	1821.
Joshua Stow,	" Nov.	1821 to Feb. 20,	1840.
E. W. N. Starr,	" Feb. 20,	1840 to Oct. 1,	1842.
Eli Wilcox,	" Oct. 1,	1842 to May 21,	1845.
Allen May,	" May 27,	1845 to June 14,	1849.
William Woodward,	" June 14,	1849.	

COLLECTORS OF CUSTOMS.

The Collection District of Middletown, was established in 1795, previously to which time the towns on Connecticut river were included in the New London District.

George Phillips,	of Middletown,	appointed,	June, 1795.
Chauncey Whittlesey,	"	"	Dec., 1797.

* All these Judges are now living with the exception of Col. Hamlin, Judge Miller, Dr. Dickinson, and Linus Coe, Esq. Mr. Coe was instantly killed, Feb. 27, 1852, as he was crossing the Railroad, between Newington and Berlin, in a wagon, "the locomotive striking the horse and the wagon, throwing him and the wagon on one side and the horse on the other."

This awful event would have produced strong sensation in any case. But Mr. Coe had a large circle of kindred and friends who greatly esteemed him, had been a prominent inhabitant of Middletown, sheriff of Middlesex County several years, judge of Probate for the District of Middletown, and at the time of his death was secretary of the Middlesex County Agricultural Society, an office which he had held sometime, and to the duties of which he had paid much attention. He was son of the late Col. Elisha Coe of Middlefield, and 60 years of age.

Alexander Wolcott, of Windsor,	appointed	Aug. 1801.
Henry Wolcott, of Middletown,	"	July, 1828.
Noah A. Phelps, of Hartford,	"	Mar.,1829.
Austin Baldwin, of Middletown,	"	April,1841.
Phillip Sage, of Portland,	"	Oct. 1844.
William D. Starr, Middletown,	"	Feb., 1849.
Samuel Cooper, "	"	June, 1849.

Lists of Deputies to the General Court from Middletown, and from the towns formed within its original limits will be given in the close of this work.

SKETCH OF UPPER MIDDLETOWN, NOW CROMWELL.

This township, while the second society in Middletown was called by different names. At first it was called the "North Society in Middletown," then "Middletown Upper Houses," or simply the "Upper Houses," and then "Upper Middletown." For a long period the first name has hardly been mentioned or known; the second was used almost solely for a great length of time, and after the third was adopted, it was of the two the most frequently used. The society being incorporated as a town and named Cromwell, in May, 1851. This distinguished and formidable name will probably soon supersede all others.

The town is bounded by Portland on the east, for the boundary in that direction extends to the eastern margin of the river; it has Rocky Hill on the north, Berlin on the west, and Middletown on the south, being separated from it, partly by the northern branch of Little River, by Little River itself and thence by a line across the Connecticut.

The lands in this town generally are good, some excellent. The lands of less value are the Plains on the north, which by judicious management may be made somewhat productive, and the wet lands along the branch of Little River, which may be improved by more thorough draining. The lands to the right and left of Prospect Hill, and onward to the meadows are fine. Some of these the elder President Adams declared to be as rich as the soil of Egypt.

Prospect Hill is thus designated by reason of the admirable southern view which it affords of the Connecticut, of the meadows and fields on either side, of Portland village, and the city of Middletown, and of the slopes, hills and mountains beyond. The view for a mile onward along the public road is softer, but charming.

The settlement commenced in Cromwell, nearly as soon as in Middletown, and the sites in both cases were selected with admirable judgment; on dry and rich grounds near the Connecticut, and as near each other as the nature of the intermediate grounds admitted.

In the Address, Nathaniel White, Samuel Stocking, George Graves, Robert Webster, Joseph Smith, Daniel Harris, John Martin, John Savage, Thomas Ranney, David Sage and John Kirby are mentioned as early settlers in this place. With these other settlers were soon united, and the settlements spread to the north and west. The sons of some of the settlers in Middletown came and settled here. Other persons came from different places and established themselves among them. Some efforts have been made in vain to find a regular catalogue of the inhabitants in 1703, at the time they were constituted the North Society in Middletown, and also to find their lists. But as the Society were about to settle their first minister, a catalogue of the taxable persons was made, together with their lists annexed, which will now be given. We have arranged the surnames alphabetically, placing those of the same name in connection.

Names.	List.	Names.	List.
James Brown.	£22 00	Samuel Frovy,	69 00
Wm. Butler,	6 00	Roger Gipson,	45 10
Joseph Butler,	13 10	Samuel Gipson,	72 00
Nathaniel Clark,	46 14	David Hurlburt,	37 00
Daniel Clark,	65 10	John Kirby,	30 00
Serj. Clark,	71 17	Samuel Lucas,	35 00
John Clark,	46 00	William Mark,	25 00
Isaac Cornwell,	24 00	Margaret Ranney,	3 10
Joseph Crowfoot,	18 00	Ebenezer Ranney,	48 18

NAMES.	LIST.	NAMES.	LIST.
Joseph Ranney,	£61 05	Thomas Stow, Jr.,	£43 00
John Ranney,	30 05	John Warner, Sen.,	77 19
Thomas Ranney,	120 15	John Warner, Jun.,	75 11
Wm. Ranney,	6 10	Joseph White,	85 00
Wm. Sage,	24 00	Ins. White,	85 10
Timothy Sage,	79 05	John White,	18 00
John Sage,	150 00	Hugh White,	42 00
Capt. Savage,	89 02	Daniel White,	49 17
Thomas Savage,	41 10	Jacob White,	88 10
William Savage,	73 00	Israel Wilcox,	148 05
Hannah Scovil,	27 10	John Wilcox,	57 05
Mary Scovil,	15 00	Francis Wilcox,	59 05
John Shepherd, Edward Shepherd, }	79 00	Samuel Wilcox,	77 00
		Joseph Whitmore,	44 00
Samuel Shepherd,	21 00		
Daniel Stocking,	59 05	Total,	£2,586 03
Samuel Stow,	39 05		
Thomas Stow, Sen.,	42 00		

What is now known as the East-street in Worthington, in the town of Berlin, belonged to this Society until 1790. Some of the foregoing inhabitants may have located themselves in that street as early as 1714. The population of Upper Middletown in 1850, was 1,275 souls. Another account says it was 1,259, which may have been the fact at a different period in the same year.

While the people generally in this place have pursued agriculture from the beginning, some in the village early began Ship-building and carried it on more or less over a century, and for about half the time vessels were built at two yards. Some individuals were considerably concerned in navigation, in the latter part of the last century, and in the beginning of the present many young men engaged in sea-faring life, and quite a number first and last had the command of vessels.*

But for some years there has been very little Ship-building and navigation in Cromwell, and few, hardly any have followed the seas. But while these branches of business have been stayed, husbandry has been more

* A notice of the building of the small Steamboat "Experiment" here in 1821, and of its peculiar construction, might be properly given in this place, but we cannot afford the space for its insertion.

thoroughly pursued, and numbers have turned their attention successfully to manufactures. [See Mr. Gorham's account pp. 129-30.]

Several neat houses were built in the village about 1804, and the place has the appearance of thrift and prosperity. There are five merchant stores in the Town, which deal principally in groceries.

It has been incidentally mentioned that the people were formed into a Society in 1703. In January of that year the town of Middletown agreed that they might be a Society, provided they settled a minister and built a meeting house within twelve months from that time, and the General Assembly incorporated them at their Session in the following May. Their thoughts and efforts were doubtless directed at once to both objects specified in the consent of the Town. And they did erect a meeting-house in 1703, or soon after, a little north of their oldest and principal cemetery, and did so much to it, that they met in it for public worship.—They also employed candidates to preach to them, hoping that their minds and hearts would be so united in some one that they might call him to be their pastor and settle him. In 1709 there was a prospect that they might settle Mr. Daniel Deming, but the prospect failed. They afterward employed Rev. Joseph Smith, and their affections were so drawn towards him, that in January 1714, "they agreed to allow him a comfortable maintainance," and expressed an intention of proceeding in a gospel way to settle him. In view of his settlement they finished their meeting-house, and January 5th, 1715, the church was organized, consisting of 23 members, 20 of whom had belonged to the church in Middletown, one to some other church, and two were received on profession. On the same occasion Mr. Smith was installed their pastor. Thus twelve years, and not merely twelve months passed away, before they had a finished meeting-house, and a minister settled among them to discharge statedly the duties of the sacred office.

When the statistical account of Middlesex County was prepared more than thirty years since, the writer was informed that Mr. Smith was a native of Concord,

Mass.; but it has since been ascertained that he was a son of Philip Smith of Hadley, who made provision in his will for his having a public education. He was graduated at Harvard College in 1695, and soon after began to instruct the Grammar School in Hadley, usually called the Hopkins Academy. He afterwards taught a school in Springfield, continuing in the two places until 1700. Subsequently he was chaplain to the garrison in Brookfield, preaching to the garrison and people of the town, and receiving his support from the Colony of Massachusetts. "In 1708 he went to Cohancy, in Cumberland county, New Jersey, and was ordained pastor of Cohancy by the Presbytery of Philadelphia May 10, 1709. Having preached there about two years he came to Greenwich, Conn., and preached there a short time, and thence he came to the Upper Houses, where he died in office Sept. 8, 1736, aged 62. His wife was Esther Parsons, daughter of Joseph Parsons of Northampton and Springfield. She died May 30, 1760, in the 89th year of her age."* Mr. Smith possessed more property than clergymen generally, and had a larger library.

Some time before the death of Mr. Smith, the thoughts of the people were directed to the preparation of a second house for the worship of God, and as their proceedings may throw some light on their circumstances, and on the customs of that period, it may be well to advert to them for a moment. Nov. 21, 1734 "two thirds of the inhabitants of the North Society, declared that it was of necessity that a new Meeting-house should be built in said Society." Again on the 28th of the same month the "Society agreed to begin to cut timber for their Meeting-house at the end of January or beginning of February." But more than a year elapsed after the last mentioned date, before they were ready to raise the frame, and that was no small concern; for the timbers were very large, and such machinery was not then used as is now employed in putting up frames. Accor-

* Foote Genealogy, by N. Goodwin, pp. 280.

dingly on the 21st of March 1735-6, (1736 as we now date,) the Society appointed Serj. Shepherd, Hugh White and Capt. John Warner to order for the providing of the dinners, for the raising of the Meeting-house, and the Society to be divided into three parts, each part to provide the dinner they are ordered to provide it."

"At the same meeting the Society agreed that what drinks are expended in raising the Meeting-house, shall be borne by the Society excepting what shall be drunk with their vituals."

This year the house was prepared for occupancy. It was 55 feet in length, and 36 in breadth, and was used as a sanctuary for more than a century.

Edward Eells, son of Rev. Edward Eells, pastor of the 2d church in Scituate, Mass., graduate of Harvard College 1733, was the successor of Mr. Smith. He was ordained Sept. 6. 1738, and died Oct. 12, 1776, aged 64. He acquired some celebrity from a pamphlet which he published respecting the "Wallingford case" in 1759. He preached at the State Election in 1767, and was trustee of Yale College from 1761 until his death.

One of his sons, Edward Eells, was a Continental Captain in the Revolutionary war. He died in his native place Dec. 8, 1787, aged 47. Three of his sons, James, Samuel and Ozias were educated at Yale, and became pastors of churches; James in East Glastenbury, Samuel in North Branford* and Ozias in Barkhamsted.

---

* Concerning Rev. Samuel Eells a recent History of North Branford says: that "being a man of much versatility of talent, he practised to some extent among his own people as a physician for the body, as well as a watchman for souls. From one incident in his life, which has been preserved in the memories of his people, it would seem that he was likewise capable, as necessity required of wielding either carnal or spiritual weapons. His ministry embraced the trying and eventful period of our Revolutionary struggle. On one occasion in the early part of the year 1777, when Washington was in the vicinity of New York, his whole force not amounting to more than fifteen hundred men, he called upon the people of Connecticut to send down with all dispatch their quota of troops.

Gershom Buckley, native of Rocky Hill, and graduate of Yale College 1770, was the successor of Mr. Eells. He was ordained pastor June 17, 1778 and dismissed, pursuant to an agreement between him and his people July 7, 1808. He died April 7, 1832, aged 84.

Joshua L. Williams, son of Rev. Joshua Williams, succeeded Mr. Buckley. He was born in Wethersfield, graduated at Yale in 1805, and ordained June 14, 1809. He was a judicious, devoted and useful minister, attended faithfully to the Schools in his parish, and taught lads in his house. He died Dec. 29, 1832, aged 48.

Zebulon Crocker, native of Willington, graduate of Yale 1827, studied theology at New Haven one year, became pastor of the church May 2, 1833, and died Nov. 14, 1847, aged 45. He stood high in his class when in College, and had the honor when he was graduated of delivering the Greek oration. He was afterward an important teacher in the "Ellington School." Thus he was happily prepared to carry forward the education of the young in his parish, which had already been advanced beyond that of parishes generally in the

---

The intelligence of this requisition arrived in this place on the Sabbath, while the people were engaged in public worship. Considering this to be one of those works of necessity which might properly receive the attention of his people on the Sabbath, Mr. Eells communicated the important intelligence from the pulpit, and requested at once that those who were willing and ready to go forth on this important mission, should parade on the Green, in front of the Meeting-house, immediately after service. The able bodied men of this Society made a ready response to this unexpected summons. At the conclusion of service a line was promptly formed on the Green, and principally through the agency and energy of Lieut. Samuel Baldwin, a company was organized. This company, including its officers, consisted finally of 60 men, a portion of whom belonged to the societies of Branford and Northford. The command of it belonged of right to Lieut. Baldwin, who with great expedition had succeeded in gathering it together in a short time. But Lieut. B. courteously waved his right in favor of his own minister, and the Rev. Samuel Eells was accordingly chosen to the captaincy, (not chaplaincy!) of the body."—His commission as captain was signed by Gov. Trumbull, Jan. 14, 1777, and he took the command, and appears to have gone with his company to the aid of Washington. The pamphlet from which this account is quoted, states further; "fortunately, he and his company had no occasion to proceed to the extremities of war, and he returned without having killed any body."

vicinity, and of taking the lead in the establishment of an Academy. As a pastor and preacher the people greatly esteemed him.

A published work of Mr. Crocker of 300 large duodecimo pages, should not be forgotten, entitled the "Catastrophe of the Presbyterian Church."

Having attended the General Assembly of the P. Church, as a delegate from the General Association of Connecticut in 1837, when the Plan of Union between the said Assembly and Association was abrogated on the part of the former, and four Synods, embracing five hundred ministers and sixty thousand communicants, were excluded from it; and deeming the exclusion unjustifiable, Mr. C. undertook to give a history of the Plan of Union and its operations, and to set aside the ground on which the Assembly acted. The work contains much matter, and is presented in a lucid style.

George A. Bryan, native of Waterbury, graduate of Yale 1843, who studied theology at New Haven, succeeded Mr. Crocker June 13, 1849.

The number of members admitted to the church by Mr. Smith, was 62, by Mr. Eells 138, by Mr. Buckley 85, by Mr. Williams 218, Mr. Crocker 137, Mr. Bryan has admitted 15. These admissions, with the 23 members at the organization make a total of 665. The communicants Jan 1, 1852, were 164.

DEACONS IN THE CHURCH.

	Elected.	*Deaths.*	*Ages.*
William Savage,	Feb. 10, 1716.		
Samuel Hall,	do.	Reelected in E.M	
Samuel Stow,		Sept. 28, 1741.	
John Wilcox,		May 12, 1751.	68.
Samuel Gipson,		March 18, 1748.	76.
Samuel Shepherd,	Dec. 3, 1745.	Dro'd Apl 9, 1750,	
Isaac White,	Jan. 15, 1749.	June 27, 1769.	71.
William Savage,		1774	74.
Thomas Johnson, Esq.,	Jan. 9, 1766.	Dec. 26, 1774.	56.
Joseph Kirby,	Nov. 29, 1770.	Sept. 12, 1783.	64.
Solomou Sage,	Jan. 26, 1775.	June 7, 1794.	74.
Timothy Gipson,	Jnn. 14, 1784.	Jan. 8, 1814.	70.
Amos Sage,	Feb 22, 1790.	Feb. 15, 1820.	72.
Jeremiah Hubbard,	Dec. 14, 1807.	Aug. 23, 1808.	63.
Bani Parmelee,	March 23, 1810.	Feb. 22, 1837.	81.
Rufus Sage,	July 1817.	March 13, 1826.	49.
Joseph R. Wilcox,	*April 6, 1822.*	*Jan. 25, 1852.*	*79.*
Isaac Sage,	Oct. 29, 1826,		
John Stevens,	Sept. 1, 1843.		

The last year the people gave about 300 dollars to public objects of christian benevolence, which may be taken as a fair average for a number of years.

The third church edifice is of brick, 69 feet by 44. It was built in 1840, and cost $7,500.

The society has a parsonage worth $2,700. It has also some lands which rent for $50 per year.

BAPTISTS IN CROMWELL.

The Society was formed Jan. 2, 1801, and the church orgaaized Feb. 2, 1802, consisting of 16 members.—Sixteen more were added in the course of that and the succeeding year. Revivals were enjoyed in 1805, '18, '31 and '43. The average number of members from 1805 may have a little exceeded 50. The number Jan. 1, 1852, was 70.

Their Meeting-house was built in 1803 in the West street, 46 feet by 36. Having been removed to the centre, it was re-opened for worship in Jan. 1833.

The people have enjoyed preaching generally, but not uniformly, and when destitute of stated preaching, unless an elder came among them for a Sabbath, they relied upon the gifts of private members of the church. The following is a list of their preachers and elders.

Eber Moffott preached to them from about the time of the organization of the church, until the latter part of 1803, or beginning of 1804, about the time of his death.

Nehemiah Dodge preached to them a part of 1804. *Daniel Wildman* a portion of the time from March 1805 until July 1811, being called about this time to the oversight of the Baptist Church in Chester, and *Frederic Wightman* preached to them from 1817 until 1832.

Charles B. Keys preached to them from Dec. 3, 1832, until the Spring of 1833, *George B. Atwell* from April 1834 until April 1835; *John R. Price* of Meriden from Nov. 1836 until April 1837, when *Frederic Wightman* preached to them again from that time until April 1839.

William Dickins, a licenciate from the Hamilton Literary Institution, preached to them from Sept. 1839 to April 1840; *William Bentley* from April 1840, about six years; *James Hepburn* commenced labors here in 1846 and continued them two years; *Joseph Bailey*, a student in the Wesleyan University supplied them with preaching afterwards six months.

George W. Hervey, native of Durham N. Y., graduate of the College in the District of Columbia 1847, who studied theology in the Union Theological Seminary New York city, began to preach to the congregation in the Autumn of 1850, and labored among them until the beginning of April 1852. He is now in New York city.

Elder Charles W. Potter, a native of Norwich, who has preached several years, succeeds him.

For four or five years the people have received assistance from the Baptist State Convention. Towards the support of Mr. Hervey during his last years service they received $25, and from their sister church in the city of Middletown $50.

The contributions of the congregation to benevolent objects for some time have been small, about 15 dollars annually, given mostly for the support of Baptist Foreign Missions.

In 1683 the inhabitants of this place were allowed their proportion of a school rate in Middletown, for the maintenance of a school among themselves. For many years they have had five school districts. This is the number at the present time. These as they are now organized are called, the Central District, including the former Nooks District, the South District, the West, North and Plain districts. The children in these districts, between 4 and 16 years of age were 313.

The influence of Mr. Crocker in the cause of education has been already noticed. The people were prepared to appreciate and second his exertions. A number of gentlemen in 1782 united together in an effort to build a new school house in the centre, and to sustain a teacher summer and winter. Their expressed design was to maintain a school which should be superior to schools generally which then existed, an object, which it is believed they in some good degree accomplished.

In 1808 a debating society was formed which was soon succeeded by the *Friendly Association*, organized on a more enlarged and efficient plan, and to which the property of the Debating Society was transferred. The objects of this association were, "the discussion of questions on various subjects, the recitation of dialogues and selected pieces, original composition and declamation, public lectures, together with a permanent library for the use of the members." The first meeting was held Feb. 20, 1810, with a prospect of success which has been fully realized. This has already existed more than forty years, and is still in vigorous operation.—Meetings are usually held weekly by the members, and a course of lectures during each winter. It has nearly 300 members and a library of between 4 and 500 volumes. The influence of the institution has been to create a taste for reading and inquiry, not only among the members, but in the families to which they belong, to elicit and strengthen talent and elevate society.

William C. Redfield, now of New York, residing here in early life, though engaged in mechanical labor manifested an ardent desire for knowledge, and sought it by every means within his reach. He was one of the most active and efficient members of the association, and while his own mind was quickened and expanded, he benefitted others. Thus he was preparing to become an acceptable contributor to the American Journal of Science and through that a benefactor to his countrymen and race. Fame has justly followed him, particularly for his development of the laws of storms, and his example is one additional proof how a youth of small means, by diligent application and good conduct, may rise to honorable distinction and eminent usefulness.

The community has felt the benefits of the Friendly Association; I repeat the idea. Thus the people were prepared to appreciate and second the exertions of Mr. Crocker in the cause of education: particularly in establishing and sustaining an academy.

The Academy building was erected in 1834, and is 41 feet by 26; its cost about $1700.

Though the institution has no permanent funds, it has hitherto been sustained mostly by the inhabitants, it has had much of the time on an average about fifty scholars, has accomplished much good and promises to accomplish much good hereafter. The resort for instructors has been to graduates of colleges, mostly to recent graduates and to such as had gone through with their classical course at Yale College; to young men, who, while possessing competent literature and science, were professors of religion, and looking forward to the ministry of the gospel as their profession. This being the case, their services as instructors were secured in most instances, only for limited periods.

Names, birth-places &c., of the successive Instructors.

Sylvester Judd, a native of Northampton, graduate of Yale 1835, taught the Academy six months. He is now a Unitarian clergyman, and was for some time pastor of a church in Augusta, Maine.

John Lord Taylor, native of Warren, graduate of Yale 1836: tutor. He taught the academy six months, and is now settled in the ministry at Andover, Mass.

Richard F. Searle, graduate of Union College 1835, taught one year. He is a Congregational clergyman.

Edgar Jared Doolittle, native of Wallingford, graduate of Yale 1836, taught one year and a half. He is now settled in the ministry in Hebron.

Israel Perkins Warren, native of Bethany, graduate of Yale 1838, taught a year and a half. Has been settled in the ministry at Granby and Hamden; is now in Plymouth.

James Hanmer Francis, native of Wethersfield, graduate of Yale 1826, taught the academy one year. (See clergymen of Westfield.)

George Thatcher, native of Hartford, graduate of Yale 1840, taught the academy one year. He was first settled in the ministry in Derby, then in Nantucket, Mass., is now pastor of the Allen street church in New York.

Jared Owen Knapp, native of Greenwich, graduate of Yale 1840, taught the academy three years. He was first settled in Plainville, Conn., and is now settled in Hatfield, Mass.

Rollen D. H. Allen, native of Middlebury, Vt., graduate of Middlebury College 1841. He taught the academy one year. Is a clergyman, not settled, resides at Terryville.

William Sturges Wright, native of Glastenbury, graduate of Yale 1839, taught the academy five years. He is the stated supply of the Congregational church of Middle Haddam.

Joseph Bardwell Lyman, native of Northampton, Mass., graduate of Yale 1850, taught the academy six months.

Julius Yale Leonard, native of Berkshire, N. Y., graduate of Yale 1851, is the present instructor.

PHYSICIANS IN CROMWELL.

Aaron Roberts. It has been said that he was a native of Portland; but this is very much doubted. He began to practice in Cromwell in 1757, and was a surgeon in the Revolutionary War. In 1783 he moved to New Britain in Berlin, to live with his son, where he died Nov. 21, 1792, in his 62d year.

Solomon Savage, practised from about 1762 until his death Jan. 29, 1783, aged 43.

Hosea Hurlburt, a native of Kensington, practised here from 1783 until 1790, moved to the town of Killingworth.

Daniel Lee, whose birth place we cannot state, practised here from 1784 until 1787, when he moved to New London.

Gideon Noble, a native of Coventry probably, practised here from 1791 to 1802, when he moved to South Glastenbury. He had a good education, pleasing manners, and acquired a respectable practice in both places. He died in 1807.

Titus Morgan, was born in Westfield, Mass. He practised here, excepting a few months spent in Guilford, from 1802 until his death, Nov. 22, 1811, aged 35. He was a gentleman of refined and poetic taste, and agreeable manners; an intelligent and respectable physician.

William Meigs Hand, born in Madison, was graduated M. D., at Dartmouth College in 1812, and probably came immediately to Cromwell. In 1816 he moved to Worthington in Berlin. He was amiable and well informed, interesting in conversation, and happy in writing sketches and essays, a successful practitioner and a man of good moral character. He published a pamphlet, entitled, "A Trip to Ohio," and a Manual of Medicine and Surgery for the family." He died in 1822, aged 32.

William Tulley. (See physicians in Middletown.)

David B. Brooks, son of Dr. David Brooks of North Guilford, Yale College M. D., commenced practice here in 1819 and remained about one year, when he settled in the city of New York, where he died July 22, 1830, aged 32. He is said to have been a popular man.

Sylvester Buckley, born in Rocky Hill, graduated at Yale 1810, was graduated M. D. at Dartmouth in 1812. He began practice in Haddam Town in 1813, and some years afterwards practised in Chester and Higganum; in Cromwell from 1821 to 1830; in Worthington from 1830 until within a recent period. He is now in practice in his native place.

Richard Warner, born in that part of Hadlyme Society, which belongs to the town of Lyme, graduate of Yale College 1817, M. D., began practice in East Haddam in 1823, moved to Cromwell in 1830, where he has constantly practiced until the present time.

NOTE. The "virtuous remains of Samuel Hurlburt Jr., M. D." rest in the old burial ground in this town, but no tradition is preserved that he ever practiced his profession, or ever lived in this place. This statement is given as received.

Russell Stow, native of Cromwell, entered Yale College in 1798, and left that institution at the close of his Freshman year: studied medicine with Dr. Ebenezer Tracy, commenced practice in Ellisburgh, Jefferson Co.

N. Y., where he continued several years: he then moved to Adams in the same county, where he still lives: he has had considerable practice in both places.

Robert Hubbard M. D., of Cromwell, entered Yale College, but left in consequence of ill-health. He afterwards studied medicine and settled as a practitioner in Bridgeport.

GRADUATES FROM CROMWELL AT YALE COLLEGE.

Stephen White, son of John, grandson of Daniel and great grandson of Nathaniel White, repeatedly mentioned as an early settler, and an highly honored inhabitant of Middletown, in the part which is now Cromwell, was born June 8, 1718, about two years before his father's family moved to New Haven, where he was graduated in 1736. He was ordained pastor of the first church in Windham, Dec. 24, 1740, and remained there in the pastoral office until his death Jan. 9, 1794.

His wife was Mary Dyer, sister of Eliphalet Dyer, a member of the Revolutionary Congress and presiding judge of the Superior Court of Connecticut. He had 13 children, the youngest of whom was the late Dyer White Esq., of New Haven, Judge of Probate.

Daniel Stocking 1748. Did not enter upon any profession, but was so much occupied in teaching school, that he acquired the title of *Master* Stocking. He died Dec. 23, 1800, aged 73.

Joseph Kirby 1765. Was licensed to preach, but being excessively diffident and very singular, he did not succeed at all as a candidate; at times his appearance and conduct were such that he was deemed by some to be partially deranged. He however married and had several children; lived some years in Granville, Mass., and then in Dorset, Vt., where he died in Sept. 1823, aged 78.

Isaac Gridley 1773. Was born in Kensington in Berlin, but lived during most of his childhood in New Haven. He came to Cromwell to teach school, and was much employed in this service in subsequent life. He was also a justice of the peace. He died Nov. 15, 1836, aged 82.

Timothy Jones Gridley 1808. Studied medicine with Dr. Nathan Smith at Dartmouth College, where he was graduated M. D.; settled as a physician in Amherst, Mass., where he held a high standing. Died March 11, 1852, aged 64.

Chauncey Wilcox 1824. Studied theology at New Haven, and was ordained pastor of the North Church in Greenwich June 25, 1828, where " he labored with great fidelity and success for eighteen years, and raised up an infant church of eighteen members among a scattered population, to number more than a hundred. Three of those converted under his ministry entered the field of Foreign Missions, and two still live to labor there; another is a useful pastor in New England. After the spring of 1847 he was 'highly useful and respected as a teacher of youth and a promoter of every good work" in Ridgefield, where he died Jan. 31, 1852, aged 55. He was a man without guile. He loved the ministry, and loved every thing pertaining to the cause of Christ.

He attended the funeral of his father, Dea. Joseph R. Wilcox in his native town, the Wednesday preceding his own death, and afterwards returned home. But though removed thus suddenly, his faith did not fail him nor waver in the least. His end was peace.*

Thomas Staughton Savage 1825, M. D. Studied at the Theological (Episcopal) School, near Alexandria, D. C., became an Episcopal clergyman; was missionary at Cape Palmas in Africa; is now rector of a church at Pass Christian, Miss.

William Kirby 1827. Studied theology in New Haven, was a Home Missionary in Illinois; has recently died in Jacksonville.

George Slocum Folger Savage, 1814. Studied Theology in Andover and in New Haven, was ordained as a Home Missionary, (in his native place,) went to St.

---

* N. Y. Observer, Feb. 12, 1852.

Charles, Kane County, Illinois, where he is now settled as pastor of a Church.

Josiah Savage, 1846. Studied law in New Haven and New York, went to California, and died at Trinity River, in Nov. 1849, aged 25.

Ebenezer Beckwith, 1847. Is teacher of an Academy at Granada, Miss.

Thomas Scranton Hubbard, 1849. Is a manufacturer in Durham.

WESLEYAN UNIVERSITY.

William A. M. Hand, 1836. Only child of Dr. William M. Hand, was a man of good talents, natural and acquired, of ardent piety and great promise; had commenced the study of theology, but was removed by death, May 16, 1839, aged 32.

Two individuals, natives of Cromwell, though not graduates of Colleges, *Jairus Wilcox*, and *William Redfield Stocking*, may be properly named in this connection.

Mr. Wilcox was engaged in secular business, beyond the usual period of preparation for the ministry before he resolved upon entering the sacred office. He was sometime member of the Bangor Seminary, and then went through with a three years course in the Theological Department of Yale College, where his studies closed in 1830. The next year he was settled in Bethany in Woodbridge, where he remained a few years. He then went to Bergen, N. Y., and thence to Victor, preaching a year or two in each place. In 1838, he went as pastor with a Church, formed in one or other of those places, to Geneseo, in Illinois, under the patronage of the Home Missionary Society. Here his health failed him, and in 1845 he removed to Chicago and became pastor of the Bethel Church, with which he was connected a considerable time. Here he was attacked by the cholera, in Sept. 1851, which produced indescribable sufferings, which closed his life on earth in twelve hours. But in these trying circumstances he was sustained by the grace of God.

William Redfield Stocking, like the worthy man after

whom he was called, with small means, has risen to an important station. To him the Friendly Association and the Academy were blessings. About 15 years ago he went out as a teacher to Oroomiah in Persia, where he is said to have become well acquainted with the language of the country and where he has been ordained a preacher of the Gospel.

CROMWELL POST-OFFICE ESTABLISHED IN 1809.

Post Masters.

Samuel Rose,	from Sept.,	1809	to Jan.	11, 1813.
Josiah Sage,	from Jan.	11, 1813	to April	16, 1839.
C. N. Cannon,	from April	16, 1839	to July	3, 1841.
N. Bushnell,	from July	3, 1841	to Oct.	1, 1845.
R. Hubbard,	from Oct.	1, 1845	to May	29, 1849.
H. Stocking,	from May	29, 1849.		

Town Clerks in Cromwell.

Samuel G. Wilcox, elected, July 16, 1851.
Lorenzo H. Treat, " Oct. 6, 1851.

Representatives.

Marvin R. Warner, elected in April, 1852.

SKETCH OF PORTLAND,

More particularly of its Ecclesiastical History, of its Ship Building and Quarries.

Very considerable settlements were made in the F rst Society of Middletown, and in Cromwell, before any were made in Portland. One reason for this delay prol ably was the danger of attacks from the Indians, particularly in the night season, and the difficulty then of fleeing across the river to their brethren, or eriving aid from them. The first two persons who settled in Portland were James Stancliff and John Gill. The former had a house on the bank of the river at the end of Portland street about 1690, perhaps a little earlier. The latter had a house not far from him about the same time. The third settler was William Cornwall, who settled back from Portland meadow. Other settlers joined them from time to time and occupied various portions of the fine arable and productive lands in the western part of the township.

There were accustomed for more than 20 years to attend public worship on the western side of the river. In May, 1714. 31 perso s, who were doubtless generally heads of families, petitioned the General Court for parish privileges. The petition was granted, and the parish was named East Middletown, a name which it retained until its incorporat on with most of Middle Haddam and East Hampton as a town, by the name of Chatham in Oct., 1767, when this parish became the first parish of Chatham, and was usually called Chatham.

The names of the petitioners were, Bariah Bacon, Shamgar Barnes, John Bevin, Samuel and Nathaniel Bidwell, Thomas Bucke, William and Jacob Cornwall, Richard Sill, John Gaines, Ebenezer and Joshua Gill, Richard Goodale, sen., Richard and Ebenezer Goodale, Thomas Hale, Samuel Hall, Walter Harris, Ebenezer Hurlbut, John Miller, Job Payne. Jonathan Sleed, Nathaniel Savage, Jonathan and Ebenezer Smith, James and William Stancliff, Joseph Warner, Joseph and Nathaniel White, and Thomas W ight. The aggregate of their list as taken the year preceeding was £1383:09.

Other persons settled there soon after by the name of Hubbard, Barney, Stocking and Wilcox. Noadiah, son of Rev. Noadiah Russell of Middletown, settled about 1720, on the site now occupied by his great grandson Daniel Russell. With these were united Lemuel Lewis from the county of Barnstable, Mass., John Penfield from Rhode Island, Joseph Blague from Saybrook, John Churchill from Wethersfield, and some others. The population and property of the parish were much increased before the incorporation of the parishes of Middle Haddam and East Hampton, the former in 1740, and the latter in 1748 Almost all the inhabitants until this time supported their families by agriculture, though long before this the free stone of Portland excited considerable attention, and ship-building was commenced.

The people having been formed into a society they built a meeting house in 1716, 40 feet by 26. This stood upon the hill, south of the present town-house.

The church was organized Oct. 25, 1721, and consisted of 29 persons, most of whom were probably recommended from the churches in Middletown and Cromwell.

At the same time *Daniel Newell*, native of Bristol and graduate of Yale College, 1718, was ordained their pastor. He is spoken of as a worthy man and some special attention to religion among his people attended his labors. He died Sept. 14, 1731, aged 31 years.

Moses Bartlett, born in that part of Guilford, which is now Madison and graduated at Yale College in 1730, studied both theology and medicine with his distinguished father-in-law, Rev. Phineas Fisk of Haddam, became the successor of Mr. Newell, June 6, 1733, and besides discharging the duties of the ministry, he was like his instructor, physician for the bodies of his people, and the only physician living within the limits of his parish. He died Dec. 27. 1766, aged 58, and his people in respect to his memory erected a monument over his grave.

Cyprian Strong, born in Farmington, graduated at Yale College, in 1763, D. D., was ordained the successor of Mr. Bartlett, Aug. 19, 1767, and died Nov. 17,1811, aged 67 years.

Dr. Strong was highly esteemed for his good sense, his thorough acquaintance with theology and his uniform and blameless life. In his private relations, as a companion and friend few have been more beloved; and though as a preacher he had not that fervency of address and brilliancy of imagination which are requisite to catch the attention of the multitude for the moment, yet his sermons were distinguished for clear reasoning and sound instruction, and his prayers for appropriateness and solemnity.

Several of his occasional sermons and controversial pieces are in print, and do honor to his understanding and his heart. The principal of these are an election sermon, and two inquiries, respecting the nature and design of christian baptism. In the midst of numerous trials he was calm and resigned. The prominent traits of his character are happily expressed upon his monument. "In morals exemplary; in doctrine uncorrupt; in reasoning profound; in declaring God's counsel perspicuous and solemn, and in death peaceful."

Eber L. Clark, native of Mansfield, graduate of William's College, 1811, was settled in Portland, Sept. 25, 1812, and dismissed Aug. 18, 1815. He afterwards settled in the parish of Turkey Hills, in Granby, and preached, alternately to the congregation in that parish, and to the convicts in the State Prison, which was then in that town. In 1820 he was settled in Winchindon, Mass., where he remained until Feb., 1835, Since June, 1838, he has been pastor of the congregational church in Richmond.

Hervey Talcott, the present pastor, born in Coventry, graduated at Yale, 1810, was settled here Oct. 23, 1816.

The constituent members of the church, as just stated were	29
Mr. Newell admitted	50
Mr. Bartlett,	114
Dr. Strong,	193
Mr. Clark,	24
Mr, Talcott has admitted	207
Total of members,	617

The number of members, Jan. 1, 1852, was 82.

Deacons of the Church.

Elected.	*Died.*		*Age.*
Samuel Hall,	Nov. 9, 1721.	March 6, 1740.	76
John Gaines,	———	July 27, 1748.	72
Joseph White, Esq.,	Jan. 22, 1724.	Dec. 14, 1770.	82
David Sage, Esq.,	Dec. 15, 1748.	Nov. 25, 1803.	86
Ebenezer White, Esq.,	April 21, 1768.	July 29, 1817.	90
Dr Moses Bartlett,	Oct. 27, 1791.	March 3, 1810.	70
Hezekiah Goodrich, Esq.,	do do	Became Epis.	
Jonathan Brown,	June 25, 1795.	March 9, 1826.	77
Daniel Shepherd, Esq.,	March 15, 1810.	Oct. 24, 1850.	97
Joel Strickland,	Nov. 2, 1821.	Dismissed, 1851.	
Job H. Payne,	Nov. 2, 1821.	" "	
Dr. G H. Gilbert,	Feb. 7, 1851.		
Franklin Payne,	do do		

On the first Sabbath in Jan., 1852, the Rev. Mr. Talcott stated to his congregation that since he came to Portland he had been called to officiate at the interment of 326 persons, that three of these were said to be 100 years old or more, one, 105—that thirteen were over 90—eighty-three over 70—one hundred and twenty-five under 20, and ninety-four, under 5.

The Congregational Society has the following funds for the support of the gospel, $8,428 77, with lands in addition, valued at $250.

The congregation for the last ten years has contributed for public benevolent objects, taking one year with another, about $150 annually. The largest amount ever contributed in a year is $184,03.

the erection of a new church edifice, on Portland street, nearly opposite the Episcopal Church, and money raised to pay the expense.

PHYSICIANS IN PORTLAND.

In the Address it is stated that the Rev. Moses Bartlett, the first minister of Portland, studied both theology and medicine with his father-in-law, Rev. Phineas Fisk of Haddam. He appears to have been the first physician in Portland as well as the first minister.

Moses Bartlett, Jun., graduated at Yale in 1763, studied medicine with Dr. Benjamin Gale of Killingworth, now Clinton. He doubtless entered upon practice before his father's death in 1766 and survived him more than forty years. He was a deacon in the church. Another son of Rev. Moses Bartlett, Phineas Bartlett, also studied medicine with Dr. Gale and was a physician in Ashfield, Mass.

Thomas Wells, acted as a surveyor as well as a physician.—He died in 1790 aged 40 years.

Elisha Phelps came from Colebrook or vicinity, to Portland as early as 1783 or 4, and practised there until about 1792, when he removed to Hanover or near there, in New Hampshire, where he died in 1819.

Isaac Smith. See onward.

Isaac Conkling. See Middletown physicians.

Newell Smith, was born in Middle Haddam, studied medicine with Dr. John Richmond, of East Hampton, practiced 25 years in Otsego and Oneida counties, N. Y. afterwards 10 years in Portland , where he died Jan. 28, 1844 aged 60.

George O. Jarvis, native of New Canaan, received his professional education in the medical department of Yale College, practiced 5 years in Torringford, 18 in Colebrook and has practiced in Portland since 1840, received the degree of M. D. from Yale College in 1846.

Gershom C. H. Gilbert, native of Mansfield, received his professional education also in the medical department of Yale College and commenced practice in 1844.

Stephen A. Fuller, from Vershire, Vt. came to East Haddam, a few years since, and more recently has come to this place.

Henry Everlin Cook, a native of this place, who studied with Dr. Sperry, of New London, commenced practice as a Thomsonian physician here about 1835, where he remained about three years, and then removed to Moodus in East Haddam.

Dr. Isaac Smith, whose name appears in the preceding list, was the son of Dea. Isaac Smith of East Hampton. He studied medicine with Dr. William B. Hall of Middletown, and commenced practice in North Killingworth, now the town of Killingworth. Having spent a few years there, he removed to Portland, where he practiced until his death, a period of 39 years.

A memoir of him was prepared by his neighbor and friend, the late Dr. Thomas Minor of Middletown, which is published in "Williams' American Medical Biography."

The surviving acquaintances and friends of Dr. Smith will be gratified by reading the following paragraphs:

"In his deportment and intercourse with the members of his profession, he was always open, candid, frank and hospitable; with the sick, upright, beloved, kind, attentive, sympathizing, always ready to sacrifice his comfort, ease and happiness for the good of his patient. His practice was plain and well adapted to the case, and his native judgment and long experience gave him a claim to confidence which was rarely disappointed. He was a regular attendant upon divine service and a communicant of the Congregational church, always appearing to rejoice in christian privileges and duties."

"Though the friends of the deceased wish not for the language of panygeric, nor do we claim for him the more distinguished talents, or that he was pre eminently skilful in *all* the diseases to which a community is incident, yet he possessed, in an eminent degree, the key to the fine sensibilities of the soul, and knew the sympathies and idiosyncracies of his subjects and would more readily address his conversation and adapt his prescription, in their case, than now can any other.

"The disease which caused his death was a fever, but so mild in its early stages that he was not prevented, but with few exceptions, from attending to his professional duties, but about a week before his death. During that week his sufferings were great, and yet he was seldom heard to complain. "With strong reliance upon the Saviour, and his soul firmly stayed on God, he bade adieu to his family his friends and the world on the night of the 19th of Dec. 1839, aged 67 years, in the full hope of an immortality beyond the grave."

LAWYERS IN PORTLAND.

Oliver Overton, son of Gen'l. Seth Overton, studied law with Judge Hosmer, commenced practice as soon as 1812, practised in Portland only one or two years, moved to Cherry-Valley, N. Y., and thence to Belfonte, or Belfontaine, Ohio, where he died, in 1825. aged 38 years.

Alfred Hall. See Middletown.

GRADUATES FROM PORTLAND,

In addition to those mentioned in the Address.

Elihu Bartlett was a son of the Rev. Moses Bartlett, and graduated at Yale in 1764. He would probably have studied theology had his health permitted, but was feeble several years. He settled in East-Guilford, now Madison, where he died in 1779, aged about 36 years.

William Payne. graduate of Trinity College, 1834, Tutor, a clergyman in Litchfield, now in Schenectady, N. Y.

Daniel Shepherd, graduate of Trinity, 1836, clergyman and teacher in Delhi, N. Y.. where he died, Sept. 29, 1846.

Nathaniel Ogilvie Cornwell, Trinity, 1839, a teacher and physician in South America.

Frederick Hall, graduate of Yale, 1841, merchant.

Richard Hart Jarvis, Trinity, 1848, studied law in New Haven and New York, and is now a practitioner in the latter city.

The question has been raised, whether Rev. Joseph Washburn was not a native of Portland. See list of Middletown graduates.

I have already had occasion to advert to the Quarrying business and the Ship-building of this town. The quarrying business has excited more or less attention from nearly or quite the time of the first settlement of Middletown, as will be shown hereafter. But for some time before the incorporation of East Middletown with most of Middle Haddam and East Hampton, as a town, ship-building was a more engrossing concern in East Middletown, and was also pursued at Middle Haddam Landing. Hence the town was called Chatham from the importance of its ship-building, in allusion to Chatham in England. The name appeared more and more appropriate for years after it was given than before.

The first vessel built in Portland was launched in Oct., 1741. This was a schooner of 90 tons, built, as is supposed, at Lewis' Yard, where very many vessels have been built since that period. Besides merchant vessels, the following ships of war and privateers have been built in Portland at different places:

The Trumbull and Bourbon were built during the Revolution near the quarries, the former of 700 tuns, 36 guns; the latter of 900 tuns, and intended to carry 40 guns, but not armed on account of the occurrence of peace. The Connecticut was built at Stevens' Wharf, in 1798 and 9, of 514 tuns, 20 guns. Ship-building was begun at Churchill's Yard in 1795, and at this yard the armed vessels and privateers about to be named were built. The Holker was built in 1813, 350 tuns, 18 guns. This was driven on shore by the English at Narragansett, and lost. Another vessel of the same name was built in 1814, of 400 tuns,

20 guns. This was cast away in a storm on the coast of Long Island. The Macedonian was built the same year, of the same tonnage and form. The Saranac and the Boxer were built in 1815, the former 373 tuns and the latter of 367, each 16 guns. The three first of the above vessels, the Trumbull, Bourbon and the Connecticut, and the two last were built for the United States. In Churchill's yard 12,500 tuns of shipping were built between the beginning of 1806 and the close of 1816. No vessels of war have been built in Portland since 1815, nor vessels of any kind to an equal amount of tunnage as before. Still there have been built since then 104 vessels, 35 by Elizur Abbey from 75 to 300 tuns and 69 by S. Gildersleeve from 75 to 700 tuns.

In the autumn of 1836, William and Joseph J. Hendley and Alexander Keith, of Middletown, and S. Gildersleeve of Portland built the schooner called the "William Bryan," which was the first vessel that ever sailed as a regular packet from New York to Texas. From that vessel has arisen the New York and Galveston line which now consists of five ships and two barques. The ships have all been built in Portland since 1847, the largest of which 700 tuns. They are called after the Texan patriots, Stephen F. Austin, Benjamin R. Milam, William B. Travis, James H. Fanning and William H. Wharton.

Ship building as well as the quarrying business has employed many hands and sustained many families; and both have stimulated husbandry. In these three great branches of industry most of the inhabitants are now occupied, though more are engaged in merchandise than formerly.

In 1814 or about that time, there were but two merchant stores in Portland, and the people then and many years afterward resorted mainly to the city of Middletown for dry goods. The same is done to a great extent now. But as the quarrying business has vastly increased within a few years, stores have been increased in number and furnished with a greater variety and amount of articles. The number of stores is 8, all dealing in groceries and some in dry goods.

There is also in the town s me increase of manufactures. About 1834 Mr. Gilbert Griswold began the manufacture of gold and silver spectacles and employed 3 or 4 hands. He is now engaged principally in making gold spectacles, and also deals in various articles such as watches, clocks, jewelry, cutlery and small arms. Within a few years a cabinet shop has been established, there is a wagon shop, and a number of other shops have been opened in which such articles as are most needed by the inhabitants are either prepared, or procured elsewhere, and kept on hand for sale.

And now let us turn our attention more particularly to the great and increasing business of the quarries.

The first quarry in Portland was opened where the stone originally rose high and hung shelving over the river; or rather perhaps for a time such stone only were taken as had been broken off from the cliffs by the action of the atmosphere and were thrown about the banks. They were sought soon after Middletown began to be settled, for building and for grave-stones. Thus they were sought not only by the inhabitants, but by persons from other places. Soon they began to be dug and raised possibly from the earth around, into which they had fallen, or in which they had been buried by the action of the waters of the river in times of freshet. Strangers thus got them as common property, it would seem, without leave from any one and without giving any thing as an equivalent. This is evident from a resolve of the Town passed in 1665, "that no one should dig or raise stones, at the Rocks, on the east side of the river, but an inhabitant of the Town, and that twelve pence should be paid to the town, for every ton of stone taken." As early as this they were carried away to other places in scows or some kind of water craft. By several subsequent resolves they appear to have been regarded as valuable and considerably sought, as is attested too by ancient tombstones, and building stones found in various towns. How soon the high and shelving rocks were removed and efforts made to procure stone further from the river and below the surface of the ground it may be impracticable to ascertain at the present time. The Quarry thus began was at length disposed of by the town and passed through various hands, among whom the names of Shaler & Hall are conspicuous. They pursued the business vigorously, secured a handsome profit and after them the quarry was long called, the "Shaler & Hall Quarry." In this, in some places there were but about five feet of earth necessary to be removed to uncover good stone, while in other places there were four or five feet of shelly rock below the earth. In this quarry for several years, between 1810 and 20, thirty hands were employed eight months in the year, and from four to six teams. The quantity of stone prepared for market and sold to the inhabitants of this and neighboring towns, and exported to distant parts of the country was then regarded as very great, though small in comparison with what is now prepared.

Some fifty rods south of this quarry another quarry was opened about 1783. There the stone were covered with about ten feet of earth. This was owned for a time by Hurlburt & Roberts. About 1814 it was purchased of the heirs of Aaron Hurlburt and two other persons, and deeded to *Erastus and Silas Brainerd*, brothers from Middle Haddam, who carried on the business jointly until the death of Silas Brainerd in 1847. The firm now owning this quarry is styled "Brainerd & Company." For some five years after the Brainerds began to work this quarry they employed only about 7, 8 or 10 hands and two yoke of oxen.

In 1819 a quarry was opened north of the Shaler & Hall

Quarry by the name of "Patten & Russell Quarry," afterwards known as the "Russell & Hall Quarry," until the year 1841, when it was united with the Shaler & Hall Quarry, and the owners were incorporated by the Legislature of the State by the name of the "*Middlesex Quarry Company.*"

Some years afterward an opening was made below the Brainerd Quarry, near the ferry from Middletown to Portland, belonging to the Shaler & Hall Company, but which since the incorporation of the Middlesex Quarry Company, is called the "Shaler & Hall Quarry."

The three quarries now spoken of stretch northward from near the ferry and a little back from the river three fourths of a mile, and the space between them and the river is generally levelled; all along against these the bank of the river is a good wharf, rising from the river at an angle of about forty-five degrees, to which vessels draw up, unload and receive their burthens. The stone found in them, spreads beyond the opening in different directions, has been discovered northward and southward in sinking drills, and to a greater distance eastward in the same way and by some small openings. Wherever found it possesses the same general properties, and lies in nearly horizontal strata with a southern dip.

The stone are not perfectly solid in the quarries, but become more so generally in large masses as they are penetrated downward. They are found in layers from *two* to *eighteen* feet in thickness, varying from *twenty* to *one hundred* in width and in length from *fifty* to *one hundred and fifty*; their direction is from *north east* to *west*.

The stone has been rising in estimation and favor with the public for many years and very rapidly for a few years; its firmness, durability and susceptibility of receiving and retaining polish are well attested. When indeed the stone began to be used, when quarrymen did not well understand their work, when they were picked up from the surface of the ground, or taken very near it, now and then a perishable stone may have found its way to market, though instances of this kind are believed to have been rare. Some chemists, who have analyzed the stone, have pronounced it to be equal in durability to granite itself.

In 1836 an association formed in Hartford, undertook to repair "the waste of time and accident among the monuments, erected as memorials of their deceased ancestors" in the old grave yard in that city, which had been abandoned about thirty years.

In doing this, all the monuments were reset, in number about five hundred, and the tables many of which had been suffered to fall were rebuilt, supported by solid masonry, and where the monuments were broken they were repaired by being fastened with iron clamps. They of course had a very favorable opportunity to see the wastes of time and accident on the monuments. During the Revolutionary War some use was made of the Bolton stone: These had decayed somewhat in the ground. All or nearly all the marble monuments of 30 years standing, by the effects of the climate and the weather, were very much decayed; the upper parts of them being decomposed and crumbling to pieces. It was found very difficult to repair such of them as were broken, as they were not strong enough to bear the force of drilling. A large proportion of the monuments were of the Portland freestone. Some of these were over the graves of such as had been dead 190 years and were not in the least affected by the weather, nor had any of this description been injured by the seasons."

These monuments were doubtless generally put up soon after the death of the person whose names they were designed to perpetuate. It is hardly possible that testimony more unexceptionable than this, could be given.

The obelisk erected in the old cemetery, in connection with these repairs, is wisely built therefore of the Portland stone, bearing the venerated names of the early settlers of Hartford; and so is the block, sent from Connecticut to grace the monument, now in the process of erection in Washington, in honor of the Father of our Country. This is already placed in the great and imposing structure.

Calls are perpetually made for this stone from different parts of our country to be used in large public buildings, and in the mansions of the wealthy, or for the fronts and ornamental parts of such edifices, also for the fronts of stores. And while two years since the companies were unable to meet the demand, it is happy that by a more perfect division as well as by an increase of labor, and other expedients, they are able now to comply with the applications made to them In 1850, the number of men employed in the three quarries was about 900, and 100 yoke of oxen. Thirty vessels were employed in carrying away stone regularly, varying from 75 to 150 tuns, making each from 20 to 30 trips in a season. Large quantities were also carried away in other vessels not belonging to the regular line and in scows. In the companies' vessels they were carried to New York and sold to persons there or to persons coming there from other places, who carried them away in vessels at their own charge. The more common practice has been for the vessels of the company merely to deliver the stone, New York excepted, at some of our large cities. New York, Albany, Philadelphia and Boston have been the principal markets. With respect to Boston, however and other eastern ports, the stone have been carried to them in vessels hired by the purchasers, as is also the case with many cargoes carried up the Hudson river and to ports south of New York. In 1851 a greater number of men and teams were employed than in 1850. This year (1852) the regular workmen are about 1200 in the quarries; about 200 more work on contract and are engaged in removing the surface of the earth and in clearing away rubbish. Within a year 12 new vessels from 120 to 200 tuns, carpenter's measure, have been purchased for transporting stone. A steam-boat also was built the last spring owned by the Middlesex Quarry Company, and Brainerd & Co., to tow quarry vessels up and down the Connecticut river, which enables the vessels to make more trips.

In some way or other the stone are carried to very many places in the country—some to very distant places, a few have been carried to Milwaukie, in Wisconsin, some even to San Francisco.

Until a period comparatively recent, efforts in all the quarries were confined to stone lying above the ordinary surface of the river, but now stone are taken many feet below it, and the opinion is somewhat current in the surrounding community that the further down the quarries are penetrated the better are the stones. The Middlesex, and the Shaler & Hall Quarries have each a steam engine of 40 horse power; and the Brainerd Quarry, has two engines, one of 40 horse power and another of about 17, by which the water accumulated in the quarries is pumped out every morning, and by which the stone are raised.

In and around these quarries a scene of activity is seen from day to day, from Monday morning until Saturday night, beyond what is seen within any equal space in the county, and the people near, all feel the influence of this activity and enterprise. It is seen in the rise of real estate, in the erection of new buildings, in the improved gardens and grounds.

While the quarrying operations are giving subsistence to many families, some Irish, some Scotch, some American and recently some English, they are as already noticed, stimulating trade and agriculture, as these families need a large amount of articles which merchants have to sell, and which farmers can raise. The teams too used about the quarries make a demand for hay straw and provender, and of the latter article far more than is now furnished in the vicinity.

As for the curious subject of birds tracks, found in these quarries, as they have been at other localities of free stone above on the river as far north as Turner's Falls, they must be left for illustration to those who have more time to spare for investigation than the writer.

The wonders of Job's Pond, so called because the pond is found on land formerly owned by Job Payne, if the facts asserted about it be admitted, constitute a more difficult subject of solution. This is against the straits, and about two miles in circumference. It is from 40 to 60 feet deep and has no outlet.—It rises and falls as much as fifteen feet, but not from such causes as affect other ponds. It is often the highest in the dryest season of the year and lowest in the wettest season. When it begins to rise, it rises regularly for six or twelve months and then falls for about the same periods.

There are in Portland 7 district schools, and the children in the districts between the ages of 4 and 16, as enumerated in 1851, were 621. In the two largest schools the older and younger scholars are instructed by different teachers in separate departments, an arrangement favorable to the more rapid improvement of both.

The oldest grave yard in the town, near the quarries, was laid out Jan. 13, 1713, the new yard as it is called, near the Central Church was laid out in 1767; a third yard back of the Episcopal Church was laid out in 1825, or about that time. In this any persons may bury their dead, whatever be the religious denomination to which they belong.

PORTLAND POST-OFFICE, ESTABLISHED IN 1827.

This office has been kept by the following persons:—

George B. Smith,	from	1827 till June 20, 1833.
His widow, Anne B. Smith,	"	June 20 1833 till Feb. 3, 1844.
Charles Henry Sage,	"	Feb. 3 1844 till Apr. 11, 1849.
John Payne, from April 11,		1849, till his death July 21; 1852.
Wm. S. Strickland,	"	July 21, 1852.

The notice of justices of the peace who lived in Portland, before the adoption of the present constitution of the State, will be found in connection with justices then in other parts of Chatham.

SKETCH OF CHATHAM.

Including the greater part of Middle Haddam Society, the whole of East Hampton, and a small section of the Society of Westchester in Colchester.

Middle Haddam Society includes Haddam Neck, a part of the town of Haddam, and stretches along the eastern bank of the Connecticut from Portland to near East Haddam Landing, terminating there in a point between the Connecticut and Salmon river. The Chatham part of Middle Haddam is generally very uneven, (as is true of Haddam Neck,) much of it rough and stoney; and on the north against the Straits, it is mountainous. Still very considerable portions of the land in the vicinity of the Connecticut possess a strong soil; most is capable of cultivation and the rest generally is valuable for pasturage or wood. The inhabitants have always had great advantages from the river, some from the shad fishery and for a long time from the salmon fishery, more from ship-building, and some from navigation.

Before any English settlements were made in this parish, there were stories going abroad of great mineral riches in Great Hill, on its northern border. These stories arose from the visits and investigation of the elder Gov. Winthrop there, though very little was known by the people as to what discoveries he actually made. Of this hill, and its mine usually called the "Cobalt Mine," we shall have occasion to speak more particularly hereafter.

About 1710 a family by the name of Goffe settled south of Middle Haddam Landing, who were the first English inhabitants in Middle Haddam. Capt. Cornelius Knowles, an early and respectable settler, built a house afterwards at the Landing directly upon the bank of the river, from whom that place and and the surrounding neighborhood was long called Knowles' Landing. There and on the rising grounds in different directions, other families settled. These sustained themselves in part by what they obtained from the river and by means of it; but principally by subduing the forests and cultivating the earth for some 40 or 50 years, when ship-building came gradually to their aid. This business was probably begun as early as 1758. The first ship was built there in 1763; and from that time ship-building was carried on generally for more than 40 years and at times to a great extent, though we are unable to specify exactly the number and the tunnage of the vessels then built. Business was drawn thither from the southern and eastern parts of Chatham and somewhat from Marlborough and Hebron. From

1805 to the close of 1838, notwithstanding the embarrassments connected with the second war with Great Britain, 51 ships were built, 24 brigs, 21 schooners, and 15 sloops, amounting in all to 27,430 tuns. Thomas Child, now approaching 90 years of age, states that he has been the master-builder of 237 vessels, and that he built the most of them at this place. For some ten or eleven years prior to 1851, ship-building was wholly abandoned; but in that year one vessel was built, and it is hoped that the business will he renewed ere long and flourish.

The Landing was more advanced by this business than by any thing else; though some of the inhabitants for many years had a considerable share in commerce, owned vessels, and followed a sea-faring life as officers or sailors. But with the loss of the West India trade from the river, navigation from this place was very much diminished

In 1819 the village contained sixty or seventy dwelling houses, four stores, and some mechanic shops. It now contains, regarding the village as co-extensive with the school districts, seventy-three houses, four stores, and seven mechanics' shops. There is also within its limits, on Taylor's Creek, a foundry for the casting of house and sleigh bells, employing about five men; a shop recently built, with the needed apparatus for pulverizing and cleansing ore from Great-Hill, and also near by a laboratory and smelting works for extracting from it its valuable contents, and four oakum factories, usually employing twenty-five hands.

The early inhabitants who lived in the Chatham part of Middle Haddam, labored under great disadvantages for attending public worship, whether they undertook to work their way through crooked paths over the Strait-Hills to the sanctuary in Portland; or, availing themselves of the Connecticut in the mild seasons of the year, went as far as they could in boats towards that sanctuary, or thus went to the churches in Middletown and Haddam. The people on Haddam Neck also, though living against Haddam Town, often found it difficult to cross the river. Nor were the people of both sections conveniently situated for meeting together, within their own limits, not so much from their distant scattered dwellings, as from the hilliness and roughness of the country, and the badness of the roads. But it being more convenient for them to meet together than to worship where they had done, they united, in Oct. 1738, in a petition to the Legislature for incorporation as a parish, and their request was granted in May 1740.

The petitioners north of the Neck were 26, and their names were Henry Atkins, Richard Bonfoey, Ebenezer, Jonathan and Nathaniel Burr, Edward Bill, Ebenezer Dart [a settler from New London], James Fowrey, Ephraim Fuller, Nathaniel Goss. Benjamin Harris, David Hebbard. John and Thomas Hubbard, David Hurlburt, Jun., Josiah Johnson, James Pelton, Noah Phelps, Thomas Rich, Benjamin and Ebenezer Smith, Samuel, Nathaniel and John Spencer, George Stocking and John Swaddle. The lists of these petitioners amounted to £1,582 2. There were three other inhabitants, Joshua Brainerd, Joshua Luther and Moses Rowley, having together a list of £109 8, who for some reason did not unite in the petition.

The petitioners on the Neck were 12, viz.: Joshua Arnold, William, James, Abijah, Josiah, Nathan and Benjamin Brainerd, William Markum, Alexander Peterson, Ebenezer and David Smith, and John Stocking. The lists of all these is not known; but it is believed that they were somewhat more in proportion to their number than the lists of those from the other part of Middle Haddam. The list of William Brainerd alone in 1739, it is ascertained, was £108 14.

The ancestors of the Freemans, Hurds, Higginses and Youngs, who united with the foregoing settlers, were from Barnstable conнty in Massachusetts. About 1750, John Eddy, from Norton, in the same state, Samuel Daniels, a native of Colchester, and a few others, settled in the east part of the parish.

The church was organized Sept. 24, 1740, and consisted of 13 male members, 7 of whom lived on the Neck.

Rev. Benjamin Bowers, a native of Billerica, Mass., and graduate of Harvard College 1733, was ordained and settled as their pastor at the same time.

At the time of this organization the people had no house erected for public worship, and must have met in a school-house or private dwelling. They had no village nor densely settled neighborhood, to plead on the ground of numbers and property, for its location in the midst of their dwellings. Knowles's Landing, now Middle Haddam Landing, indeed began to be a place of some business not long afterward; but it did not attain its present size till that generation, and many of succeedings ones had gone to the grave. The people therefore united in a local centre, or one that was nearly so, and built a meeting-house in 1744, 44 feet by 36, in which they worshipped until 1712; several years longer than they would have done had they been united in views as to the site of a second Meeting-house.

Mr. Bowers died May 11, 1761, aged 45, having obtained the reputation of a pious and faithful minister.

Rev. Benjamin Boardman, a native of Westfield in Middletown, a graduate of Yale 1758, Dean scholar and tutor in that institution, was ordained Jan. 5, 1762: In his ministry, if not before, some families, living on Moromus street, on the West side of the Connecticut and near its bank, became accustomed to attend worship more or less in Middle Haddam; and in Jan. 1775 the First Society granted them liberty to pay half their society tax into the treasury of Middle Haddam. The heads of these families were Israel Carrier, Francis Clarke, John Cone, Simeon and Richard Morgan, Stephen and John Sears, Samuel Simmons and John Swaddle. During this year Mr, Boardman went as chaplain with a company of cavalry to the vicinity of Boston. He was chaplain there, during that year, for a number of months. Difficulties afterwards arising between him and his people from two or three causes, he was dismissed in 1783. On the 5th of May in the following year he was installed pastor of the South church in Hartford, where he died Feb. 12, 1810, aged 70.

Rev. David Selden, native of Haddam Neck, graduate of Yale 1782, studied theology with Dr. Lockwood of Andover, Conn. and was licensed to preach by Hartford South Association, June 3, 1783. Soon after this he preached in Hebron and was invited to settle as colleague with Dr. Pomeroy; he preached also in other places, but was settled in Middle Haddam Oct. 19, 1785, where he died in office, esteemed by his people and his brethren in the ministry, Jan. 18, 1825, aged 64.

Rev. Charles Bentley, native of New Marlborough, Mass. graduate of Amherst College, 1824, was ordained successor to Mr. Selden Feb. 15, 1826 and dismissed May 22, 1833. Since his dissmission Mr. Bentley has been settled at Salmon Brook, in Granby, in Harwinton, and in Green's Farms, in Fairfield, where he is now pastor.

Rev. Stephen A. Loper, native of Guilford and graduate of Bangor Theological Seminary, was first settled in Hampden, a little below the city of Bangor, in Maine. He was installed in Middle Haddam June 11, 1834 and dismissed Nov. 1, 1841. He was afterwards settled in Hadlyme several years; but since July 1, 1850 has preached to the congregation in Higganum in Haddam.

In the interval between the dismission of Mr. Loper from Middle Haddam, and the settlement of another pastor, the people were supplied by *Rev. William Case*, who had been pastor of the church in Chester, by *Mr. Samuel Mosely*, a candidate for the ministry, since dead, and by *Rev. Philo Judson*, who had been pastor of the church in Ashford and of the church in North Stonington.

Rev. James Colburn Houghton, native of Lyndon, Vt., but who spent most of his youth in Putney in that State, graduate of Dartmouth College 1837, and who studied theology in East Windsor, was installed at Storrsville, now Dana, Mass. Dec. 23, 1840. After leaving that place, he preached as stated supply in East Hartland, and in Granby, Conn. for a short time. He began to preach in Middle Haddam in May 1847 and was installed there on the 15th of Sept. following. He was dismissed from this charge the 1st. of November 1850, and installed over the South Church in New Hartford Dec. 31, 1851.

Rev. William Sturgess Wright, native of Glastenbury and graduate of Yale College 1839, who studied theology two years in New Haven, and taught the Academy in Cromwell 5 years, has been stated supply in Middle Haddam since Jan. 1851. He was ordained after he commenced services in this place, but not installed as pastor.

DEACONS IN THE CHURCH.

	Elected.	Died or moved away.	Ages.
Ebenezer Smith,	Nov. 8, 1740.	Feb. 11, 1752	81
Gideon Arnold,	" " "	Mar. 1772	
Benjamin Harris,	Mar. 14, 1748.	Apr. 11, 1775.	75
Daniel Arnold,	Nov. 27, 1771.	May 27, 1774.	43
Ezra Brainerd, Esq	" " "	Apr. 7, 1837.	93
David Smith,	June 1, 1774.	Nov. 25, 1795,	52
Dr Thos. Brainerd,	Dec. 10, 1795.	Moved to Ludlow, Mass.	
Selden Gates,	July 27, 1810.	" L. I. died at Brooklyn.	
Jesse Hurd,	Sept. 18, 1818.	July 22, 1831.	66
Edward Root,	June 1827	Moved to Middletown, 1849.	
Levi Mitchell,	" "	" " " 1839.	
Samuel B. Butler,	Jan. 3, 1840.	Moved to Stonington, 1841	
David Dickinson,	June 30, 1843.		
Anson Strong,	June 29, 1849,		

Those whose names are in italics lived in the Chatham part of Middle Haddam.

It has been stated that the number of members in the church at its formation was 13.

Mr. Bowers, admitted,	171.
Mr. Boardman, "	162.
Mr. Selden, "	221.
Mr. Bentley, "	95.
Mr. Loper, "	19.
The number admitted since Mr. Loper's dismission, is	44.
	725.

The number of communicants Jan. 1. 1852, is not ascertained, but the number reported to the Gen. Association for Jan. 1. 1851, was 133.

The 2d Meeting-house, to which reference has been made, was built in 1812 and is 50 feet by 40.

The society own a parsonage. They have also two pieces of land, given by the late Dea. Ezra Brainerd, worth about $200; the rents of which are about 9 or 10 dollars annually.

The annual average of contributions by the people for public benevolent objects for the last five years has not been less than $160. During the three years of Mr. Houghton's ministry they were not less than $200 per year.

EPISCOPAL CHURCH AT MIDDLE HADDAM LANDING.

A small Episcopal Church was formed in the eastern part of Middle Haddam in 1771, which held meetings a few years and was dissolved. Their house of worship built in 1772, 26 feet by 24, was taken down.

The church at the Landing was formed April 25, 1785, and their church edifice was built in 1786 or 7, 47 feet by 36. The church belonged to the care of *Mr. Jarvis* of Middletown until

1791. The two succeeding years *Rev. Tillotson Bronson*, afterwards preceptor of Cheshire Academy, divided his labors equally between this church and the church in Portland, and then they reverted to the care of Mr. Jarvis. From 1795 or 6 till 1810 *Rev. M. Smith Miles*, ministered here one half of the time. From 1811 till 1821 *Rev. Jasper D. Jones* ministered here one third or fourth of the time, with the exception of about two years, (1815 and 16, it is believed,) when the church was supplied by *Rev. Solomon Blakeslee*, and *Rev. R. Ives*. Mr. Jones was succeeded by *Rev. Nathan Burgess*, who preached here a quarter of the time in 1822 and 3. He removed to Vermont. *Rev. Edward T. Ives*, born and educated in Cheshire, and who studied theology in New Haven, took charge of the parish about two years. He removed to Peekskill, N. Y. From 1825 to 1826 *Rev. Orson V. Howell*, then connected with the Military Academy in Middletown, ministered to the parish one half the time. From 1826 to 1829 or 30, *Rev Ashbel Steel*, a native of Waterbury, educated at Cheshire Academy, a very devoted and good man, ministered to the people. *Rev. Alpheus Geer*, became rector in 1831 and preached to them till the spring of 1837, being connected during that period with the church in Hebron. *Rev. James Sunderland*, came into the parish in 1837 and preached till the spring of 1838. He was succeeded by *George Augustus Sterling* who preached two years. He was a native of Sharon, educated at West Point, and studied theology in New York city. *Rev. Benjamin S. Huntington* took charge of the parish July 5, 1840, and resigned in the autumn of 1841. He studied theology in New York, and it is believed was born and educated classically in that city. *Rev. Charles W. Bradley*, preached in Middle Haddam about 5 months in the close of 1841 and beginning of 1842. He is a native of New Haven, has been Secretary of State of Connecticut, and is now a consul in China. *Rev. Sylvester Nash* succeeded him in May 1842 and resigned Nov. 1, 1845. He is a native of Ellington. His classical education was private—his theological at the P. Episcopal Seminary in New Haven and New York, being a member of it at its removal. *Rev. F. B. Woodward* took charge of the parish in April 1846 and is the present rector. He became first a physician, and still practices medicine. His theological education was in the Eastern Diocese while under the supervision of Bishop Griswold.

The number of communicants in this church prior to 1840 cannot be definitely ascertained. The correspondent who has furnished many of the foregoing facts thinks it safe to put the average at 50. There were 51 in May 1842; the number Jan. 1, 1852 was from 40 to 45.

Contributions are taken up in the church for the Bible Society and Tract cause, and for Missions, Domestic and Foreign. To the Bible and Tract cause $150 are given annually; though in justice it should be added that the greater part of all the contributions are given by three or four individuals.

METHODISTS IN MIDDLE HADDAM, CHATHAM PART.

They held meetings here as early as 1792, and in 1796 or 7 built them a small church at the Landing, 24 feet by 23 At one time they had fifty communicants, but the number of professors among them afterwards greatly diminished; for some time their church has been closed.

I have already said that we should have occasion to speak more particularly of Great Hill and its Cobalt Mine. The situation of this hill, the size of which is indicated by its name, is towards the northwest corner of Middle Haddam Society. That the elder Gov. Winthrop believed that there were mines and minerals in Middletown, and that he had become so convinced of their value as to think seriously of setting up works for improving them, is evident from the following grant made to him a few years after the first settlement of Middletown.

"The inhabitants of Middletown, for the encouragement of the designs of our much honored governor, Mr. John Winthrop, for the discovery of mines and minerals, and for the setting up of such works as shall be needful for the improvement of them, do hereby grant unto our said much honored governor any profitable mines or minerals that he shall find or discover upon any common land within the bounds of our Town, and such woodland as may be convenient for the use of the same, to the value of 500 or 1,000 acres, as it may lie so that it be not nearer than two or three miles from the present dwelling houses of the Town, as the Town shall judge to be least prejudicial to themselves for their necessary fire-wood, provided the Town shall have free liberty of commonage, as far as our Town bounds go, until the improvers shall see good to impropriate the same with inclosures—provided further, that said governor, and such as may be co-improvers with him, will set up the works to improve such mines and minerals as he shall find, within these 5 years and let us know whether he doth accept of this our grant within two years; and so it be to him and his heirs and associates from the time of setting up such works, else at two or five years, and to be in the liberty of the Town to grant the same to any other. May 25, 1661."

At the time of this grant the people of Middletown dwelt mostly within the limits of the city, and in the lower part of the present village of Cromwell. There is no probability that Mr. Winthrop had any very strong impression of finding valuable mines and minerals, excepting on the hills near the Straits, where lead on the west side of the Connecticut, and cobalt on the eastern were afterwards more seriously sought, and these localities were sufficiently away from the existing settlements. That his thoughts were mainly, if not entirely, turned to Great Hill, is probable from the fact that this Hill was long called the "*Governor's Gold Ring*," a name derived from the impression which people around had, that the governor, from explorations and labors there, had actually found gold, which might at least be made into rings. From the correspondence of the governor with learned men in England, it is possible that some knowledge of this locality crossed the Atlantic in his time.

Be this as it may, no considerable efforts appear to have been made to find gold or any other mineral in this hill, for about a century after this grant was made. But about 1762 Dr. John Sebastian Stephauney, a German, employed a number of men, and made a horizontal opening into the hill in search of hid treasures. He continued his exertions but a short time. About 1770 he renewed them, in connection with two other Germans, John Knool and Gominus Erkelens; but at length it appears that he made over the management of the concern to his associates, reserving to himself only a portion of the profits, and there was an agreement that what metals and minerals were sent to Great Britain should be consigned to Knool's friends, and those sent to Holland to Erkelens'. A large opening was made into the hill, and the superincumbent matter was prevented by stanchions from falling upon the laborers. Many casks of ore were obtained and sent to Europe, and it is probable some were carried to China. But as all the persons, laborers as well as principals, were foreigners, and as the ore was exported, little was known of its character or value. Various conjectures were made as to what it contained; the better informed, however, believed that Cobalt was the object sought. Erkelens seems finally to have been the principal manager. This appears from a passage in the diary of Pres. Stiles of Yale College. The president writes:

"1787. Jan. 1. Mr. Erkelens visited me, full of his Cobalt mine and China voyage. He some years ago bought the Governor's Ring, as it is called, or a mountain in the N. W. corner of East Haddam, [Middle Haddam,] comprehending about 800 acres, or about a square mile area. Here he finds plenty of Cobalt, which he manufactures into smalt, with which is made the beautiful blue on China ware, &c."

"Gov. Trumbull has often told me that this was the place to which Gov. Winthrop of N. London used to resort with his servant, and after spending three weeks in the woods of this mountain, in roasting ores and assaying metals and casting gold rings he used to return home to New London with plenty of gold. Hence this is called the Gov. Winthrop's ring to this day. Gov. Winthrop was an adept, in intimate correspondence with Sir

Kenelm Digby, and the first chemical and philosophical characters of the last century—as may be seen in the dedication of 40th vol. Phil. Transactions 1740."

"Mr. Erkelens about 1775 being a projector, erected a distillery in Haddam [Middle-Haddam,] 6 miles from Middletown, on a stream, descending from this mountain—he also purchased the Cobalt mine there. He has been at £2,000, sterling expense to no profit. He is going on a voyage to China, carrying with him 20 tuns of Cobalt ore."*

Much is recorded on the books of the Town of Chatham respecting the lands which Erkelens secured.

His object in building a distillery probably was, as at that time the regular trade with the West Indies was liable to be greatly interrupted, that he might supply his workmen more conveniently with a beverage which they loved, and have wherewithal to supply exposed and suffering soldiers, who, in the current opinion of that period, would hardly be expected to live and fight bravely, without the aid and stimulus of strong drink.

Whether he actually carried his Cobalt ore to China in 1787, or soon after, and if he did, how it was disposed of, we are not informed. But from the time he left, operations at the mine were suspended, and nothing more was done there for about 30 years. The opening in the hill remained a considerable period, but at length the stanchions giving way, the mass above fell and filled it.

When Pres. Stiles visited the hill in 1787, he sketched the Governor's Gold Ring, and a map showing the country from New London to Middle-Haddam and Middletown.† This he was doubtless prompted to do by the prospect which Great Hill afforded, which strictly considered is a hill of no inconsiderable size and elevation, resting on the range of the Strait Hills. The Cobalt mine is near the bottom of this hill, running so far as discovered a short distance from it, taking a semicircular course in accordance with its form, beginning at the west south-west and gradually bending round towards the south and south-east, being at an elevation on the range of hills of about 400 feet above the level of the Connecticut, the top of the hill, rising two or three hundred feet more. From the summit the view was fine in all directions then, except the north-east where a range of hills stretches far into the interior. It is finer now, as the lands are more generally cleared, and the country more densely settled. Besides the windings of the river directly under the eye, you often see vessels moving upon it propelled by wind and steam, and on the numerous hills and ranges of hills on either side, many churches and habitations of men. In a clear day, Long

* Literary Diary of Pres. Stiles, Ms. v. 13, p. 34.

† Idem, p. 35.

Island Sound with its moving navigation, and Long Island shore are distinctly visible. Not far from you, you contemplate the birth-place of *David Brainerd*, and very near you the birth-place of *James Brainerd Taylor*, while in the line towards N. London you have the birth-place of *Dr. Emmons*, and further on that of *Dr. Griffin*; and in the entire view the birth-places, or residences, of many other men. distinguished in their day, some in civil and some in military life. This prospect alone is worth a visit to Great Hill, and if persons wish to ramble, a mile and half east of this hill is Clark's Hill, from which the Sound can be seen.

But as to the Mine, Mr. Seth Hunt, from New Hampshire, commenced operations at Great Hill in the autumn of 1818 and continued them about two years. Anticipating great results, he expended liberally and exhausted his own resources. In these circumstances he sold interests in what he had done and obtained, say one sixteenth to one friend and one eighth to another, until he had gathered around him six associates, only one of whom is now living. This survivor states that Mr. Hunt expended about $20,000; that his main outlay in mining was in following the vein opened by the Germans downwards, but that he also opened the earth and traced near a quarter of a mile eastward, where he found more mica and the absence of hornblend, and that he expended much in repairing the old glass furnace in Glastenbury and in fitting it to smelt, in carting ore thither, (where most was sent,) stamping it by hand and reducing by potash. This survivor further states, that though Mr. Hunt read books on mining, he did not well understand his work, and that he doubts whether the man on whom he relied for chemical and scientific information, knew more than he did himself; that he obtained as he supposed 1000 lbs. of Cobalt which was proved in England to be nickel, containing from 3 to 4 parts of Cobalt. This proof induced an entire suspension of operations.

In the summer of 1844 the mine was opened again by Prof. Shepherd, author of the "Report on the Geological Survey of Connecticut." He employed only a few hands for a short time, but what disposition he made of the ore, and what discoveries he or others obtained from it, have not been ascertained, and it is a remarkable fact, after all that has been done at different periods in and about Great Hill by the first Gov. Winthrop, by the Germans, Mr. Hunt and Prof. Shepherd, that so little is really known to the public as yet as to the worth of the minerals, and whether the mine can be so wrought as to render much profit to the undertakers. It is evident however that the great object which has been sought is Cobalt, which has long been the name of the supposed mine.

"Cobalt," says Prof. Johnston of the Wesleyan University, "is a rare metal and is not used in the arts in a metallic state, but its oxid is used largely in preparing the beautiful blue coloring matter for painting glass and porcelain ware."

"This locality," (the one about Great Hill) he adds, "is the only one known in this country, where this peculiar ore of the metal is obtained, but in two or three places the oxid is found associated with oxid of manganese. At mine La Motte in Missouri it occurs in sufficient quantity to be extracted from the ore for use in the arts."

In March 1850, Mr. Edmund Brown in conjunction with some friends began operations about the base of Great Hill, a little eastward from the place where the previous operations had been made. He employed many hands and sunk a shaft. 7 by 9, 38 feet deep, and wrought from the shaft for some 50 to 60 feet, and took from the opening a large amount of ore. They then commenced a tunnel seven hundred feet east of the shaft at a ravine, and proceeded with it some 35 feet westerly with a view of meeting the opening from the shaft, in the meanwhile putting up the stamping works, laboratory and smelting works already mentioned. But after doing thus much, in the course of fifteen months, and expending a large amount of money, the company failed, or stopped operations, and Mr. Brown has since died.

Dr. Franckfort, a French physician and chemist, mentioned on page 160 of this work, was employed sometime in examining and testing the ore taken from about the shaft, before the company failed, and he is full in the opinion that a leader only was struck and not the vein, though he thinks he has discovered the vein himself. But the leader contains an ore of Cobalt, which he analysed, and as his analysis has been pronounced correct by some of the best chemists, I am authorized to publish it in his own words. "Analysis of an ore found in Chatham, Middlesex County, Conn. by E. Franckfort, M. D."

Arsenic,	80,04
Sulphur,	4,47
Iron,	9,03
Cobalt,	2,50
Nickel,	3,75
Bismuth trace.	
	99,79

From this analysis he observes, that the ore is, properly speaking, an arsensical pyrites containing some cobalt and nickel, and not a cobalt ore."

In a communication by Dr. Franckfort from which a quotation is made in connection with his name, he observes in regard to operations made about Great Hill by the Germans and others prior to Mr. Brown, that they "worked in the micaceous shale of that region, with a view of obtaining the smaltine or Cobalt Pyrites, a silvery white fine grained ore found here. The black peroxyd of Cobalt, extensively used in the manufacture of blue pottery, fine smalt, &c. &c. was the object which those who mined here wished to prepare. This mineral, he adds, is very rare in the United States and there is no doubt whatever that the regular vein of it, which the writer, [Dr. Franckfort,] thinks to have discovered, will pay amply for mining. There has also, formerly, a mineral of copper red color, called *Copper Nickel*, been found, but I have never been able to discover a vestige of it, though looking after it diligently. Nickel is a metal used in the manufacture of German Silver."

It is understood that the regular vein, believed to contain much more Cobalt than the leader which Mr. Brown struck, will soon be opened again, and it is hoped for the benefit of the community as well as that of the undertakers, that the next effort will be attended with great and known success.

PHYSICIANS IN MIDDLE-HADDAM.

In the address page 96, mention is made of three physicians in Middle Haddam, *Drs. Joshua Arnold*, *Jeremiah Bradford* and *Amos Skeele*.

Dr. Arnold, lived on the Neck, but doubtless practiced among the inhabitants north of it, and probably much in the town of Haddam after the death of Rev. Phineas Fiske in 1738, who had been physician both for the souls and bodies of his people. He died in 1753 aged 66. There is a tradition that the Red Cedar, found abundantly in some lands, not far from his residence, were introduced by him.

Jeremiah Bradford, was the son of Gershom and Priscilla (Wiswalk) Bradford, first of Kingston, Mass. and then of Bristol R. I., grandson of Samuel and Hannah (Rogers) Bradford, of Duxbury, Mass. Samuel Bradford, was son of William Bradford, a distinguished inhabitant and Lieut. Governor of Plymouth Colony, and grandson of Gov. William Bradford. Where Dr. Bradford studied medicine is not ascertained. He settled in Middle Haddam probably as early as 1754 or 5, and practised until old age, dying in 1814, aged 80. He was a man of good sense and an able practitioner.

Amos Skeele, a native of Woodbury, at the commencement of of the Revolution, entered the American army by a temporary enlistment and was in the battle at White Plains. Upon a sudden call in 1777, he went in pursuit of the English as they were retreating from Danbury, and while engaged in attack upon them was wounded by a bullet in his right arm, and was so injured as to unfit him for the pursuit of agriculture in which he had before engaged, and he turned his attention to the study of medicine. For a time he studied in Litchfield, but during the greater part of his preparations he was under the instructions of Dr. Hastings in Bethlem. While in this town he had the privilege of sitting under the preaching of Rev. Dr. Bellamy which contributed much to the formation of his religious character. He entered upon practice in Hampton in 1783, and moved to Middle Haddam in 1787. He lived in the north-eastern part of the parish, in the house afterward owned by Capt. Stephen Griffith, whence it was convenient for him to visit patients in the northern part of Middle Haddam, and also the western part of East Hampton. He removed to Somers in 1795, where he continued a number of years, and then removed again to Chicopee, Mass. where he practised until he was about 80, and where he died March 2, 1843 aged 93. For a very long period he discharged the duties of piety to God and beneficence to men with remarkable fidelity. For many years he was deacon in the church in Chicopee, and was very active and successful in promoting its religious interests,

Dr. Nathaniel Freeman was contemporary for a time with both Dr. Bradford and Dr. Skeele. He was a native of the parish, and was a smart active man, but did not acquire an extensive practice. He died probably not far from the commencement of this century, perhaps a few years previously.

Dr. Thomas Brainerd, a native of Middle Haddam, lived upon the Neck, but doubtless practised somewhat among the inhabitants of the Society further north. His practice was limited, and some years before his death he moved to Ludlow, Mass.

David B. Hollister, a native of Glastenbury, first settled in Middle-Haddam as a merchant. He had previously studied surgery, and afterwards made himself acquainted with medicine. He accordingly commenced the practice of medicine among the people and was regarded as skilful. He died Aug. 8, 1821, in the 56th year of his age.

Ebenezer Munger, native of Madison, graduate of Yale College 1814, studied medicine partly in New York, practised a short time in Middle Haddam, moved to Haddam in 1818 or 19 and thence about 1823 to Bainbridge, N. Y., then to Homer where he has lived some 20 years.

Samuel Simons, born in Hampton, was brought up by ex-Governor Peters of Hebron, studied medicine and was taken into partnership with him, came to Middle Haddam in 1821 or 2, moved to Bridgeport in the spring of 1824, received the degree of M. D. from Yale College in 1827, was elected a member of Congress from the 4th Congressional District of Connecticut in 1843, died at Bridgeport in 1847.

Frederic Morgan, native of Groton, graduate of Yale College 1813, Tutor, M. D. studied medicine principally with Dr. Nathan Smith; began practice in Colchester in Jan. 1820, succeeded Dr Simons in Middle Haddam in 1824, moved to Middletown in the spring of 1826; and remained there until Feb. 1829, when he moved to Ellington; in Oct. 1830 he returned to Colchester where he has since practised.

Charles Smith, son of Col, Chester Smith of North Stonington studied medicine with Dr. Eleazer B. Downing of Preston City, commenced practice in East-Hampton in the spring of 1823, where he remained until March 27, 1826, (the day on which his successor there took his place,) when he moved to Middle Haddam, where he died March 13, 1848, aged 47.

Albert B. Worthington, native of Colchester, studied with Dr. John P. Fuller, formerly of Providence, R. I., then of Salem, Ct. now of Norwich. He also attended lectures in New York. He came to Middle Haddam a little before the death of Dr. C. Smith and is still practising there.

Frederic B. Woodward, mentioned as rector of the Episcopal church at the Landing, was born in the parish of North Litchfield, received his medical education at New Haven, and practised in Woodbury generally from 1824 untill 1836. He now both preaches, and practises medicine.

Eugene A. Franckfort, a native of France, but who received his education in Germany, being graduated at the Medical University of Bonn, and also at the Chemical School of Giessen, came to Middle Haddam in March 1851, at first to test the ores which Mr. Brown had collected from Great Hill, in which service he was engaged until the subsequent June. Upon the suspension of operations by Mr. Brown, he resumed the practice of medicine; for he had before practiced medicine in Newtown, Bucks County, Penn., and also in Philadelphia. He has very recently moved his family to Middletown and is now working the mine usually called the Lead Mine, and which is described by him on pp. 160 and 61 of this work.

LAWYERS IN MIDDLE HADDAM.

Asahel Hooker Strong, son of Rev. Cyprian Strong D. D. of Portland, was graduated at Yale College in 1796, and was one of the best scholars in his class. He studied law with the Hon. Sylvester Gilbert of Hebron, and began to practice as early as 1802. He was greatly esteemed by his brethren of the bar and by the judges of the courts, for his good sense, his clear and discriminating knowledge of law, and his fair and able pleas; he was an excellent counsellor and a good special pleader.

John Hugh Peters, was the son of Jonathan Peters of Hebron, and brother of John T. Peters, late a judge of the Superior Court of the State, and of Samuel A. Peters, judge of the County Court in the County of New London, was graduated at Williams College in 1798, and having studied law with the brother first named, began practice in Middle Haddam as early as 1803, and practised law there until his death in Oct. 1811, aged 35. He was a well read lawyer, but not distinguished as an advocate, more modest than brilliant, and more correct than forcible. When the post-office was established in 1804, he was appointed postmaster and held the office through life.

Abiel A. Loomis—Ebenezer Force. See list of lawyers in Middletown.

Asahel Utley, native of Wilbraham, Mass., was admitted to the bar in 1822, spent a year or two in Middle Haddam, then went to East Haddam, where he remained until the spring of 1831, when he went to Middletown, where he died on the 27th of July following, aged 35.

Constans F. Daniels, came to Middle Haddam form Waterford in 1822, left in 1825 and now lives in New London.

Mark Moore, came from Boston to Middle Haddam in 1822, moved to Bridgeport in 1825, where he died in the spring of 1850.

Horace Foote, native of Marlborough, graduate of Yale College 1820, studied law with Seth P. Staples, Esq., of New Haven, was admitted to the bar in 1822, moved to Cleveland in Ohio about 1835.

Linus Parmelee, native of Guilford, whose parents moved to Haddam, when he was about six years of age, studied law with Levi H. Clark, Esq. He was admitted to the bar in 1808 or 9, practised in Haddam until 1842, since which time he has practised in Middle Haddam.

GRADUATES FROM MIDDLE-HADDAM AT DIFFERENT COLLEGES.

Jeremiah Bradford, Yale College 1779. Son of Dr. J. Bradford, born in Nov. 1758. He studied medicine but never practised as a physician. He resided for some time at Middle Haddam, and about the year 1806, moved to Berlin, Vt. where he was more or less occupied in Agricultural pursuits, and where he died Dec. 25, 1835, aged 77 years.

Sylvester Selden, Williams College 1807. Son of Rev. David Selden, studied theology at Andover, was pastor of the Congregational Church in Westbrook from June 10, 1812 until 183 and of the Congregational Church in Hebron from Sept. 30, 1835 until his death Oct. 4, 1841, at the age of 55. His remains are interred in a cemetery in Middle Haddam, near the grave, residence and church of his father.

Hiram Foot Mather, Yale 1813. Studied law and settled in Auburn, N. Y.

Ashbel Dart, Yale 1816, M. D. Studied medicine in Middletown and in New Haven, and attended lectures in New York; settled and practised in Conneought, Ohio, where he died in Nov, 1844 aged 51.

James Brainerd Taylor, son of Col. Jeremiah Taylor was born in Middle Haddam, April 15th 1801. He was a graduate at Nassau-Hall, Princeton, N. J., in 1826. He read theology at New

Haven, and at Prince Edward, Virginia. He died at the early age of 28. His memoirs written by the two Doctors Rice, of Virginia, present him as one of the most remarkable of men for his religious character and successful effort in religious action, during his short career. He died at the residence of John Holt Rice, D. D., in Virginia, and was interred in the burial ground not far from the Union Theological Seminary, at Prince Edward.

Fitch Welwyn Taylor, son of Col. Jeremiah Taylor and brother of James Brainerd Taylor, was born at Middle Haddam. He was graduated at Yale College in 1828. He read theology, as resident graduate, at New Haven, and in Alexandria, Virginia. He was Rector of William and Mary Parish, Charles Co., Maryland, for four years, and then made a voyage around the world in the U. S. Frigate Columbia. He received an appointment in the U. S. Navy in 1841, and is still in the service. He is author of several works: "The Flag Ship," "A voyage around the World," "The Broad Pennant," "Ella V—, or the July Tour," and "A New Tribute to the Memory of James Brainerd Taylor."

William Wright. Yale 1835, studied theology in New Haven, was settled in Jewett City, in Griswold, Nov. 18, 1832, where he was pastor about four years; was installed in Plainville, in Farmington, Nov. 8. 1843, where he was pastor a much longer period: Feb. 15, 1852 he was constituted pastor of the church at Chicopee, Mass.

Thomas Tallman, Yale 1837. Graduate of the Theological Department in that institution; was installed pastor of the church in the society of Scotland, in Windham, March 20, 1844.

MIDDLE-HADDAM POST-OFFICE,
ESTABLISHED IN 1804.

Post Masters.

John Hugh Peters,	from	1804 to 1811.
John Stewart,	"	1811 " 1830.
John Stewart, formerly Jr.,	"	1830 " 1832.
Henry Stewart,	"	1832 " 1841.
Huntington Selden,	"	1841 "

Cobaltville Post-Office in the north part of Middle-Haddam, established in 1851—Charles Rich, postmaster.

SKETCH OF EAST-HAMPTON.

It was mentioned in the address that the first settlers in East Hampton were attracted thither in 1743 by the fine mill site at the outlet of Powtopogue pond where a forge was erected. This pond is a beautiful as well as a very important sheet of water. The circumference following the curves of the shore is about nine miles. The waters are generally ten feet deep and inclose several islands, one of which was the favorite resort of a clan of Indians. It is fed by low springs, for rains which fall so gently as not to run off from the earth do not alter its height. For several miles the outlet is known by the name of the Powtopogue stream, and then by that of Pine Brook, which after a course of six or seven miles in East-Hampton and Middle-Haddam empties itself into Salmon River, three miles from the entrance of that river into the Connecticut at East Haddam Landing.

At the time the forge was erected, iron was very much needed by the inhabitants in the surrounding country, and it was soon needed in Ship-building, to which the attention of numbers on the Connecticut was turned in a few years. How much business was done at the forge for the first forty years it would be difficult now to ascertain. Probably much was done. The property passed into the hands of various individuals and companies. For a time at least it was held by Abijah Hall. About 1784 it passed into the hands of his son Abijah Hall, Jun., and from that time until about 1810 or 12, when the forge was given up, about 8 hands on an average were employed in it, and two lads.

Ore was brought to the forge from West Point, and from this iron was made for use in ship-building. The best iron for general purposes was made from pigs, procured in the city of New York and from Salisbury, and for these purposes that from Salisbury was preferred. Much iron was made for the vessels built at Middletown, and in places below on the river. In 1825 a new forge was built on the site of the old forge, and a scythe factory, and at these, business was done several years. Both are dilapidated.

The factories and mills now existing below are as follows, and in the order they are named, viz:

Buell & Veazey's Bell Factory, which employs from a dozen to fifteen hands. The principal building is 38 feet by 22, two stories; to which an iron foundry is attached, one story, 40 feet by 20.

Beven Brothers' Bell Factory. The casting shop is 110 by 18 with a turning shop connected, 30 feet by 18. There is also a blacksmith and finishing shop 55 feet by 22. They employ on an average about 20 hands.

BUELL & SEARS' SAWMILL, in full operation is on the east side of the stream, on the opposite side they have a batting mill.

J. S. HALL & Co's. BELL FACTORY. Shop 47 feet by 26; eleven or 12 hands on an average.

BELL FACTORY OWNED BY THE EAST HAMPTON BELL COMPANY. Foundry and finishing shop 91 feet by 25, 2 stories; 19 feet head and fall. wheel 16 feet. Employs 15 hands. This is on the ancient site of Cook's grist mill.

NOAH S. MARKUM'S HOE FACTORY. The building is 36 feet by 26, the fall of water 14 feet. Seven hands are employed and 1200 dozen of hoes made annually. These are the concave hoe, entirely of cast steel and highly polished. They are much admired at the north for all the purposes for which hoes are needed. For this fine article a silver medal has been awarded to Mr. Markum by the American Institute in the city of New York.

NILES, PARMELEE & Co's. BELL FACTORY. The building is 36 feet by 20, the fall of water 14 feet, turning an overshot wheel of 12 feet diameter. Ten hands are employed.

BARTON & CLARK'S FACTORY. The building is 36 feet by 18, with two wings 18 by 14. The fall of water is 14 feet, and the wheel, (a breast wheel) 16 in diameter. This manufactures brass kettles of various sizes, which are useful for all purposes in which iron material is not needed.

SKINNER'S SAWMILL. This has a fall of water of 16 feet. It is new and in full operation. Connected with this is a large building in which is a grain mill, and in which manufacturing operations are expected to be carried on.

All the above factories and mills are within two miles of the Powtopogue Pond. Further on are:

ABEL'S SAW & GRAIN MILLS. These are in operation, but out of repair.

PINE BROOK FACTORY, 38 feet by 26. There has not been much done in this factory, and it is now undergoing repairs.

WEST'S SAW MILL. This has a fall of 16 feet, but the building is so much decayed as not to be fit for use.

JOHNSON'S PISTOL FACTORY, 24 feet by 20, 7 feet posts, not in operation.

JUSTIN SEXTON & SONS' SATINET FACTORY, 36 by 26 with an ell 22 by 20, fall of water 18 feet, the wheel 14. This employs 5 hands, cards wool and manufuctures cloth for customers. With this factory a saw mill is connected.

Northeast of the Pond, on Chatham and Marlborough Turnpike, H. & W. Veazey, have a bell factory moved by horse power, which employs on an average 16 hands.

Nearly all the bell factories manufacture ship and house bells, cow, sheep, hand and sleigh bells. Various articles of iron are also manufactured in them to some extent, particularly waffle irons.

It is a remarkable fact that sleigh bells are manufactured here, and in the factory mentioned as being in Middle-Haddam, almost exclusively for all those parts of the United States in which such bells are used, and also in Canada. With the exception of a small quantity made in a factory in New Britain, it is said, they are entirely. The manufacturing enterprize and general prosperity of East Hampton are very much owing to Mr. William Barton, who was born in Wintonbury, a society of Windsor, now the town of Bloomfield, Nov. 26, 1762. He labored with his father, whose name he bore, and who was armorer at Springfield in the Revolutionary war. At the close of the war he returned to Wintonbury and manufactured pistols and other warlike implements until 1790, when he went to New York and engaged in the manufacture of andirons and articles of brass. From that city he came to East Hampton in the spring of 1808, and commenced the manufacture of hand and sleigh-bells. Others acquired skill from him and engaged in the same concern. Liberal minded himself, he was happy in benefitting others and the community soon began to flourish around him. In May 1826 he removed to Cicero, in the state of New York, where he exerted a happy influence, but after 20 years returned to spend the residue of his days with his children and friends in East Hampton, where he died July 15, 1849, universally respected and lamented.

In connection with the foregoing factories and mills it might have been mentioned, that further south on Pine Brook, are Rand's Oakum Factory and House's Paper Mill. But the former is not now in operation, and both are in a part of Middle Haddam, belonging to the town of Haddam.

Salmon River for some distance washes the south-eastern border of East Hampton parish. The principal sources of this stream are in Hebron and Lebanon; it passes through a part of Colchester. It is much larger than that flowing from the pond. On this are several sites where factories might be built. But as the river is liable to sudden and great rises, as dams of much strength and cost are needed, and as they are further from navigable water, than the sites on the other stream, they are not yet occupied. But should the contemplated rail road through Middletown on to Boston be soon built, it is probable men of the requisite capital would secure the sites and erect upon them large establishments. There are however, many unoccupied privileges on Pine Brook, where men of small capital may invest property to advantage. A good road opened along near the stream would hasten their occupation.

East Hampton was settled more rapidly than any part of Middletown east of the Connecticut. There was a rush of inhabitants there upon the erection of the forge at the outlet of the Pond about 1743.

The names of the inhabitants and their lists as taken that year, and as stated on the colony records. were as follows:

Name	£	Name	£
Azariah Andrews,	£ 30	George Hubbard,	33
* Jonathan Bailey,	48,16	* James Johnson,	86
* David Bailey,	27	Wm. Johnson,	0
* John Beven. Jun.	34,06	* Seth Knowles,	58,10
* William Beven,	20	* John Markum,	21
John Bozworth,	18	* William Norcot,	41
* Jabez Clark,	39.09	* William Norcot, Jun.	20
* Ebenezer Clark,	42.13	* Joseph Parker,	100.16
* John Clark,	143.10	* Hezekiah Russ,	30
* Josiah Cook,	32.06	* Isaac Smith,	26
Samuel Eggleston,	30	John Stephens,	26
* Stephen Griffith,	47	* Samuel Wadworth,	40
Nathan Harding,	27	* Isaac Williams,	18
Daniel Hills,	31	* Daniel Young,	22
Total			1100.06.

All those whose names are starred. together with Caleb Johnson, William Clark, Shubael and Thomas Lewis, became afterwards applicants for society privileges. and the reason that the others named did not, is probably owing to death, removal or some other circumstance of which we have no information.

A Mr Miller early settled in the society, from whom the hill where he lived, over which the Chatham and Colchester Turnpike passes, is called Miller's Hill. John Parmelee from Branford was also an early settler. James Bill from Lebanon, and Joseph Buell from Colchester came here afterwards.

The parish was incorporated in May 1746, the church was organized Nov. 30, 1748. at which time Rev. John Norton, a native of Berlin and graduate of Yale College 1737, was installed their pastor.

He was settled before. Nov. 25. 1741 over a small church and congregation at Falltown, now Bernardston, Mass., but the people being greatly disturbed by the occurrence of the first French war, he took a dismission in 1745, and became chaplain at Fort Massachusetts, in Adams. He was there at the time it was attacked, Aug, 20, 1746, by an army of about 900 French and Indians under Gen De Vaudruil. Sergt. Hawks, afterwards Col. Hawks. who commanded the fort at that time, had only 22 effective men with him, and but 33 persons, men, women and children, and was miserably supplied with ammunition. Notwithstanding these unfortunate circumstances, he defended the fort 28 hours, and probably would never have given it up had not his ammunition failed. He was finally obliged to capitulate and offered such articles as were accepted. One special article was, that none of the prisoners should be delivered into the hands of the Indians. The next day however, Vaudruil delivered one half of them to the Indians, on the plea that there was danger of mutiny in his army, the Indians being irritated that they were cut off from the profits of the conquest. The savages immediately killed one of the prisoners, because being sick, he was unable to travel, for the prisoners were destined to march into Canada as captives. In the siege, Col. Hawks lost but one man, while the enemy as near as could be ascertained, lost 45 men, who were either killed outright or died of their wounds.

Mr. Norton wrote an account of his captivity and that of his companions, which was published, and fills a duodecimo pamphlet of 40 pages. From this it appears that when the prisoners were marched as far as Crown Point, on their way to Quebec, a party of the Indians, who went off from Adams with a view of attacking Deerfield, returned with 6 scalps and one captive, and that afterwards, while in Quebec, a sickness broke out among the English prisoners; that Mr. Norton himself was repeatedly sick, and that 15 belonging to the company from Adams died, 10 men, 3 women and 2 children, and that on the 27th of Aug. 1747, they sailed under a flag of truce from Quebec, and on the 16th of September arrived in Boston.

In 1755, in the 2d French war, while pastor at East Hampton, Mr. Norton went as chaplain in the expedition to Crown Point, and the members of the Hartford South Association, to which he belonged, agreed to supply his pulpit from Oct, 12th, in that year, till Feb. 2d. 1756, He died of the small pox, March 24, 1778 aged 62.

Rev. Lemuel Parsons, native of Durham, graduate of Yale 1773, succeeded Mr. Norton as pastor Feb. 10, 1779 and died in Feb. 1791, two days after he had closed the 12th year of his ministry, aged 37.

Rev. Joel West, native of Lebanon. graduate of Dartmouth College 1789 was ordained Oct. 17, 1792, and died in the pastoral office Oct. 26, 1826, aged 60.

Since his death the people have had the following pastors;—*Rev. Messrs., Timothy Stone, Samuel J. Curtis, Rufus Smith* and *William Russell.*

Mr. Stone, was the son of Rev. Timothy Stone of the society of Goshen, in Lebanon, and was early prepared to enter some class in college, but by reason of disease abandoned literary pursuits for some time, and studied the art of painting with the celebrated John Trumbull, a native of the same town with himself. After this, becoming a subject of grace, he resolved to enter the ministry and placed himself under the instruction of President Dwight, living in his family, and under his guidance pursuing both classical and theological studies. Nov. 10, 1803 he was ordained pastor of the church in South Cornwall, and at the commencement in 1804 the Corporation of Yale College conferred upon him the degree of Master of Arts. He was dismissed from this charge in 1827 or the beginning of 1828, and on the 4th of June in the last mentioned year was installed pastor of the church in East Hampton. He was dismissed a second time Feb. 7, 1832, and soon after returned to his family in South Cornwall where he died April 14, 1852 aged nearly 78.

Mr. Curtis, a native of Meriden, was settled in East Hampton Nov. 1, 1832 and dismissed Nov. 21, 1837 After his dismission he was stated supply at West Woodstock and at Union; at the latter place he has been pastor since April 12, 1843. On fast day March 25, 1842, he was called to the sudden and aggravated affliction of parting with his wife and a daughter who were killed by lightning.

Mr. Smith is a native of Chaplin, and was sometime a physician in Griswold, but afterwards studied theology and was licensed to preach. He was settled in East Hampton, Sept. 19, 1838 and was dismissed Aug. 1, 1845. He now lives in East Hartford.

Mr. Russel is a native of Stratford, graduate of Yale 1837. Studied theology at New Haven. He was first settled in Wakeman, Huron Co., Ohio, in Dec. 1842. He was installed in E. Hampton Oct, 14, 1846.

The early records of the church are lost, and of course it cannot be told of how many the church consisted at its formation, nor how many were admitted to it by Mr. Norton.

Mr. Parsons, admitted		58
Mr. West,	"	128
Mr. Stone,	"	16
Mr. Curtis,	"	40
Mr. Smith,	"	22
Nr. Russell has admitted,		37
The number of members Jan. 1, 1852, was		118

DEACONS.

	Elected.	*Deaths.*	*Age.*
Ebenezer Clarke,		Moved away.	
Isaac Smith,		July 29, 1802.	85.
John Clarke, Esq.		Aug. 8, 1809.	94.
James Bill, Esq.	July 5, 1795,	July, 23, 1825.	87.
Gideon Arnold,	do.	Feb. 17, 1807.	72.
Moses Cook,	May 16, 1805,	May 15, 18[illegible]8,	75.
Isaac Smith,	do.	Oct. 28, 18[illegible]5,	70.
Joseph Sage,	July 24, 1815,	Feb. 20, 1818,	60,
David Clarke, Esq.	July 1816,	Mar. 20, 1843,	88.
Warren A. Skinner,	May 1, 1818,		
Diodate B. West,	1824,		

The society have the following funds for the support of the ministry :—

A bequest made by Mr. Silas Smith in Aug. 1840	$878.
One hundred dollars raised by the society.	100.
	978.

The annual contributions of the people to the great objects of

Christian benevolence have been for several years past about $200.

BAPTIST CHURCH IN EAST HAMPTON.

A few families of this denomination by the name of Morgan, Webb and Welsh, originally from Colchester, but who had lived for a time in Nova Scotia, came to this place and settled about 1775. Among these a church was formed Sept. 10, 1784. The Strict Congregationalists in the southern part of Haddam in 1792 professed themselves Baptists and united with them. The two branches maintained public worship separately. Elder William Welsh, who labored more or less in both branches, lived in East Hampton. He died in 1824, and the branch there is extinct.

METHODIST EPISCOPAL CHURCH.

The Methodists in East Hampton began to have week-day preaching about 1815; from 1828 to 1847 they had preaching once in two weeks on the sabbath, and from 1847 they have had preaching from sabbath to sabbath. In 1830 they built a meeting-house on Miller's Hill, 48 feet by 36, which cost $1800. Twenty-eight of their members withdrew from them in 1848. The number belonging to the church Jan. 1, 1852 was 30; and 6 persons were on probation.

FREE METHODISTS.

The twenty-eight persons who withdrew from the Methodist Episcopal Church in 1848 were formed into a free or independent church. They built a house for the worship of God, which was dedicated April 10, 1851. Its dimensions are 40 feet by 30. Their members Jan. 1, 1852 were 48.

PHYSICIANS IN EAST HAMPTON.

Dr. Robert Usher, who practised medicine in East Hampton and also in Westchester, is spoken of in the address, and nothing farther need to be stated here respecting him, except that his residence was in the southeast part of Chatham, in a neighborhood called Waterhole, and attached to the parish of Westchester in Colchester, separated from the parish of East Hampton by Salmon river.

John Richmond was from Brookfield, Mass. He studied medicine with Dr. Timothy Hall of East Hartford. and was introduced into East Hampton by Dr. Coleman of Glastenbury about 1792. He died Dec. 16, 1821 aged 54. Besides attending professional duties, he guided the studies of several young men who were contemplating the same services. Richard Mayo Smith, who became his successer was his pupil; Newell Smith already mentioned in the notice of Portland physicians, Abner Clark, who is now living near Dunkirk, N. Y., and Elijah Root who died in Marlborough in the autumn of 1827, were also his pupils.

Richard Mayo Smith, native of Chaplin, was attending medical lectures at New Haven at the time of Dr. Richmond's death. He commenced practice in East Hampton in the spring of 1822, and died on the 22d. of December following, aged 26. The church records say he died Dec. 23d.

Charles Smith, See physicians of Middle Haddam.

Francis Griswold Edgerton, born in Norwich, studied medicine for a shorter or longer period with Drs. George Hazard of South Kingston, R. I, Philemon Tracy of Norwich Town, and William P. Eaton of Norwich Landing, and attended medical lectures in New Haven in 1824 and 5. He commenced practice in East Hampton on the 27th of March 1826, and has ever since practised in this place.

To this notice it may be properly added that *Elias Norton* a son of Rev. John Norton, studied medicine with Dr. Thomas Mosely of East Haddam and was surgeon's mate with Dr. Robert Usher in the Revolutionary war, by an appointment made Jan 29. 1776. He afterwards settled as a physician at Machias in Maine, where he died some years since.

Dan Arnold, also a native of East Hampton, studied medicine with Dr. John R. Watrous of Colchester and settled in Hebron, where he has practised about 60 years.

GRADUATES FROM EAST HAMPTON.

Amasa West was long a member of one of the New England Colleges, it is believed of Williams College, and he is spoken of in East Hampton as being a graduate, and as having taught school there after he was graduated, but as his name is not on the Triennial catalogue of Williams College, nor of any other college which the writer has consulted, it is doubted whether he went wholly through with his college course. He studied theology, and went, it is believed as early as 1812 or 13 to the county of Chatauque, and preached in several places about the centre of that county for many years. He is now in the State of Michigan.

Ephraim Tucker Barstow, Yale 1841. Died while engaged in the study of law at Rochester, N. Y., in 1845.

Rufus Smith, son of Rev. Rufus Smith, was born in Griswold, and graduated at Yale 1846. He taught school in Powelton, Hancock Co., Georgia, about a year; and then on due consultation and advice started for Texas, with the view of opening a school in that State, but on his way fell sick with the yellow fever at New Orleans, where he died Oct. 15, 1847 aged 26. He held a very respectable rank in his class, and had been an exemplary professor of religion a number of years.

Shaler Hall, G. of Michigan University 1847, is engaged in manufacturing.

Adonijah S Welsh, G of Michigan University 1847, is employed in teaching at Jonesville, Michigan.

Edwin H. Cole, W. U. 1851. Is teaching in Armenia, N. Y.

EAST HAMPTON POST-OFFICE,

ESTABLISHED IN 1817.

Post Masters.

Franklin G. Comstock, from June	1818	to the spring of	1821.
David Buell, from the spring of	1821	"	1845.
William G. Buell, "	1845	May 21,	1850.
Noah S. Markum, from May 21,	1850		

Chatham Post-Office, also in East Hampton, established in 1851, Moses Warren Comstock, postmaster.

ADDITIONAL ITEMS.

Within the society of East Hampton there are 177 tenantable dwelling houses and 188 families. About 80 of the houses have been built within 26 years, and during that time about half as many have been torn down or abandoned as dwellings.

The small section of land, belonging to Chatham, which is attached to the society of Westchester, lies to the southeast of East Hampton, and is separated from it by Salmon river. The section is part of a school district called Waterhole, and in this section there are 8 houses and 9 families.

The number of school districts in East Hampton is 7; the children in them between the ages of 4 and 16 in 1851 was 236, and there were 6 more in the Chatham part of Waterhole.

There are two merchant stores in East Hampton.

The grave-yards in the society are 3, and there is a 4th in Waterhole within the limits of Chatham. The deaths in E. H. for 10 years prior to Jan. 1, 1852 were 91.

JUSTICES IN CHATHAM

UNTIL THE ADOPTION OF THE PRESENT CONSTITUTION OF THE STATE,

Inclusive of those who lived in what was at the time the First

Society in Chatham, but has since become the Town of Portland. The justices who are not indicated as living in Middle Haddam or East Hampton by the letters M. H. and E. H., affixed to their names, are to be regarded as having lived within the present limits of the new Town.

Names.	*Deaths.*			*Ages.*
Joseph White,	Dec.	14,	1770.	82.
Nathaniel Freeman,	Sept.	6,	1791.	78.
David Sage,	Nov.	25,	1803.	86.
Ebenezer White,	July	29,	1817.	90.
Joseph Dart, M. H.	May	5,	1791.	53.
John Clark, E. H.	Aug.	8,	1809.	94.
Jonathan Penfield,	July	23,	1794.	69.
Bryant Parmelee, E. H.	Jan.	6,	1817.	84.
James Bill, E. H.	July	25,	1825.	87.
Hezekiah Goodrich,	April		1817,	72.
Chauncey Bulkley, M. H.	May	10,	1818.	75.
Daniel Shepherd,	Oct.	24,	1850.	97.
David White,	Sept.	18,	1833.	79.
Gen'l. Seth Overton,				
Dea. David Clark, E. H.	May	20,	1843.	88.
Stephen Griffith, M. H.	About		1839.	76.
John Parmelee, E. H.	June	20,	1827.	62.
Nathaniel Cornwall,	March	22,	1823.	73.
William Dixon,	March	20,	1826.	81.
Cyrus Bill, M. H.	Moved from the county			
Asahel H Strong, M. H.	Jan.	7,	1818.	41.
Joseph Dart, M. H.				
Ralph Smith, M. H.	Jan.		1838.	77.
George White,	June	1,	1848.	84.
Amasa Daniels, Jun. M. H.			1847.	70.
Sparrow Smith, E. H.	July	14,	1842.	82.

TOWN CLERKS IN CHATHAM.

This town was incorporated Oct. 1757, and held its first meeting for the choice of officers on the 7th of December following. The office of clerk has been held by the following persons:

Jonathan Penfield,	from	Dec. 7, 1767	till	July 23, 1794.
Daniel Shepherd, jr.	"	Sept. 15, 1794	"	Dec. 6, 1802.
Zebulon Penfield,	"	Dec. 6, 1802	"	Oct. 3, 1836.
Edward A Penfield,	"	Oct. 3, 1836	"	June 1841.
John Markham, jr.	"	July 10, 1841	"	Oct. 11, 1841.
Nathaniel C Smith,	"	Oct. 11, 1841	"	

CHATHAM PROBATE DISTRICT.

Was established May 1824. It still includes Portland. Haddam Neck belonged to it until 1830, when the town of Haddam was constituted a district.

1824, Benjamin Hurd, appointed Judge. Constant F. Daniels, Clerk July, 12.

1829, Franklin G. Comstock, Esq. appointed Judge, officiated without a clerk.

1833, Ira Lee Esq. appointed Judge. Horace Foot Esq. was appointed Clerk, June 1833.

1835, Philip Sage appointed Judge, June 29, Daniel Penfield, Clerk.

1838, Ezra Foot Esq., appointed Judge, and officiated without a clerk.

1839, Philip Sage appointed Judge.

1844, David Cornwall appointed Judge, Linus Parmelee Clerk.

1846, Braddock Strong Esq., appointed Judge, and officiated without a clerk.

1847, David Cornwall appointed Judge, Linus Parmelee Clerk.

1850, Cyrus Hurd was appointed Judge, and officiates without a clerk.

MIDDLETOWN DEPUTIES TO THE GENERAL COURT.

The Town was first represented in Sept. 1652.

William Smith,	Sept., 1652.	William Cheney,	Oct. 1663.
John Hall, jr.	May, 1653.	Nathaniel White,	May, 1664.
William Smith,	do	Robert Warner,	do
Robert Webster,	Sept. 1653.	William Cornwell,	Oct. 1664.
William Smith,	do	William Cheney,	do
Robert Webster,	May, 1654.	Nathaniel White,	May, 1665.
Wm. Cornwall,	do	Samuel Stocking,	do
Robert Webster,	Sept. 1654.	Robert Warner,	Oct. 1665.
Thomas Whitmore,	do	Samuel Stocking,	do
Robert Webster,	May, 1655.	Nathaniel White,	May. 1666.
William Smith,	do	Mr. Hamlin,	do
William Smith,	Oct. 1655.	Nathaniel White,	Oct. 1666.
Robert Webster,	May 1656.	Mr. Hamlin,	do
Thomas Allyn,	do	Giles Hamlin,	May. 1667.
Robert Webster,	Oct. 1656.	Nathaniel White,	do
None recorded,	May 1657.	Giles Hamlin,	Oct. 1667.
Robert Webster,	Oct. 1657.	William Cheney,	do
George Graves, jr.	do	Giles Hamlin,	May, 1668.
George Graves, jr.	May, 1658.	Nathaniel White,	do
Samuel Stocking,	do	Mr. Hamlin,	Oct. 1668.
Robert Webster,	Oct. 1658.	Nathaniel White,	do
George Graves, jr.	do	Nathaniel White,	May, 1669.
Robert Webster,	May, 1659.	Samuel Stocking,	do
Samuel Stocking,	do	Nathaniel White,	Oct. 1669.
Nathaniel White,	Oct. 1659.	Samuel Stocking,	do
Samuel Stocking,	do	Nathaniel White,	May, 1670.
William Cheney,	May, 1660.	William Cheney,	do
Robert Warner,	do	Giles Hamlin,	Oct. 1670.
William Cheney,	Oct. 1660.	Nathaniel White,	do
Robert Warner,	do	Giles Hamlin,	May, 1671.
Robert Warner,	May, 1661.	Nathaniel White,	do
Nathaniel White,	do	Giles Hamlin,	Oct. 1671.
Robert Warner,	Oct. 1661.	Nathaniel White,	do
Nathaniel White,	do	Nathaniel White,	May, 1672.
Nathaniel White,	May, 1662.	William Cheney,	do
William Cheney,	do	Samuel Collins,	Oct. 1672.
Nathaniel White,	Oct. 1662.	William Cheney,	do
Robert Warner,	do	Giles Hamlin,	May. 1673.
Nathaniel White,	May, 1663.	Nathaniel White,	do
Robert Warner,	do	Giles Hamlin,	Oct. 1673.
Nathaniel White,	Oct. 1663.	William Cheney,	do

Giles Hamlin,	May, 1674.
Nathaniel White,	do
Nathaniel White,	Oct. 1674.
Samuel Sto king,	do
Giles Hamlin,	May, 1675.
Nathaniel White,	do
Nathaniel White,	Oct. 1675.
William Cheney,	do
Nathaniel White,	May, 1676.
William Cheney,	do
Nathaniel White,	Oct. 1676.
John Grave,	do
Nathaniel White,	May, 1677.
William Cheney,	do
Nathaniel White,	Oct. 1677.
Samuel Stocking,	do
Giles Hamlin,	May 1678.
Nathaniel White,	do
Daniel Harris,	Oct. 1678.
William Cheney,	do
Nathaniel White,	May, 1679.
William Cheney,	do
Giles Hamlin,	Oct. 1679.
Nathaniel White,	do
Giles Hamlin,	May, 1680
Nathaniel White,	do
Giles Hamlin,	Oct. 1680.
Nathaniel White,	do
Giles Hamlin,	May, 1681.
Nathaniel White,	do
No names recorded.	Oct. 1681
Giles Hamlin,	May. 1682.
Nathaniel White,	do
Giles Hamlin.	Oct. 1682.
Nathaniel White,	do
Giles Hamlin.	May, 1683.
Nathaniel White,	do
Giles Hamlin.	Oct. 1683
Nathaniel White,	do
Giles Hamlin.	May. 1684
Nathaniel White,	do
Daniel Harris.	Oct. 1684.
William Cheney,	do
William Cheney,	May. 1685.
Nathaniel White,	Oct. 1685.
William Cheney,	do
Nathaniel White,	May, 1686.
William Cheney,	do
Nathaniel White,	Oct. 1686.
Robert Warner,	Oct. 1686.
Nathaniel White,	May. 1687.
Robert Warner,	do
William Harris,	Oct. 1687.
William Cheney,	do
No election—Usurpation, of Maj. Andros,	May, 1688.
Do	Oct. 1688.
Nathaniel White,	May, 1689.
Nathaniel White,	Oct. 1689.
William Ward,	do
Nathaniel White,	May. 1690.
William Cheney,	do
Nathaniel White,	Oct. 1690.
John Hamlin.	do
Nathaniel White,	May, 1691.
John Hamlin,	do
Nathaniel White,	Oct. 1691.
John Hamlin,	do
Nathaniel White,	May, 1692.
John Hamlin,	do
Nathaniel White,	Oct. 1692.
John Hamlin,	do
Nathaniel White,	May, 1693.
John Hamlin.	do
Nathaniel White,	Oct. 1693.
John Hamlin.	do
Nathaniel White,	May. 1694.
No names recorded.	Oct. 1694.
Nathaniel White,	May. 1695.
William Cheney,	do
Nathaniel White,	Oct. 1695.
William Cheney,	do
Capt. White.	May. 1696.
Nathaniel Bidwell,	do
William Cheney,	Oct. 1696.
John Hall.	do
Nathaniel White,	May. 1697.
Samuel Stowe.	do
Nathaniel White,	Oct. 1697.
Samuel Bidwell.	do
Nathaniel White,	May. 1698.
Samuel Bidwell,	do
Nathaniel White.	Oct. 1698.
Samuel Bidwell,	do
Nathaniel White,	May. 1699.
John Hall.	do
Nathaniel White,	Oct. 1699.
Nathaniel White,	May, 1700

John Hall,	May. 1700.	William Ward,	Oct. 1712.
Nathaniel White,	Oct. 1700.	Joseph Rockwell,	May. 1713.
John Hall,	do	William Ward,	do
Nathaniel White,	May, 1701	Joseph Rockwell,	Oct. 1713.
John Hall,	do	William Ward,	do
Nathaniel White,	Oct. 1701.	Joseph Rockwell,	May, 1714.
William Sumner.	do	William Harris,	do
Nathaniel White,	May, 1702.	Joseph Rockwell,	Oct. 1714.
William Sumner,	do	William Harris.	do
Capt. White,	Oct. 1702.	Joseph Rockwell,	May, 1715.
William Sumner,	do	William Harris.	do
Capt White,	May, 1703.	Joseph Rockwell,	Oct. 1715.
William Sumner,	do	William Savage,	do
Nathaniel White,	Oct. 1703.	Joseph Rockwell,	May, 1716.
Samuel Bidwell,	do	William Savage,	do
Nathaniel White,	May, 1704.	Joseph Rockwell,	Oct. 1716.
Nathaniel White,	Oct. 1704.	William Savage,	do
John Hall,	do	Joseph Rockwell,	May, 1717.
Nathaniel White,	May, 1705.	Samuel Hall,	do
John Hall,	do	Azariah Wetmore,	Oct. 1717.
Nathaniel White.	Oct. 1705.	John Sage	do
Samuel Bidwell,	do	Azariah Wetmore,	May, 1718.
Nathaniel White,	May, 1706.	William Savage,	do
Thomas Ward,	do	Azariah Wetmore,	Oct. 1718.
Nathaniel White,	Oct. 1706.	William Savage,	do
Thomas Ward,	do	Joseph Rockwell,	May, 1719.
Nathaniel White,	May 1707.	William Savage,	do
Thomas Ward,	do	Joseph Rockwell,	Oct. 1719.
Nathaniel WLite.	Oct. 1707.	William Savage,	do
John Hall,	do	William Harris.	May. 1720.
Nathaniel White,	May, 1708.	Wiliam Savage,	do
John Hall,	do	William Savage,	Oct. 1720.
Nathaniel White,	Oct. 1708	William Harris,	do
John Hall,	do	William Harris,	May, 1721.
Nathaniel White,	May. 1709.	William Savage,	do
John Hall,	do	Azariah Wetmore,	Oct. 1721.
Nathaniel White,	Oct. 1709.	John Sage,	do
John Hall,	do	Azariah Wetmore,	May. 1722.
Nathaniel White,	May, 1710.	John Sage.	do
John Hall,	do	William Harris,	Oct. 1722.
Joseph Rockwell,	Oct. 1710.	William Savage,	do
William Ward,	do	Azariah Wetmore,	May, 1723.
Edward Shepard,	May, 1711.	William Savage,	do
William Ward,	do	Azariah Wetmore,	Oct. 1723.
John Hall,	Oct. 1711.	William Savage,	do
Thomas Ward,	do	Azariah Wetmore,	May, 1724.
Thomas Ward,	May, 1712.	William Savage,	do
John Warner, jr.	do	Azariah Wetmore,	Oct. 1724.
Joseph Rockwell,	Oct. 1712.	William Savage,	do

Name	Session
Azariah Wetmore,	May. 1725.
William Savage,	do
Azariah Wetmore,	Oct. 1725.
William Savage,	do
Azariah Wetmore,	May. 1726.
John Sage.	do
Azariah Wetmore,	Oct. 1726.
William Savage,	do
Giles Hall,	May, 1727.
John Andrews,	do
Giles Hall,	Oct. 1727.
John Andrews,	do
Azariah Wetmore,	May, 1728.
John Andrews.	do
William Harris,	Oct. 1728.
John Andrews,	do
Joseph Wetmore,	May. 1729.
John Andrews,	do
George Phillips,	Oct. 1729.
John Andrews,	do
Giles Hall,	May, 1730.
John Andrews,	do
Giles Hall,	Oct. 1730.
George Phillips,	do
Giles Hall,	May 1731.
George Phillips,	do
George Phillips,	Oct. 1731.
Jabez Hamlin,	do
George Phillips,	May 1732.
Jabez Hamlin,	do
Giles Hill.	Oct. 1732.
Thomas Allyn,	do
George Phillips,	May, 1733.
Joseph White,	do
George Phillips,	Oct. 1733.
Jabez Hamlin,	do
George Phillips,	May, 1734.
Jabez Hamlin,	do
George Phillips,	Oct. 1734.
Jabez Hamlin,	do
George Phillips,	May, 1735.
George Phillips,	Oct. 1735.
Jabez Hamlin,	do
George Phillips,	May, 1736.
Jabez Hamlin,	do
George Phillips,	Oct. 1736
Jabez Hamlin,	do
George Phillips,	May, 1737.
Jabez Hamlin,	do
George Phillips,	Oct. 1737.
Jabez Hamlin,	do
Jabez Hamlin,	May. 1738.
George Phillips,	do
Jabez Hamlin,	Oct. 1738.
Seth Wetmore,	do
Jabez Hamlin,	May. 1739.
Thomas Johnson,	do
Jabez Hamlin,	Oct. 1739.
Thomas Johnson,	do
Jabez Hamlin,	May. 1740.
Seth Wetmore,	do
George Phillips,	Oct. 1740.
Jabez Hamlin,	do
Jabez Hamlin.	May. 1741.
Seth Wetmore,	do
Jabez Hamlin,	Oct. 1741.
Seth Wetmore,	do
Jabez Hamlin,	May. 1742.
Seth Wetmore,	do
Jabez Hamlin,	Oct. 1742.
Seth Wetmore,	do
Jabez Hamlin,	May, 1743.
Seth Wetmore,	do
Jabez Hamlin,	Oct. 1743.
Seth Wetmore,	do
Jabez Hamlin,	May. 1744.
Thomas Johnson,	do
Jabez Hamlin,	Oct. 1744.
Seth Wetmore,	do
Jabez Hamlin,	May. 1745.
Seth Wetmore,	do
Jabez Hamlin,	Oct. 1745.
Seth Wetmore,	do
Jabez Hamlin,	May. 1746.
Seth Wetmore,	do
Jabez Hamlin,	Oct. 1746.
Seth Wetmore,	do
Jabez Hamlin,	May 1747.
Seth Wetmore,	do
Jabez Hamlin,	Oct. 1747.
Return Meigs,	do
Jabez Hamlin,	May. 1748.
Seth Wetmore,	do
Jabez Hamlin,	Oct. 1748.
Seth Wetmore,	do
Jabez Hamlin,	May. 1749.
Seth Wetmore,	do
Jabez Hamlin,	Oct. 1749.

Seth Wetmore,	Oct. 1749.
Jabez Hamlin,	May, 1750.
Seth Wetmore,	do
Jabez Hamlin,	Oct. 1750.
Joseph Southmayd.	do
Jabez Hamlin,	May, 1751.
Joseph Southmayd,	do
Jabez Hamlin,	Oct. 1751.
Joseph Southmayd,	do
Jabez Hamlin,	May, 1752.
Joseph Southmayd,	do
Joseph Southmayd,	Oct. 1752.
Jabez Hamlin,	do
Jabez Hamlin,	May, 1753.
Joseph Southmayd,	do
Jabez Hamlin.	Oct. 1753.
Seth Wetmore,	do
Jabez Hamlin,	May, 1754.
Joseph Wright,	do
Jabez Hamlin,	Oct. 1754.
Seth Wetmore,	do
Jabez Hamlin,	May. 1755.
Seth Wetmore,	do
Jabez Hamlin,	Oct. 1755.
Seth Wetmore,	do
Jabez Hamlin,	May. 1756.
Seth Wetmore,	do
Jabez Hamlin,	Oct. 1756.
Michael Burnham,	do
Jabez Hamlin,	May 1757,
Seth Wetmore,	do
Jabez Hamlin,	Oct. 1757.
Seth Wetmore,	do
Jabez Hamlin,	May. 1758.
Seth Wetmore,	Oct. 1758
Matthew Talcott,	do
Seth Wetmore,	May. 1759.
John Fitch,	do
Seth Wetmore,	Oct. 1759
Matthew Talcott,	do
Seth Wetmore,	May. 1760.
Matthew Talcott,	do
Seth Wetmore.	Oct. 1760.
Matthew Talcott,	do
Seth Wetmore,	May, 1761.
Matthew Talcott,	do
Seth Wetmore,	Oct. 1761.
Matthew Talcott,	do
Seth Wetmore.	May, 1762.
Matthew Talcott.	May, 1762.
Seth Wetmore,	Oct. 1762.
Matthew Talcott,	do
Matthew Talcott,	May, 1763.
Seth Wetmore,	Oct. 1763.
Matthew Talcott,	do
Seth Wetmore,	May, 1764.
Matthew Talcott,	do
Seth Wetmore,	Oct. 1764.
Richard Alsop,	do
Seth Wetmore,	May. 1765.
Richard Alsop,	do
Seth Wetmore,	Oct. 1765.
Richard Alsop,	do
Seth Wetmore,	May. 1766.
Richard Alsop,	do
Jabez Hamlin,	Oct. 1766.
Seth Wetmore,	do
Jabez Hamlin,	May. 1767.
Richard Alsop,	do
Jabez Hamlin,	Oct. 1767.
Richard Alsop,	do
Jabez Hamlin,	May, 1768.
Seth Wetmore,	do
Jabez Hamlin,	Oct. 1768.
Seth Wetmore,	do
Jabez Hamlin,	May. 1769.
Seth Wetmore,	do
Jabez Hamlin,	Oct. 1769.
Seth Wetmore,	do
Jabez Hamlin,	May, 1770.
Richard Alsop,	do
Jabez Hamlin,	Oct. 1770.
Seth Wetmore,	do
Jabez Hamlin,	May, 1771.
Seth Wetmore,	do
Jabez Hamlin,	Oct. 1771.
Richard Alsop,	do
Jabez Hamlin,	May. 1772.
Matthew Talcott,	do
Jabez Hamlin,	Oct. 1772.
Richard Alsop,	do
Jabez Hamlin,	May, 1773.
Richard Alsop,	do
Richard Alsop,	Oct. 1773.
Titus Hosmer,	do
Richard Alsop,	May. 1774.
Titus Hosmer,	do
Matthew Talcott,	Oct. 1774.

Titus Hosmer,	Oct. 1774.	Ebenezer Bacon,	May, 1786.
Matthew Talcott,	May, 1775.	Comfort Sage,	Oct. 1786.
Titus Hosmer,	do	Ebenezer Bacon,	do
Titus Hosmer,	Oct. 1775.	George Phillips,	May, 1787.
John Dickinson,	do	Elijah Hubbard,	do
Titus Hosmer,	May, 1776.	George Phillips,	Oct. 1787.
Comfort Sage,	do	Elijah Hubbard,	do
Titus Hosmer,	Oct. 1776.	Asher Miller,	May, 1788.
John Dickinson,	do	George Phillips,	do
Titus Hosmer,	May, 1777.	Asher Miller,	Oct. 1788.
Comfort Sage,	do	Elijah Hubbard,	do
Titus Hosmer,	Oct. 1777,	Asher Miller,	May, 1789.
Titus Hosmer,	May, 1778.	Ebenezer Bacon,	do
John Dickinson,	do	Samuel W. Dana,	Oct. 1789.
John Dickinson,	Oct. 1778.	Elijah Hubbard,	do
Ebenezer Bacon,	do	Asher Miller,	May, 1790.
Matthew Talcott,	May, 1779.	Samuel W. Dana,	do
Comfort Sage,	do	Elijah Hubbard,	Oct. 1790.
John Dickinson,	Oct 1779.	Asher Miller,	do
Ebenezer Bacon,	do	Elijah Hubbard,	May, 1791.
Comfort Sage,	May, 1780.	Asher Miller,	do
Matthew Talcott,	do	Elijah Hubbard,	Oct. 1791.
John Dickinson,	Oct. 1780.	Asher Miller,	do
Ebenezer Bacon,	do	Elijah Hubbard,	May, 1792.
Matthew Talcott,	May, 1781.*	Asher Miller,	do
Dr. J. Dickinson,	do	Elijah Hubbard,	Oct. 1792.
Comfort Sage,	Oct. 1781.	Asher Miller,	do
Matthew Talcott,	do	Elijah Hubbard,	May, 1793.
Comfort Sage,	May, 1782.	Asher Miller,	do
Matthew Talcott,	do	Elijah Hubbard,	Oct. 1793.
Comfort Sage,	Oct. 1782.	Samuel W. Dana,	do
Matthew Talcott,	do	Elijah Hubbard,	May, 1794.
Comfort Sage,	May, 1783	Samuel W. Dana,	do
Ebenezer Bacon,	do	Elijah Hubbard,	Oct. 1794.
Comfort Sage,	Oct. 1783.	Samuel W. Dana,	do
Ebenezer Bacon,	do	Elijah Hubbard,	May, 1795.
Comfort Sage,	May, 1784.	Samuel W. Dana,	do
Samuel H. Parsons,	do	Elijah Hubbard,	Oct. 1795.
Comfort Sage,	Oct. 1784.	Samuel W. Dana,	do
Samuel H. Parsons,	do	Elijah Hubbard,	May, 1796.
Asher Miller,	May, 1785.	Samuel W. Dana,	do
Samuel H. Parsons,	do	Elijah Hubbard,	Oct. 1796.
Comfort Sage,	Oct. 1785.	Samuel W. Dana,	do
Ebenezer Bacon,	do	Stephen T. Hosmer,	May, 1797.
Comfort Sage,	May, 1786.	Elijah Hubbard,	do

* The Roll of Representatives for May 1781 is not given in the Records in the State House at Hartford, but the roll as kept by Gov. Jonathan Trumbull is deposited in the Rooms of the Ct. His. Society.

Andrew Campbell, Oct. 1797.
Amos Church, do
Andrew Campbell, May, 1798.
Asher Miller, do
Andrew Campbell, Oct. 1798.
Ebenezer Bacon, do
Elijah Hubbard, May, 1799.
Ebenezer Bacon, do
John Pratt, Oct. 1799.
Elijah Hubbard, do
Stephen T. Hosmer, May. 1800.
Elijah Hubbard, do
Ebenezer Bacon, Oct. 1800.
Jehosaphat Starr, do
Elijah Hubbard, May, 1801.
Jehosophat Starr, do
Elijah Hubbard, Oct. 1801.
Enoch Parsons, do
Elijah Hubbard, May, 1802.
Abijah Savage, do
Elijah Hubbard, Oct. 1802.
Abijah Savage, do
Elijah Hubbard, May, 1803.
Enoch Parsons, do
Elijah Hubbard, Oct. 1803.
Asher Miller, do
Elijah Hubbard, May, 1804.
Asher Miller, do
Elijah Hubbard, Oct. 1804.
Asher Miller, do
Elijah Hubbard, May, 1805.
Joshua Stow, do
Elijah Hubbard, Oct. 1805.
Joshua Stow, do
Elijah Hubbard, May, 1806.
John Pratt, do
Elijah Hubbard, Oct. 1806.
John Pratt, do
Elijah Hubbard, May, 1807.
John Pratt, do
Elijah Hubbard, Oct. 1807.
John Pratt, do
Elijah Hubbard, May, 1808.
John Pratt, do
Lemuel Storrs, Oct. 1808.
Jozeb Stocking, do
John Pratt. May, 1809.
Chauncey Whittlesey, do
John Pratt, Oct. 1809.
Chauncey Whittlesey, do
E. Sage, May, 1810.
Chauncey Whittlesey, do
E. Sage. Oct. 1810.
Chauncey Whittlesey, do
E. Hubbard. May, 1811.
Chauncey Whittlesey, do
E. Hubbard, Oct. 1811.
Chauncey Whittlesey, do
E. Hubbard, May, 1812.
S. Wetmore, do
Elijah Hubbard, Oct. 1812.
S. Wetmore, do
Elijah Hubbard, May, 1813.
S. Wetmore, do
Elijah Hubbard, Oct. 1813.
S. Wetmore, do
Elijah Hubbard. May, 1814.
S. Wetmore, do
Elijah Hubbard, Oct. 1814.
Alexander Collins, do
Elisha Coe, May. 1815.
Arthur W. Magill, do
Samuel Gill. Oct. 1815.
Jozeb Stocking, do
Samuel Gill. May. 1816.
Jozeb Stocking, do
Elisha Coe, Oct. 1816.
C Whittlesey, do
Elisha Coe. May. 1817.
Nathan Starr, jr. do
Elisha Coe, Oct. 1817.
Nathan Starr, jr. do
John Alsop, May, 1818.
Nathan Starr, do
John Alsop, Oct. 1818.
Horace Goodrich. do
Present Constitution in operation. Henceforward but one election yearly.
John Alsop, May. 1819.
Elisha Coe, do
John Alsop, May. 1820.
Elisha Coe, do
Seth Paddock, May, 1821.
Elisha Street. do
Samuel W Dana, May 1822.
Josiah Savage, do

John Alsop,	May, 1823.
Josiah Savage,	do
Minor Hotchkiss,	May, 1824.
Daniel Rand,	do
Daniel Rand.	May, 1825.
Minor Hotchkiss,	do
Daniel Burrows,	May, 1826.
Samuel W. Dana,	do
Wm. L. Storrs,	May, 1827.
Elijah Paddock,	do
W. L. Storrs,	May, 1828.
E. Paddock,	do
W. L. Storrs,	May 1829.
E. Jackson, jr.	do
E. Jackson. jr.	May, 1830.
H. Woodward,	do
E. Jackson, jr.	May, 1831.
H. Woodward,	do
E. Jackson jr.	May, 1832.
Joseph Coe,	do
Elijah Paddock,	May, 1833.
Samuel Russell,	do
W. L. Storrs,	May, 1834.
Jedediah Wilcox,	do
S. K. Wightman,	May, 1835.
Wm. Plumb,	do
S. K. Wightman,	May, 1836.
Wm. Plumb. 2d.	do
S. K. Wightman,	May, 1837.
Timothy Savage,	do
Richard Hubbard,	May, 1838.
Eben Wilcox,	May, 1838.
Charles Woodward,	May. 1839.
Henry D. Smith,	do
No choice,	May, 1840.
Noah A. Phelps.	May, 1841.
Wm. Plumb, 2d.	do
S. K. Wightman,	May. 1842.
Alexander Sage,	do
Daniel C. Crowell,	May, 1843.
One vacancy,	do
Elihu Spencer,	May, 1844.
Alfred Hubbard,	do
No choice,	May, 1845.
Ebenezer Jackson,	May, 1846.
Samuel Russell,	do
Charles Woodward,	May. 1847.
Henry D. Smith,	do
Edwin Stearns,	May, 1848.
Elihu Spencer,	do
Edwin Stearns,	May. 1849.
Earl Cooley,	do
Noah A. Phelps,	May, 1850.
Joseph Coe,	do
Elihu Spencer,	May. 1851.
Bulkley Edwards,	do
Daniel H. Chase,	May. 1852.
Elisha S. Hubbard,	do

REPRESENTATIVES TO THE GENERAL ASSEMBLY FROM CHATHAM.

In the incorporation of this town in Oct. 1767, it was enacted that the town should send only one representative at the public expense, and but one was sent at the sessions the next year.

David Sage, May, 1768.
David Sage, Oct. do
David Sage, May, 1769.
Nathaniel Freeman, do
Ebenezer White, Oct. 1769.
Elisha Cornwall, do
Ebenezer White, May, 1770.
Nathaniel Freeman, do
Ebenezer White, Oct. 1770.
Nathaniel Freeman, do
David Sage, May, 1771.
Nathaniel Freeman, do
Ebenezer White, Oct. 1771.
Nathaniel Freeman, do
Ebenezer White, May, 1772.
David Sage, do
Ebenezer White, Oct. 1772.
Silas Dunham, do
Ebenezer White, May, 1773.
Silas Dunham, do
Ebenezer White, Oct. 1773.
Silas Dunham, do
Ebenezer White, May. 1774.
Silas Dunham, do
David Sage, Oct. 1774.
Silas Dunham, do
David Sage. May, 1775.
Ebenezer White, do
David Sage. Oct. 1775.
Ebenezer White, do
Ebenezer White, May, 1776.
John Penfield. do
Ebenezer White, Oct. 1776.
John Penfield, do
Ebenezer White, May, 1777.
John Penfield, do
Ebenezer White, Oct. 1777.
Ebenezer White, May. 1778
John Penfield, do
Silas Dunham, Oct. 1778.
Jeremiah Bradford, do
John Penfield, May. 1779.
Joseph Kellogg, do
Ebenezer White, Oct. 1779.
Joseph Kellogg, do
Ebenezer White, May, 1780.
Joseph Kellogg, do
John Penfield, Oct. 1780.
Silas Dunham, do
Gov. Trumbull names Mr, Jonathan Penfield and Mr. Eber White, as the representatives in May, 1781. but Col. John Penfield and Mr. Ebenezer White. were probably the persons intended.
Ebenezer White, Oct. 1781.
Chauncey Buckley. do
Ebenezer White, May. 1782.
Chauncey Buckley, do
Moses Bartlett, Oct. 1782,
James Bill. do
Ebenezer White, May. 1783.
James Bill. do
Ebenezer White, Oct. 1783.
Chauncey Buckley, do
Ebenezer White, May, 1784.
Chauncey Buckley, do
Ebenezer White, Oct. 1784.
James Bill, do
Joseph Blake, May, 1785.
Chauncey Buckley, do
Ebenezer White. Oct. 1785.
Bryan Parmelee, do
Ebenezer White, May. 1786.
Elijah Smith. do
Ebenezer White, Oct. 1786.

Chauncey Buckley,	Oct. 1786.
John Penfield,	May, 1787.
James Bill,	do
John Penfield,	Oct. 1787.
James Bill,	do
Ebenezer White,	May, 1788.
Chauncey Buckley,	do
Ebenezer White,	Oct. 1788.
Chauncey Buckley,	do
John Penfield,	May, 1789.
James Bill,	do
Ebenezer White,	Oct. 1789.
John Penfield,	do
Hezekiah Goodrich,	May, 1790.
James Bill,	do
Hezekiah Goodrich,	Oct. 1790.
James Bill,	do
Ebenezer White,	May, 1791.
Chauncey Buckley,	do
Hezekiah Goodrich,	Oct. 1791.
Chauncey Buckley,	do
Hezekiah Goodrich,	May, 1792.
James Bill,	do
Hezekiah Goodrich,	Oct. 1792.
Chauncey Buckley,	do
Hezekiah Goodrich,	May, 1793.
Chauncey Buckley,	do
Hezk. Goodrich,	Oct. 1793.
Timothy Rogers,	do
Hezk. Goodrich,	May, 1794.
Timothy Rogers,	do
Hez'k. Goodrich,	Oct. 1794.
Hez'k. Goodrich,	May, 1795
Joseph Sage,	do
Hez.k. Goodrich,	Oct. 1795.
James Bill,	do
Hez'k. Goodrich,	May, 1796.
Chauncey Buckley,	do
Hez'k. Goodrich,	Oct 1796.
Moses Cook,	do
Hez'k. Goodrich,	May, 1797.
Moses Cook,	do
Daniel Shepherd. jr.	Oct. 1797.
Chauncey Buckley,	do
Dan'l. Shepherd, jr.	May, 1798.
James Bill,	do
Hez'k. Goodrich,	Oct, 1798.
James Bill,	do

Hez'k. Goodrich,	May. 1799.
Chauncey Buckley,	do
Seth Overton,	Oct. 1799,
Stephen Griffith,	do
Seth Overton,	May, 1800.
Robert Usher,	do
Hez'k. Goodrich,	Oct. 1800.
Chauncey Buckley,	do
Hez'k. Goodrich,	May, 1801.
Moses Cook,	do
Hez'k. Goodrich,	Oct. 1801.
Charles Buckley,	do
The S. Records say Charles but Chauncey Buckley is probably intended.	
Hez'k. Goodrich,	May. 1802.
Bryant Parmelee,	do
Hez'k. Goodrich,	Oct. 1802.
David Clarke,	do
Hez'k. Goodrich,	May, 1803.
David Clarke,	do
Enoch Sage,	Oct. 1803.
John H. Strong,	do
Enoch Sage,	May, 1804.
John H. Strong,	do
Enoch Sage,	Oct. 1804.
Robert Usher,	do
Hez'k. Goodrich,	May. 1805.
Robert Usher,	do
Hez'k. Goodrich,	Oct. 1805.
Benjamin Hurd,	do
Hez'k. Goodrich,	May, 1806.
Benjamin Hurd,	do
Enoch Sage,	Oct. 1806.
Nathaniel Markum,	do
Daniel Cheeney,	May, 1807.
Nathaniel Markum,	do
Daniel Cheeney,	Oct. 1807.
Jonathan Bowers,	do
Isaac Conkling,	May, 1808.
Jonathan Bowers,	do
Abel Penfield,	Oct. 1808.
Jesse Hurd,	do
Abel Penfield,	May, 1809.
Benjamin Hurd,	do
Hez'k. Goodrich,	Oct. 1809.
Constant Welch,	do
Hez'k. Goodrich,	May, 1810.

Benjamin Hurd, May, 1810.
Hez'k. Goodrich, Oct. 1810.
Benjamin Hurd, do
Hez'k. Goodrich, May, 1811.
Jabez Comstock, do
Hez k. Goodrich, Oct. 1811.
James Comstock, do
Hez'k. Goodrich, May, 1812.
Benjamin Hurd, do
Abel Penfield, Oct. 1812.
Benjamin Hurd, do
Asahel H. Strong, May, 1813.
Jesse Hurd, do
Asahel H. Strong, Oct. 1813.
David Churchill, do
Asahel H. Strong, May. 1814.
Stephen Griffith. do
No representatives recorded on S. Records from Chatham. Oct. 1814.
Samuel Hall, May, 1815.
Joseph Dart, do
Samuel Hall, Oct. 1815.
Joseph Dart. do
Enoch Sage, May, 1816.
Nehemiah Gates, do
Enoch Sage, Oct. 1816.
Nehemiah Gates, do
Enoch Sage, May. 1817.
Benjamin Hurd, do
Enoch Sage, Oct. 1817.
Benjamin Hurd, do
Enoch Sage, May, 1818.
Nehemiah Gates, do
The delegates to the Convention which formed the present Constitution of the State, meeting in Aug. this year were,
Enoch Sage, and
Benjamimin Hurd,
Enoch Sage. Oct. 1818.
Nehemiah Gates, do
Delegates to the Assembly under the new constitution, one regular session annually.
Enoch Sage, May, 1819.
Benjamin Hurd, May, 1819.
Enoch Sage, May. 1820.
Nehemiah Gates, do
George White, May, 1821.
Ira Lee, do
Nathan.l. Markum, May, 1822.
Guy Cooper, do
Guy Cooper, May. 1823.
Ralph Smith, do
Philip Sage, May, 1824.
Nathaniel Markum, jr.
Philip Sage, May, 1825.
Ralph Smith, do
F. G. Comstock, May, 1826.
Ralph Smith, do
Elijah Colton, May, 1827.
Nathaniel Markum. jr.
Guy Cooper, May, 1828.
John Stewart, jr. do
Guy Cooper. May, 1829.
Nathaniel Markum, do
Philip Sage, May, 1830.
John Stewart, do
Joseph Hall, May, 1831.
Nathaniel Markum, do
David Williams, May, 1832.
John Markum, do
David Williams May, 1833.
Nathaniel C. Smith, do
Selden Co k, May, 1834.
John Markum, jr. May, 1834.
Selden Cook, May, 1835.
Lazarus Watrous, do
Guy Cooper, May, 1836.
John Markum, jr. do
Edward Lewis, May, 1837.
Lazarus Watrous, do
Edward Lewis, May, 1838.
John Markum, do
William R Smith, May, 1839.
Francis Young, do
William R. Smith, May. 1840.
Braddock Strong, do
Ralph Goodrich, May, 1841.
Elijah Clark, do
Braddock Strong, May. 1842.
Elijah Clark, do
Cyrus Hurd, May. 1843.

Dan B. Niles,	May, 1843.	Nathaniel C. Smith,	May, 1848
Cyrus Hurd,	May, 1844.	Levi Bunce,	May. 1849.
Lewis Utley,	do	Nathaniel C. Smith.	do
Hiram Markum,	May, 1845.	Levi Bunce,	May. 1850.
William Bevin,	do	Nathaniel C. Smith,	do
Hiram Markum,	May, 1846.	John Markum, jr.	May. 1851.
William G. Buell,	do	Amasa Carpenter,	do
Charles Jacobs,	May, 1847.	Martin Roberts,	May. 1852.
William G. Buell,	do	William Bevin,	do
Alfred Brooks,	May, 1848.		

REPRESENTATIVES TO THE GENERAL ASSEMBLY FROM PORTLAND.

Portland, made a town in Oct. 1842, has sent the following representatives.

Kellogg Strong,	May, 1843.	Alfred Hall,	May, 1848.
Erastus Brainerd,	do 1844.	Joseph Hall,	do 1849.
Archibald Kinney,	do 1845	William H. Bartlett,	do 1850.
Russell Penfield,	do 1846	Alfred Hall,	do 1851.
Russell Penfield,	do 1847.	Alfred Hall,	do 1852.

In these catalogues we have a large proportion of the prominent and influential men in Middletown, Cromwell, Chatham and Portland, Some of these are mentioned in the address and some in the notes. Robert Warner, one of the first settlers, held many offices of trust. He died April 10, 1690. Many were in the commission of the peace, as appears from lists of justices already given, not a few held their commissions by successive and long continued appointments. Jabez Hamlin and Seth Wetmore were justices of the Quorum for Hartford county before Middlesex County was formed. John Hamlin and Jabez Hamlin were judges of that court as stated in the sketches of them. Lemuel Storrs, Ebenezer White. Seth Overton and F. G. Comstock were justices of the Quorum for Middlesex County. John Stewart has been a judge of the County court. and a representative in the Congress of the United States. A large number of the representatives were honored with miltary commissions and their titles are very generally given on public records, while the people were exposed to attacks from the Indians and to colonial wars. High military titles appear on records in the Revolution and years afterwards. In early times military men passed slowly from one grade to another. So Nathaniel White, the patriarch of the Upper Houses is titled ensign in 1667, lieutenant 1679, and captain in Oct. 1690.

The absence of the Author of this "Address," his distant residence and the consequent difficulty in having the proofs critically read, have occasioned some errors, especially in dates. The publisher therefore, being fully aware of the value of accuracy in this respect, has been induced to append the following list of

ERRATA.

Page 139, fourth name from bottom for Mamphahelh, read Wamphaneh.
" 159, 11th line from bottom, after Nov. 5th insert *five thousand*.
" 166, 15th line from top, for 1813 read 1713.
" 176, for P*, read Pp 180,81,
" 181, 10th line from top, for 1052 read 1852.
" 189, 8th line from bottom, for 1286 read 1836.
" 194, 13th line from bottom, for 1312 read 1812.

Note to page 100. Mr. Dana died July 21, 1830, at the age of 70.
" " " 243. Dr. Hand practised in Upper Middletown, about five years; from 1811 to 1815 inclusive.

Page 253, for Shamga read Shamgar.
" 233. The name of the great pond in East Hampton, has been generally spelt *Pocct-pogue*.

www.ingramcontent.com/pod-product-compliance
Lightning Source LLC
LaVergne TN
LVHW020232110826
845151LV00003B/897

* 9 7 8 1 4 2 5 5 3 0 5 1 8 *